CONSTRUCTING GRIEVANCE

CONSTRUCTING GRIEVANCE

Ethnic Nationalism in
Russia's Republics

Elise Giuliano

CORNELL UNIVERSITY PRESS   **ITHACA AND LONDON**

First published 2011 by Cornell University Press
Printed in the United States of America

Library of Congress Cataloging-in-Publication Data

Giuliano, Elise, 1968–
    Constructing grievance : ethnic nationalism in Russia's republics / Elise Giuliano.
       p. cm.
    Includes bibliographical references and index.
    ISBN 978-0-8014-4745-7 (cloth : alk. paper)
  1. Minorities—Political activity—Russia (Federation)   2. Russia (Federation)—Ethnic relations.   3. Nationalism—Russia (Federation)   4. Self-determination, National—Russia (Federation)   5. Russia (Federation)—Politics and government—1991–   I. Title.
    JN6693.5.M5G58   2011
    320.54089'00947—dc22   2010038701

Cornell University Press strives to use environmentally responsible suppliers and materials to the fullest extent possible in the publishing of its books. Such materials include vegetable-based, low-VOC inks and acid-free papers that are recycled, totally chlorine-free, or partly composed of nonwood fibers. For further information, visit our website at www.cornellpress.cornell.edu.

Cloth printing   10 9 8 7 6 5 4 3 2 1

Contents

Figures

Tables

Preface

This book began as a microstudy about why people in the Russian republic of Tatarstan threw their support behind nationalist movements in the early 1990s. It developed into an investigation comparing all of Russia's republics. Why did people with minority ethnic identities in some other republics—which were analogous to Tatarstan in so many ways—pass through this period with so little interest in movements calling for national revival? Why didn't the Russian Federation mimic the Soviet Union's implosion along ethnic lines? Investigating these questions prompted a set of inquiries into the relationship between mass and elite, individual identity and nationalist ideology, and the role of economic structures versus human agency in the formation of political preferences.

Contrary to popular expectations as well as to the broad attention the subject has received among scholars, nationalism very often fails to take root. Russia, with its fluctuating and ultimately failed nationalist mobilizations across its republics, is a case in point. Throughout the book I show that the usual suspects—cultural difference, religion, language, demographic crises, and levels of regional wealth or poverty—do not lead to nationalism. What does inspire people to respond to leaders calling for nationalist transformation? I argue that people must develop a group grievance—a feeling of resentment about important aspects of their present situation—that they share with other people with the same ethnic affiliation. Grievances are not simply present (or absent) among people with ethnic identities; rather, they develop out of an interaction between people's lived experiences and the specific messages that nationalists articulate to make sense of those experiences. For grievances to develop, it is not enough for nationalists to define current conditions as unjustly oppressing people with a particular ethnic identity; they must also convince individuals that their personal interests in material success and social status are tied to the fate of the nation. Nationalist leaders try, in other words, to create a sense of nationhood among people by stoking a sense of outrage that current conditions (the status quo) ignore their interests on the basis of their ethnicity.

The nationalist message cannot exist at a purely rhetorical level. It must describe, with a certain degree of plausibility, people's experience of existing realities. Where nationalism emerged in Russia's republics, nationalist entrepreneurs depicted an ethnic injustice: inequality in local labor markets. Their message was not entirely accurate, for the labor situation in Russia's republics actually privileged titular minorities vis-à-vis ethnic Russians in many ways. But the nationalist message resonated with central experiences of the time: rising job insecurity and fear of unemployment in the crisis-ridden economy of the late Soviet era. Thus, nationalism develops out of a dynamic interaction between economic structures, the discourse of political entrepreneurs, and the experiences of ordinary people. This combination suggests that mass nationalist mobilization is far from easy and that the sustained politicization of mass ethnic populations is actually more of a rare than a regular occurrence. This book joins several other recent approaches to the subject of nationalism and ethnic politics to chip away at the expectation—often found among policymakers and other interested observers—that people with ethnic affiliations form distinct interest groups ready to mobilize behind nationalist leaders at a moment's notice.

A project that undergoes as many evolutions as this one has incurs a lot of debts along the way. First, I acknowledge the Department of Political Science of the University of Chicago, where this project began, for providing a remarkably stimulating environment. I was very fortunate to have had a trio of brilliant advisers: David Laitin, Ronald Suny, and John Padgett not only offered support through the various phases of the project but also provided specific, valuable, and very diverse criticisms and insights. It is no exaggeration to say that I cannot imagine a better experience, and I am grateful to each of them. I express particular appreciation to David Laitin. He provided an example of how to "do" political science in so many respects, from conducting field research to carrying out fine-grained, well-documented comparative research across the Soviet space. I am grateful for his consistent support over the years.

I acknowledge and express appreciation to the various institutions that have supported the research and writing of this book, including Harvard University's Davis Center for Russian and Eurasian Studies, Columbia University's Harriman Institute, the University of Notre Dame's Kroc Institute, the Kennan Institute of the Woodrow Wilson International Center for Scholars, and the University of Miami. I am also grateful for financial support provided by IREX and the American Political Science Association, the United States Institute of Peace, the Fulbright-Hays Doctoral Dissertation Research Fellowship, the Mellon Foundation–University of Chicago Dissertation Year Fellowship, and the MacArthur Foundation Council for the Advanced Study of Peace and International Cooperation Dissertation Fellowship.

Colleagues and scholars have offered comments on various aspects of my research and book, for which I am very appreciative, including Rawi Abdelal, Dominique Arel, John Breuilly, Dawn Brancati, Tim Colton, Kathleen Collins, Jim Fearon, Tim Frye, Cora Sol Goldstein, Dmitry Gorenburg, Stephen Hanson, Yoshiko Herrera,

John Kenny, Tomila Lankina, Alena Ledeneva, Stathis Kalyvas, Cynthia Kaplan, Pal Kolsto, Harris Mylonas, Phil Roeder, Blair Ruble, Gulnaz Sharafutdinova, Tom Simons, Oxana Shevel, Louise Davidson-Schmich, Stephen Saidemann, Jack Snyder, Josh Tucker, Pieter Van Houten, and Lucan Way. Particular thanks to Dominique Arel and Blair Ruble for their support and suggestions throughout the Kennan Institute's Workshop series on Multicultural Legacies in Russia, Ukraine, and Belarus and the publication of an edited volume from that workshop. The Laboratory in Comparative Ethnic Processes (LiCEP) provided an unparalleled workshop setting for stimulating discussions with other people who care deeply about ethnic politics. I am grateful to all its members for those discussions. In particular I acknowledge the supportive and excellent advice I received about writing and publishing a book from Elisabeth Wood and Michael Hechter. I am also indebted to my research assistants: Alevtina Gavrilova, Antonio Lupher, Garrett Ho, Albert Petichenskiy, and Nick Voitsekhovitch.

Conducting research in Russia would not have been possible without the many kind hosts I met in both Tatarstan and Moscow. I am grateful especially to Guzel Stoliarova, Damir Iskhakov, and Rosa Musina—scholars in Kazan who shared their time and expertise, from recommending interviewees to consistently providing a sounding board when I would return to their offices to discuss the latest information I had learned about Tatarstani politics. Guzel in particular offered her friendship and skilled assistance with my large survey project. I also thank Galia Zakirova of the Tatarstan National Library for stimulating conversations, as well as research assistants and friends: Gulfiya, Marat, Natasha, Deborah Ballard, and Larissa, Julia, and Lev Sumskii. I was particularly lucky to have shared a period of time during my field research in Kazan with my friend and colleague Kate Graney who was always ready to discuss Tatar politics if our telephone lines could maintain a connection. I thank Jeff Kahn for sharing his Kazan interview notes. My research at Moscow libraries and institutes was improved immeasurably by the research assistance of Boris Rubanov and the guidance of Mikhail Guboglo of the Institute of Ethnology and Anthropology of the Russian Academy of Sciences, as well as Tania Guboglo.

I express sincere appreciation to Roger Haydon of Cornell University Press for his advice, supervision, and patience throughout the publication process. I am also very grateful to my incredibly constructive anonymous reviewers whose suggestions were both useful and practical. My friends and family eased the book-writing process by always being willing to listen. In particular, Yoshiko Herrera, through Moscow, Chicago, and Boston, offered comments, support, and above all, good friendship. Thanks also to Merike Blofield, Dawn Brancati, Cora Sol Goldstein, Lara Nettelfield, Sherrill Stroschein, Tracy Regan, Nancy Scherer, and my sisters, Rachel and Michelle Giuliano.

Finally, but not least, my family's encouragement throughout my career made it possible for me to write this book. I am grateful to my parents Rachel and Francis Giuliano for their unstinting moral support and also for providing examples of an engaged professional life. I thank my husband, Grey Seamans, for his optimism, continuous patience and encouragement, and above all for convincing me that our newborn twins, Olivia and Simone, did not really constitute an obstacle to finishing a book. This book is dedicated to him.

ETHNIC ENTREPRENEURS, ORDINARY PEOPLE, AND GROUP GRIEVANCE

This era no longer wants us! This era wants to create independent nation-states! People no longer believe in God. The new religion is nationalism. Nations no longer go to church. They go to national associations.

—Joseph Roth, *The Radetzky March*

In the late 1980s ethnonationalist movements were springing up all over Eastern Europe and the Soviet Union. Initiated by intellectuals but carried out by mass publics through protest cycles, popular referenda, and elections for independence, nationalist movements sought to gain political control of their region away from rulers they considered foreign. As the states of Eastern Europe suddenly dislodged communist rule and union republics in the Soviet Union unexpectedly acquired independent statehood, the federal integrity of the new Russian state balanced precariously. Home to sixteen *autonomous republics* (ARs) that were ranked just below the *union republics* (URs) in the USSR's ethnoterritorial administrative hierarchy, Russia shared the same ethnofederal structure as the Soviet Union and was experiencing the same colossal upheaval.[1] Entrenched ideologies were thrown to the wind, central economic planning was disassembled, and the Communist Party—with its system of political appointments at every level of state administration—disintegrated. Amid these transformations, opposition nationalist movements in the republics were attracting growing levels of popular support. When a struggle for power developed in Moscow between the proreform executive and the conservative legislature, several republics took advantage of central state weakness to accelerate their quest for sovereignty.

Throughout the early 1990s the Russian Federation faced a serious threat of dissolution along ethnic lines. In nearby Yugoslavia, violent ethnic conflict and

---

1. Philip Roeder popularized the term "ethnofederalism" in "Soviet Federalism and Ethnic Mobilization," *World Politics* 43, no. 2 (January 1991): 196–233.

war loomed. The Russian state, for its part, identified—and as part of the Soviet Union had itself reified over time—more than one hundred ethnic minorities. Russia also contained over twenty ethnically defined subfederal territories. An outbreak of ethnic violence there, given the country's enormous nuclear arsenal, could have produced untold destruction. At the time, Russian leaders and Western observers alike feared that Russia would follow the disintegration of the Soviet Union along ethnic lines.[2] Yet such fears were proven wrong. Within a few years ethnofederal implosion had become increasingly unlikely as nationalist separatism in Russia's republics faded away, with the exception of the Republic of Chechnya. Why did mass publics mobilize behind nationalist movements in certain Russian republics but fail to do so in others?[3] Why did some republics mount strong secessionist campaigns against Moscow while others remained quiescent? In this book I examine variation in mass nationalist mobilization and regional secessionism across Russia's republics in order to address one of the thorniest and most undertheorized issues in the literature on nationalism: why ordinary people respond to the appeals of nationalist leaders calling for radical transformation of the status quo.

There is no shortage of studies on the phenomenon of nationalist mobilization, yet most overestimate the power of ethnicity as a basis of political action. Some accounts view ethnic masses as passive actors who automatically respond to the manipulations of ethnic elites; others treat masses as highly likely to support elites when the right combination of economic and political variables is present. They view people with ethnic identities as members of ethnic groups— and ethnic groups as political actors with interests distinct from those of other actors in the same society. In this approach, ethnic groups exist in multiethnic societies as bounded, self-aware actors *prior to* an episode of political mobilization. Thus they respond automatically when a political entrepreneur asserts that national independence serves the interest of the group. In this view, nationalist mobilization is a relatively common outcome.

Yet ethnic groups in plural societies are not simply "there." People may come to develop a sense of solidarity with others and feel that they are part of an ethnic group, but ethnic groups are not entities in the world with a bounded set of

---

2. Boris Yeltsin wrote in his memoirs that "the specter of discord and civil war" threatened Russia and the former USSR. *Prezidentskii marafon* (Moscow: Izdatel'stvo AST, 2000), 62.

3. I rely on John Breuilly's definition of a nationalist political movement as one "justifying [its] action with nationalist arguments." A nationalist argument "is a political doctrine built upon three basic assertions: (a) There exists a nation with an explicit and peculiar character. (b) The interests and values of this nation take priority over all other interests and values. (c) The nation must be as independent as possible. This usually requires at least the attainment of political sovereignty." John Breuilly, *Nationalism and the State* (Chicago: University of Chicago Press, 1994), 2.

interests.[4] Because ethnic identities are socially salient categories for the subjects of study and because those subjects themselves reify ethnic groups, analysts tend to take ethnic groups as social givens; they tend to adopt their subjects' categories as their own.[5] Ethnic identities are a social reality for many people and have real effects on outcomes, but this does not mean that people with ethnic affiliations constitute a group with common interests and a sense of political destiny prior to a moment of political mobilization. Instead, a sense of "groupness"[6] comes into being as a result of a political process. The process of nationalist mobilization transforms previous meanings of ethnic identity in a particular society into something that denotes a cultural community deserving control of its own state. It is political mobilization itself that makes people start to categorize themselves as being on one or another side of a group boundary and to perceive information in terms of how it affects their group.[7]

This means that whereas certain political and economic conditions may establish an environment that offers incentives for political leaders to play the ethnic card, mass nationalism does not automatically spring from these conditions. Rather, nationalist mobilization occurs when political and economic conditions become imbued with particular kinds of meanings at the microlevel. These meanings are not self-evident; it takes intentional action by political entrepreneurs to portray a given set of conditions in a way that connects to the lived experiences of ordinary people. Nationalist entrepreneurs must define the ethnic group that they seek to represent as an organic body that is a victim of forces beyond its control. They must attribute blame for that victimization to current circumstances or political authorities. Nationalists must articulate a position that makes the solution to the problem—establishing a nation-state—look like the only and essential way to redress group victimization and an unjust status quo. Finally, this message has to resonate with people's lived experiences. When it does, a sense of nationhood can develop rapidly and nationalist mobilization may occur. But it is also possible, or even likely, that people who identify with a particular ethnic identity never come to see themselves as part of a victimized

---

4. As Rogers Brubaker states, nations should not be understood as "real entities...as substantial, enduring, internally homogenous and externally bounded collectivities." See "Myths and Misconceptions in the Study of Nationalism," in *The State of the Nation,* ed. John A. Hall (Cambridge: Cambridge University Press, 1998), 292.

5. Rogers Brubaker, *Ethnicity without Groups* (Cambridge, Mass.: Harvard University Press, 2004).

6. Brubaker employs this term ibid., 4.

7. As Craig Calhoun argues, "[I]dentity is not a static pre-existing condition that can be seen as exerting a causal influence on collective action; at both personal and collective levels, it is a changeable product of collective action." "The Problem of Identity in Collective Action," in *Macro-Micro Linkages in Sociology,* ed. Joan Huber (London: Sage, 1991), 51.

group. They do not place blame on other actors for conditions facing the group and thus do not view control of the state as a necessity. In this case, support for nationalism never gets off the ground. Both of these phenomena—mass nationalist mobilization and the absence of mass mobilization despite the appeals of nationalist leaders—took place in Russia's republics. In short, mass nationalism is a political process, not a fixed set of preferences on the part of people who maintain ethnic identities. Nationalism can come and go while ethnic identities remain strong and deeply felt.

In several of Russia's republics, mass nationalism developed out of the interaction between people's experiences in local labor markets and issue framings articulated by ethnic entrepreneurs. Nationalist entrepreneurs articulated issues about what I call *ethnic economic inequality*. They described obstacles to economic achievement facing members of titular ethnic groups[8] by claiming that ethnic Russians held the most prestigious jobs and enjoyed access to desirable resources, while titulars were concentrated in low-status jobs or rural economies. At first glance this looks like a standard story of nationalist politics: inequality develops among communities in a given society; one community becomes aware of its subordinate position and mobilizes to rectify the inequality by establishing its own nation-state. A closer look at labor markets and Soviet state policies, however, indicates that not only did people with titular identities face relatively few obstacles to achievement, but in fact titulars had achieved considerable occupational success during the Soviet era. Thus titular nationalities in the late 1980s could be considered either subordinate to or more privileged than Russians. On the one hand, titulars were subordinate: they held a larger portion of rural agricultural jobs than ethnic Russians while Russians occupied the most prestigious positions in republican economies. On the other hand, titulars were privileged: they had undergone significant socioeconomic mobility as a result of the Soviet state's *korenizatsiia*, or affirmative action policies, and had moved into urban factory jobs and white-collar positions. So economic conditions in the republics during the late glasnost period and early post-Soviet period can be (and were) interpreted in multiple ways.[9]

In republics where nationalist entrepreneurs articulated issues concerning ethnic economic inequality, they were able to attract a substantial degree of popular support even though their claims did not accurately portray the socioeconomic opportunities open to titular nationalities. However, in republics where nationalists focused on articulating other issues, including cultural and language

---

8. The term "titular" denotes the ethnic group for which the republic is named—e.g., Tatars in Tatarstan.

9. *Glasnost* refers to Gorbachev's policy of intellectual openness.

issues, they failed to win popular support. Mass nationalist mobilization took place only in those republics where nationalist entrepreneurs put forward ethnified framings of economic issues.

The experience of nationalist leaders in Russia suggests that ethnic entrepreneurs face considerable constraints. They cannot easily or mechanically attract support from ordinary people who share their ethnic identity by assuming that as coethnics they have common interests. Yet at the same time, economic issues do not work mobilizational magic. There are limits to the kinds of claims nationalists can make about economic inequality. Nationalist leaders in Russia were able to attract mass support in certain republics because their framing of issues of ethnic economic inequality resonated with people's anxieties about job insecurity in an economy undergoing severe crisis.

In the late 1980s the Soviet economy entered a massive recession. Economic production began to contract throughout the country. At the same time, perestroika-era reforms introduced shortages of consumer goods, long lines for food, and the beginnings of unemployment.[10] Soviet citizens who had become accustomed to state-provided educations, jobs, and occupational security in an expanding economy found the new conditions tremendously unsettling. As more citizens than ever before were obtaining education and training to work in an industrialized economy, people began to sense a tightening of labor opportunities. Massive fear of unemployment set in. Against this background, the nationalists' story of titular underrepresentation and blocked opportunity in local economies persuaded people with titular identities to interpret their experiences and feelings of job insecurity in ethnic terms—as something related to the fortunes of the ethnic group. Nationalist entrepreneurs alleged that titulars were socioeconomically subordinate to Russians and depicted them as *victims*. Then they placed the *blame* for this situation on a discriminatory state. Finally they offered a *solution* by claiming that attaining republican sovereignty would eliminate oppression and restore justice.[11] Nationalists connected people's ethnic identity to their material interest in a desirable job and to their sense of self-worth concerning their socioeconomic status. They helped to define individual interests by linking personal life chances to the fate of the nation. Even though the frame of ethnic economic inequality was not entirely accurate, the fact of rising job insecurity

---

10. Perestroika refers to Gorbachev's policies of economic and political restructuring.

11. The social movements literature identifies these three dimensions of victimhood, blame, and solution as critical to issue framing. See David A. Snow and Robert D. Benford, "Master Frames and Cycles of Protest," in *Frontiers in Social Movement Theory,* ed. Aldon Morris and Carol McClurg (New Haven: Yale University Press, 1992), 137; and Robert D. Benford and David A. Snow, "Framing Processes and Social Movements: An Overview and Assessment," *Annual Review of Sociology* 26 (2000): 611–39.

in a contracting, centrally planned economy made people receptive to it. Thus a group grievance developed, crystallizing a sense of ethnic nationhood among people with titular identities and inspiring them to support the call to replace the status quo with a new, national order. The framework developed in this book focuses on how a dynamic interaction between economic structures, the experiences of ordinary people, and the discourse of political entrepreneurs produces group grievances that inspire support for nationalist transformation.

The Puzzle of Nationalism in Russia's Republics

On a campaign swing through Kazan, Tatarstan, in 1990, Boris Yeltsin told that republic's residents, "Take as much sovereignty as you can swallow."[12] At the time, demands for sovereignty were radiating from the autonomous republics inside the Russian Soviet Federative Socialist Republic (RSFSR) to Moscow. The Soviet Union collapsed a year later, and Yeltsin, who had since become president of the new Russian Federation, inherited one of Mikhail Gorbachev's most intractable problems. As he struggled to consolidate control of the central state, several of Russia's republics stepped up their demands on Moscow for sovereignty. They asserted control over natural resources, defied federal laws, and introduced republican presidencies. The decisions some republics made to boycott federal elections, stop paying federal taxes, and hold referenda on "state" sovereignty lent momentum to a process that seemed likely to end in Russia's disintegration.

In several republics, opposition nationalist movements were attracting rising levels of popular support. Crowds grew at street demonstrations, the status of nationalist opposition leaders was rising, and local parliaments adopted legislation that directly challenged Moscow's sovereignty. Nationalist organizations in some of the republics announced that they sought nothing less than independent statehood. Soon radical wings broke off from the main nationalist organizations to promote ethnically exclusivist agendas, sometimes hostile to Russians living in the republics. It looked as if an ethnic outbidding scenario was under way in which ethnic politicians would win mass support by advocating a more ethnically exclusivist program than other politicians and then, once in power, oppress ethnic minorities. Russia's republics seemed about to transform from peaceful, multiethnic societies into ethnically divided, conflict-ridden ones.

The Republic of Tatarstan was one of Russia's most nationalist republics in the early 1990s. With its large population and relatively high level of economic

---

12. E. Chernobrovkina, "Reshat' vam samim" [Decide for Yourselves], *Vecherniaia Kazan'*, August 10, 1990, 1.

development, it was home to a very popular nationalist organization, the Tatar Public Center (TOTs), which had explicitly modeled itself on the Baltic popular-front organizations. TOTs began by calling for the protection of Tatar culture and ended up championing full independence for Tatarstan. In 1991 a radical wing broke off from TOTs and formed Ittifak (Alliance), which promoted an exclusivist nationalist agenda openly hostile to Russians in Tatarstan. As Ittifak attempted to win support away from the moderate Tatars, pro-Russian federalist groups organized in response. Ethnic outbidding by nationalist leaders was taking place, and within Tatarstan secession was being debated as a serious option. Moscow politicians feared that the separation of this republic would produce a domino effect leading to the ethnic unraveling of the fledgling federation. At one point, rumors circulated within Tatarstan that federal troops were being massed at its borders. Yet despite Tatarstan's early and strong mass nationalist mobilization, neither ethnic outbidding nor nationalist secession ultimately took place. Popular support for the nationalist movement weakened. By the mid-1990s, Mintimir Shaimiev, a Soviet-era communist leader, born again to some extent as a Tatar nationalist, managed to consolidate control over republican politics. With the 1994 conclusion of a bilateral treaty between Tatarstan and Moscow, the republic backed away from national secession.

In addition to Tatarstan, only a few of Russia's republics—Tuva and Chechnya, and to a lesser degree Bashkortostan and Yakutia—experienced nationalist mobilization at the mass level. In other republics very little popular nationalist mobilization took place at all. Why? What can account for the short-lived development of mass nationalist mobilization in certain republics, and its virtual absence in others? This book examines these questions through both an in-depth analysis of politics in Tatarstan and a comparative analysis of Russia's fifteen other autonomous republics. Soviet leaders had established the ARs as homelands for certain ethnic groups, although large populations of ethnic Russians lived there as well. The republics looked considerably more like states than the ethnic regions ranked lower in the Soviet Union's administrative hierarchy—the *autonomous oblasts* (regions) and *autonomous okrugs* (districts)—because they had their own legislatures, executives, and judiciaries, as well as flags, constitutions, and some national language education.[13] Also, compared with the lower-ranked ethnic territories, the ARs were allowed greater, albeit symbolic, representation in the federal government and limited rights to set local administrative policy. In this book I compare only those Russian regions that held the status of AR before 1991 in order to hold constant these factors of rights, privileges, and institutional

---

13. In total, twenty-six of Russia's administrative territories were associated with particular ethnic categories, or nationalities, in Soviet parlance.

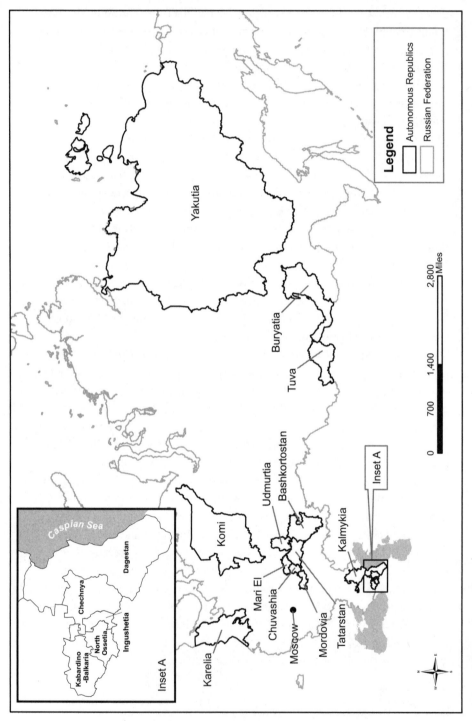

MAP 1.1 Autonomous areas in Russia

development. I also focus on the ARs because they, like Russia's oblasts, were politically more important than lower-level ethnic territories. Thus, I exclude republics that were elevated from autonomous oblast to republic in 1991: Adygei, Gorni Altai, Khakassia, Karachai-Cherkessia, and Ingushetia, which split off from Checheno-Ingushetia in 1992. These republics displayed very little nationalism and therefore add no variation to the original sixteen ARs. The republics analyzed in this book are depicted in Map 1.1.[14]

Competing Explanations of Nationalism in Russia

Political scientists have devoted much attention to explaining the emergence of ethnonationalist separatism across the Soviet space, as well as its ultimate failure in Russia. Historical institutionalist explanations, for example, demonstrate how the Soviet state's nationality policies and ethnofederal structure created ethnic elites in the republics and furnished them with identities, territories, and institutional resources that they would use to forge campaigns for autonomy against Moscow.[15] Another set of studies focuses on macroeconomic factors to explain variation in nationalist separatism across the republics. In this approach, leaders of resource-rich, economically developed republics were motivated by

14. The period of nationalist mobilization analyzed in this book (1989–94) spans the Soviet Union and Russian Federation. Several of the names of the Soviet autonomous republics changed when they became republics in the Russian Federation. For clarity and consistency, I use the post-Soviet names of the republics except when referring to Checheno-Ingushetia before Ingushetia separated from the republic in 1992 and when referring to the republic of Yakutia. Yakutia changed its name to the Sakha Republic (Yakutia) when it declared sovereignty in 1990. I employ the more widely known terms Yakutia and Yakuts.

15. Rogers Brubaker, *Nationalism Reframed: Nationhood and the National Question in the New Europe* (Cambridge: Cambridge University Press, 1996); Valerie Bunce, *Subversive Institutions: The Design and the Destruction of Socialism and the State* (New York: Cambridge University Press, 1999); Svante E. Cornell, "Autonomy as a Source of Conflict: Caucasian Conflicts in Theoretical Perspective," *World Politics* 54, no. 2 (January 2002): 245–76; Carol Skalnik Leff, "Democratization and Disintegration in Multinational States: The Breakup of the Communist Federations," *World Politics* 51, no. 2 (January 1999): 205–35; Juan Linz and Alfred Stepan, "Political Identities and Electoral Sequences: Spain, the Soviet Union, and Yugoslavia," *Deadalus* 122, no. 2 (Spring 1992): 123–39; Philip Roeder, *Where Nation-States Come From: Institutional Change in the Age of Nationalism* (Princeton: Princeton University Press, 2007); "Soviet Federalism," 196–233, and "The Triumph of Nation-States: Lessons from the Collapse of the Soviet Union, Yugoslavia and Czechoslovakia," in *After the Collapse of Communism: Comparative Lessons of Transition,* ed. Michael McFaul and Kathryn Stoner-Weiss (New York: Cambridge University Press, 2004); Ronald Suny, *The Revenge of the Past: Nationalism, Revolution and the Collapse of the Soviet Union* (Stanford, Calif.: Stanford University Press, 1993). Henry Hale also emphasizes institutional structure, arguing that the existence of a core ethnic region—the Russian republic—facilitated the USSR's collapse, while the lack of a core ethnic region ensured Russia's survival. "The Makeup and Breakup of Ethnofederal States: Why Russia Survives Where the USSR Fell," *Perspectives on Politics* 3, no. 1 (March 2005): 55–70.

their republics' wealth to demand greater sovereignty, while leaders of poorer, economically dependent republics remained quiescent.[16] One variant of these "wealth" hypotheses argues that the Russian Federation, unlike the Soviet Union, survived as an ethnofederal state because Moscow appeased the wealthiest, most separatist republics with economic transfers and bilateral treaties granting increased autonomy.[17] Still other studies account for the weak degree of nationalism in most Russian republics by pointing to factors such as ethnic demography and the administrative status of federal regions. Demographic explanations maintain that the proportionally larger number of ethnic Russians in Russia's republics than in the union republics made the former less likely to support nationalism.[18] The administrative-status approach contends that Russia's lower-status ARs had fewer privileges, rights, and ethnic institutions than the URs and thus were less likely to identify as independent states.[19]

---

16. Kisangani Emizet and Vicki Hesli, "The Disposition to Secede: An Analysis of the Soviet Case," *Comparative Political Studies* 27, no. 4 (January 1995): 493–536; Daniel Treisman, "Russia's 'Ethnic Revival': The Separatist Activism of Regional Leaders in a Postcommunist Order," *World Politics* 49 (January 1997): 212–49; Henry Hale, "The Parade of Sovereignties: Testing Theories of Secession in the Soviet Setting," *British Journal of Political Science* 30 (2000): 31–56; Henry Hale and Rein Taagepera, "Russia: Consolidation or Collapse?" *Europe-Asia Studies* 54, no. 7 (November 2002): 1101–25; Kathryn Stoner-Weiss, "Federalism and Regionalism," in *Developments in Russian Politics 4*, ed. Stephen White, Alex Pravda, and Zvi Gitelman (Durham, N.C.: Duke University Press, 1997), 239; James Hughes, "From Federalism to Recentralization," *Developments in Russian Politics 5*, ed. Stephen White, Alex Pravda, and Zvi Gitelman (Durham, N.C.: Duke University Press, 1998), 134. For a new, more nuanced approach that emphasizes the importance of regions' assessments of the risks and benefits of integration versus separation see Henry Hale, *The Foundations of Ethnic Politics: Separatism of States and Nations in Eurasia and the World* (New York: Cambridge University Press, 2008).

17. Steven Solnick, "Will Russia Survive? Center and Periphery in the Russian Federation," in *Post-Soviet Political Order: Conflict and State-Building*, ed. Barnett R. Rubin and Jack Snyder (London: Routledge, 1998), 58–80; Mikhail Alexseev, "Decentralization Versus State Collapse: Explaining Russia's Endurance," *Journal of Peace Research* 38, no. 1 (2001): 101–6; Daniel Treisman, *After the Deluge: Regional Crises and Political Consolidation in Russia* (Ann Arbor: University of Michigan Press, 1999).

18. Gail Lapidus and Edward W. Walker, "Nationalism, Regionalism, and Federalism: Center-Periphery Relations in Post-Communist Russia," in *The New Russia: Troubled Transformation*, ed. Gail Lapidus (Boulder: Westview, 1995), 79–113; Gail Lapidus, "Asymmetrical Federalism and State Breakdown in Russia," *Post-Soviet Affairs* 15, no. 1 (1999): 74–82. Also see Hughes "From Federalism to Recentralization," 131–34.

19. Mikhail A. Alexseev, "Asymmetric Russia: Promises and Dangers," in *Center-Periphery Conflict in Post-Soviet Russia: A Federation Imperiled*, ed. Mikhail A. Alexseev (New York: St. Martin's, 1999), 247–79; Lapidus, "Asymmetrical Federalism," 75; Hale, "Parade of Sovereignties," 48–49; Treisman, "Russia's 'Ethnic Revival,'" 229–30. In a different vein, Stephen Hanson argues that the ideological shift from Marxism-Leninism to democracy as the Russian Federation formed made it harder for people in Russia's republics to oppose Moscow than during the Soviet era. He also argues that secessionism in Russia was hampered by a lack of support from international actors, especially the United States. "Ideology, Interests, and Identity: Comparing the Soviet and Russian Secession Crises," in Alexseev, *Center-Periphery Conflict*, 15–46.

Although most of these explanations have advanced our understanding, they share three main shortcomings. First, many studies focus on the presence or absence of structural variables, arguing that the right combination of variables or the correct set of economic and political conditions will spark mass nationalism. This approach reifies ethnic groups and overestimates the likelihood of nationalist mobilization. Second, most accounts focus almost exclusively on elite actors and especially on the role of regional leaders. They valuably delineate how regional leaders manipulated ethnic identify for strategic reasons yet assume that these leaders acted autonomously within the republics and fomented mass nationalism to strengthen their negotiating position with Moscow. In this view, leaders act strategically while masses act out of a sincere commitment to nationalism—an approach that essentializes ethnic populations. Third, few studies sufficiently account for empirical variation in levels of separatism across all the ethnic republics of either the Russian Federation or the Soviet Union.[20] Studies that focus on structural economic and political variables to explain empirical variation fail to recognize how the massive political transformations occurring at the time affected both mass and elite actors within the republics and therefore republican relations with Moscow. They overlook how popular mobilization in certain republics pressured regional leaders and drove secessionist campaigns toward Moscow.[21] Finally, virtually no existing studies offer a comparative account of the rise of mass nationalism across all the republics, though ethnic politics continues to be a central issue in Russia.[22]

Much of this critique is not unique to post-Soviet politics. Generally, in analyses of multiethnic societies, observers tend to naturalize the existence of bounded ethnic groups and view them as easily triggered into political action along ethnic lines. Though most observers now recognize the constructed origins of ethnic groups, some erroneously treat these groups as coherent actors moving forward through time from the moment of their "construction," typically thought to have occurred in the early twentieth century. My argument in this book, by contrast, is that people with ethnic affiliations do not constitute an interest group that endures over time.

---

20. I provide evidence for each of these claims in chapter 2.

21. I elaborate on this point in chapter 7. Some accounts also assume that the union republics were more nationalist than the ARs, when actually popular support for nationalism was stronger in certain Russian republics than in Belarus and Central Asia.

22. An important exception is Mark Beissinger's study that addresses variation in nationalist mobilization in the ARs, although it focuses principally on the union republics of the USSR. *Nationalist Mobilization and the Collapse of the Soviet State* (Cambridge: Cambridge University Press, 2002). Dmitry Gorenburg examines mass nationalism in Russia but concentrates on explaining the origins of mobilization in four republics. See *Minority Ethnic Mobilization in the Russian Federation* (New York: Cambridge University Press, 2003).

In Russia, people with Russian and titular identities were not separate, self-enclosed communities who got along at some points in time and came into conflict at others. Like most ethnically heterogeneous societies around the world, Russian republics were not societies divided along ethnic lines. To assert that boundaries enclosing ethnic groups are porous and blurry means, first, that individual "members" of ethnic groups have many experiences in common with "members" of other groups. For example, titulars and Russians attended the same schools, lived in the same neighborhoods,[23] and shopped for the same consumer goods.[24] They worked in the same factories,[25] traveled to work on the same public transportation, and listened to the same state-controlled media. In the cities of most republics, linguistic differences did not reinforce a boundary between Russians and titulars since many titulars had learned Russian by the 1970s and 1980s.[26]

Second, porous group boundaries allow members of ethnic groups to maintain other kinds of social identities besides ethnicity. Soviet citizens were categorized, for example, by class and profession, gender, region of birth, generation, and Communist Party membership. They identified variously as World War II veterans; *shestidesyatniki,* or members of the 1960s generation; *odnokursniki,* or classmate cohort; and rural dweller—an important social category in Soviet society.[27] Rural dwellers themselves held multiple identities, some of which overlapped with ethnicity (village of birth; *te'ip,* or clan, in the Caucasus; linguistic and religious affiliation) and some of which did not (*kolkhozniki,* or state farm workers; teachers, doctors, or other representatives of the creative intelligentsia; and religious affiliation). Additionally, in the late 1980s, glasnost offered people new kinds of identities: environmentalist, feminist, antinuclear activist, democrat, and of course nationalist.

The fact that Soviet citizens with ethnic affiliations had multiple identities and shared many experiences with Russians and others does not mean that they had assimilated to a Soviet nation (*Sovetskii narod*). Ethnicity was socially salient, and generally people were aware of one another's ethnic affiliations—even

---

23. For example, even in the so-called Tatar neighborhood of Kazan, Russians, Tatars, and other nationalities lived side by side. That designation referred to the distant past when Tatars lived and worshipped at mosques there.

24. There were exceptions in rural regions in certain republics where titulars lived in concentrated numbers. However, in most rural areas in most republics, Russians lived alongside titulars.

25. Soviet work collectives generally were not divided along ethnic lines. Exceptions consisted of specialized institutions created to promote titular art, knowledge, and culture and some shops in the cities where titular clerks worked after migrating from rural areas.

26. There is some variation on this dimension among Russia's republics—a subject I address in chapter 3.

27. Rural dwellers were sometimes referred to as representatives of "a different culture." Field notes, Kazan, Tatarstan, 1997. I discuss rural identity and culture in chapter 3.

when physical appearance or linguistic and cultural practices did not obviously mark differences. In many places people held stereotyped views of minority nationalities, and marriage across ethnic boundaries rarely occurred. In short, ethnicity was felt, recognized by others, and expressed in various ways, a fact that demonstrated the success of the Soviet state in constructing and reifying ethnic categories.

But this does not mean that titulars and Russians experienced political and economic conditions differently. Thus an exogenous event like the opening of political opportunity that took place during glasnost or a dramatic downturn in the economy did not cause titulars to suddenly realize that they were subjugated and could "do better" in a sovereign state. In other words, structural conditions shape individuals' experiences and emotions but do not spontaneously establish ethnic groups with systematically opposed interests and preferences.

A sense of groupness comes into being as a result of the process of political mobilization itself. Mobilization transforms the meaning of ethnic identity in a particular society into a shared sense of nationhood defined by a belief that the nation deserves to control its own state. People start to categorize themselves as being part of a nation and to perceive information in terms of how it affects that nation. As a result, support for nationalism develops. A sense of groupness or nationhood, however, is fragile and can rapidly fall apart.

Why Ordinary People Respond to Nationalist Leaders

Nationalism entails a radical reordering of society and state; it "redefines the nature of legitimate political authority," in Breuilly's words.[28] Nationalist movements seek to mobilize the masses behind a *new* national community with *new* political leadership. Thus nationalist mobilization means that people act in opposition to something—the ethnic other, the central state, or the current political order. In order to act *against,* people must have a strong sense of grievance, or resentment and dissatisfaction concerning important aspects of their present situation. A grievance may be described as the feeling of having been wronged, as distinguished from the actual or supposed circumstances, acts, or events that are believed responsible for that feeling.

Several influential theories of political mobilization assume that group grievances directly reflect objective economic and political conditions, historical

---

28. Breuilly, *Nationalism and the State*, 25.

events, or other social structures, and therefore they do not analyze the formation of those grievances. Social scientists have focused much attention, for example, on economic inequality as the basis of group grievance and people's desire for sovereign statehood.[29] Ernst Gellner points to the effect of uneven modernization on groups that are culturally different from the economically dominant or state-bearing population.[30] Michael Hechter shows how internal colonialism and a cultural division of labor raise people's awareness of discrimination and central state economic exploitation.[31] Resource competition theorists argue that industrialization encourages competition for common resources such as jobs, which increases group solidarity among cultural minorities.[32] Recent accounts of nationalism in Russia that emphasize the variable of republican wealth make the same kind of argument: that the uneven distribution of economic resources in society arouses discontent, inspiring groups to support nationalism.[33]

More broadly, recent research on rebellion and ethnic civil war also views grievances as a direct response to objective conditions in society but discounts their causal influence in motivating rebel leaders and their followers.[34] Cross-national studies by Paul Collier, Anke Hoeffler, David Laitin, and Jim Fearon measure grievance by observing the presence of specific structural factors such as income inequality, autocracy, and state regulation of religious activity.[35] This

---

29. Political science has a long tradition of explaining mass mobilization in general by emphasizing economic adversity. For example, Samuel Huntington argued that inequitable land ownership and poverty produce suffering and discontent, which lead to peasant revolution in *Political Order in Changing Societies* (New Haven: Yale University Press, 1968), 375. Also see Edward N. Muller and Mitchell A. Seligson, "Inequality and Insurgency," *American Political Science Review* 81 (1987): 425–52.

30. See Ernst Gellner, *Thought and Change* (London: Weidenfeld and Nicolson, 1964) and *Nations and Nationalism* (Ithaca: Cornell University Press, 1983).

31. Hechter, *Internal Colonialism: The Celtic Fringe in British National Development, 1536–1966* (Berkeley: University of California Press, 1975), and "Group Formation and the Cultural Division of Labor," *American Journal of Sociology* 84 (1978): 293–318. Similarly, Donald Horowitz made strong claims about the likelihood of a backward group in a backward region to secede. Horowitz, "Patterns of Ethnic Separatism," *Comparative Studies in Society and History* 23 (1981): 165–95, and *Ethnic Groups in Conflict* (Berkeley: University of California Press, 1985).

32. Francois Nielsen, "Toward a Theory of Ethnic Solidarity in Modern Societies" *American Sociological Review* 50 (1985): 133–49, and "The Flemish Movement in Belgium after World War II: A Dynamic Analysis," *American Sociological Review* 45 (1980): 76–94.

33. See Emizet and Hesli, "The Disposition to Secede," Treisman, "Russia's 'Ethnic Revival,'" and Hale, "Parade of Sovereignties." I discuss these accounts in chapter 2.

34. James D. Fearon and David D. Laitin, "Ethnicity, Insurgency, and Civil War," *American Political Science Review* 97, no. 1 (February 2003): 79; Paul Collier and Anke Hoeffler, "Greed and Grievance in Civil War," *Oxford Economic Papers* 56, no. 4 (October 2004): 563–95.

35. For example, Collier uses the Gini coefficient as a proxy measure of the grievance of income inequality and whether a state is an autocracy as a proxy measure of political repression in examining 161 states with 78 civil wars. Collier and Hoeffler, 570–72. Fearon and Laitin conceptualize grievance as resentment produced by state discrimination and measure it using state regulation of religious and

approach treats grievance as both objective structures *and* people's attitudes about those structures without considering what people themselves make of conditions in their society.[36] The authors find that the structural factors (i.e., grievances) are present in many states and are not correlated with rebellion. They therefore conclude that since all societies have groups with grievances, it is not the grievances that explain mass mobilization.[37] Their investigations turn away from analyzing grievance and toward other explanations. Resource mobilization theory makes similar assumptions about grievances, viewing discontent and psychological alienation as constants that help to motivate mass mobilization or social movement participation. Since resource mobilization theory considers grievances background conditions, it focuses analytical attention on how access to resources, organizational skills, and the political opportunity structure influences mobilization.[38]

These accounts devote little analytical attention to grievances because they assume that people react in an unmediated way to inegalitarian economic realities. They assume that people who are subject to, for example, economic inequality or political exclusion perceive their situation the way an outside observer would. Conceptualizing grievance in this way ignores the content of mass beliefs and attitudes or worse, accepts statements made by nationalist leaders as direct representations of mass attitudes.[39] It fails to observe how the people in a given society

missionary activity and state denial of official recognition to minority languages, as well as the Gini coefficient to indicate income inequality. Fearon and Laitin, *Ethnicity, Insurgency and Civil War,* 79.

36. Paul Collier, "Doing Well out of War: An Economic Perspective," in *Greed and Grievance: Economic Agendas in Civil Wars,* ed. Mats R. Berdal and David M. Malone(Boulder: Lynne Rienner, 2000), 91–111.

37. David Laitin argues elsewhere that latent ethnic grievances *do* motivate insurgents toward violent rebellion against the state but only when they become "vital and manifest." Grievances exist in latent form everywhere, he argues (e.g., resentments or hatreds among Russian speakers in both Transdniestria in Moldova and northeast Estonia) but only sometimes are associated with ethnic violence. It is the various effects of central state weakness that cause latent grievances to become manifest and spark ethnic violence. See Laitin, *Nations, States, and Violence* (New York: Oxford University Press, 2007), chapter 1.

38. See Craig J. Jenkins and Charles Perrow, "Insurgency of the Powerless: Farm Worker Movements (1964–1972)," *American Sociological Review* 42 (1977): 249–68; John D. McCarthy and Mayer N. Zald, "Resource Mobilization and Social Movements: A Partial Theory," *American Journal of Sociology* 82 (1977): 1212–41; Anthony Oberschall, *Social Conflict and Social Movements* (Englewood Cliffs, N.J.: Prentice-Hall, 1973); and Charles Tilly, *From Mobilization to Revolution* (Reading, Mass.: Addison Wesley, 1978), cited in David Snow, E. Burke Rochford, Jr., Steven K. Worden, and Robert D. Benford, "Frame Alignment Processes, Micromobilization, and Movement Participation," *American Sociological Review,* 51, no. 4 (August 1986): 464–81.

39. Ted Gurr's relative deprivation framework—though it recognizes that the existence of economic deprivation does not always produce a perception of inequality among people—codes the presence of group grievance by observing statements made by movement leaders. See Gurr and United States Institute of Peace, *Minorities at Risk: A Global View of Ethnopolitical Conflicts* (Washington, D.C.: United States Institute of Peace Press, 1993), 61, 68–72; Gurr, *Peoples versus States:*

actually understand the conditions in which they find themselves and thus over-estimates or miscalculates the likelihood of mass nationalism.

Inequality and hierarchy among collectivities are ubiquitous; events occur, and economic, political, and social arrangements exist in most societies that outside observers would characterize as unequal and unjust. But do people living in those societies also see their situation in this way? There are many places with impoverished groups and highly inegalitarian conditions where people do not feel that things have become intolerable, do not blame the state or another group, and do not mobilize for change.[40] Group grievances, in other words, do not unproblematically arise from all manner of structurally unequal conditions. To assume that aggrieved groups are found everywhere that inequalities exist "avoids the enormous variability in the subjective meanings people attach to their objective situations."[41]

In order to understand why group grievances develop that inspire support for nationalism, we need to know more than the objective political and economic conditions that leave certain people disadvantaged. We need to know how actors themselves—both mass and elite—understand their situation. People do not have automatic, unmediated understandings of economic and political conditions, historical events, or other social structures. There are numerous ways in which they may interpret a given set of circumstances in their society.

The argument that there are multiple interpretations of economic and political realities is not a new one. Social theorists have long argued that experience cannot be apprehended apart from interpretation. The constructivist turn in the nationalism literature has focused on how elites construct a nationalist discourse around invented national histories and symbolic events.[42] Social movement theorists have shown how movement leaders frame ideas to influence mass behavior.[43] But few studies of nationalism have investigated how economic

---

Minorities at Risk in the New Century (Washington, D.C.: United States Institute of Peace Press, 2000); and Gurr and Woodrow Wilson School of Public and International Affairs, *Why Men Rebel* (Princeton: Princeton University Press, 1970), 24.

40. Assimilation rather than mobilization by poor, discriminated-against minority immigrants in the United States suggests just one example.

41. Social movements theorists Snow, Rochford, Worden, and Benford, "Frame Alignment Processes," 465–66, make this criticism of the resource mobilization approach.

42. Eric Hobsbawm and Terence Ranger, eds., *The Invention of Tradition* (New York: Cambridge University Press, 1992); Breuilly, *Nationalism and the State;* M. Crawford Young, *The Politics of Cultural Pluralism* (Madison: University of Wisconsin Press, 1976), and "The National and Colonial Question and Marxism: A View from the South," in *Thinking Theoretically about Soviet Nationalities,* ed. Alexander Motyl, 67–97 (New York: Columbia University Press, 1992); Jack Snyder, *From Voting to Violence: Democratization and Nationalist Conflict* (New York: Norton, 2000).

43. For example, see Mayer N. Zald, "Culture, Ideology and Strategic Framing," in *Comparative Perspectives on Social Movements, ed.* Doug McAdam, John D. McCarthy, and Mayer N. Zald (Cambridge: Cambridge University Press, 1996), 262–74.

conditions and structures are themselves subject to interpretation by ordinary people and elites. Thus they miss an opportunity to investigate how elite framing of economic conditions shapes mass-level group grievances that create a sense of nationhood.[44]

How, then, do ethnic grievances develop? I argue that they are constructed through an interactive process between elite actors and ordinary people in which elites imbue economic conditions and structures with ethnic meanings. Ethnic entrepreneurs depict economic conditions as unfairly consigning people with ethnic identities to a subordinate position in society. They place blame for that inequality on current political authorities, and they suggest that the solution to the injustice entails acquiring state sovereignty or independence. Ordinary people, however, are not automatically convinced by elite declarations that conditions in their society are unequal and discriminate against a particular ethnic group. Rather, they begin to view economic inequalities in ethnic terms when the particular way in which an issue is framed resonates with experiences that concern their occupations, social mobility, and socioeconomic status.

Why are these kinds of experiences in particular related to ethnic grievance and political mobilization? Jobs, professional mobility, and socioeconomic status fundamentally concern individuals' material interests and, in the context of late-twentieth-century industrialized society, their sense of self-worth. Many people around the world care deeply about these forms of self-interest. Thus they are likely to be receptive to a framing of local economic conditions that links personal material achievement to the fate of the ethnic nation. Nationalist entrepreneurs—in claiming that current conditions do not offer equal economic opportunity to the ethnic nation—convey to individuals that they are denied material success because of their ethnic identity. Nationalists argue that the future life chances of individuals will be determined by whether the existing order can be replaced with one in which their group faces no obstacles to socioeconomic achievement. An ethnic grievance develops when people with ethnic identities come to share the belief that the economic inequality the nationalists describe exists and harms them personally because of their ethnic affiliation.

Can ethnic entrepreneurs construct group grievances that are utterly divorced from objective conditions? I argue that the answer to this is no; there are limits to the creative abilities of elites. If a large empirical disconnect exists between people's experiences and elites' descriptions of ethnic economic inequalities, individuals will not be convinced that their personal interests are tied up with the

---

44. This is not true of Mark Beissinger's framework, which emphasizes human agency and event, as well as preexisting structures to explain the contingent nature of mass nationalism. See *Nationalist Mobilization.*

position of the ethnic group, and the nationalists' narrative will seem an irrelevant (or even ridiculous) depiction of local conditions. Nationalists will lose credibility, and group grievances will fail to emerge. Therefore, both the *kinds* of issues entrepreneurs articulate and the way in which they frame those issues matter to the construction of group grievance because the issues must plausibly map onto central experiences in people's lives. As with economic issues, if elites describe inequality and discrimination related to religious or cultural issues associated with an ethnic minority, people will not necessarily respond unless those issues map onto some aspect of their lived experiences. In Russia's republics, given the particular legacies of Soviet secularization, cultural homogenization, and Russification, issues of economic inequality were generally more likely to resonate with a greater number of citizens than were those concerning the denial of religious and cultural rights.[45]

The fact that nationalist leaders cannot automatically attract support by describing just any issue as an instance of ethnic discrimination drains them of some of the power they are often thought to exert over ethnic masses. It also suggests that nationalists should not necessarily be viewed as exclusively strategic actors, cynically manipulating issues that they know will evoke a response. They often earnestly believe in the ideas they articulate and communicate them to the masses as sincere descriptions of the way they understand societal conditions. In Russia, nationalist leaders acted both expressively and strategically.

Ethnic entrepreneurs in the republics perceived titulars to be subordinate to Russians in local labor markets and overlooked titular mobility for several reasons. First, as titulars, nationalists could base their understanding of current conditions on their interpretation of their own family history. They could think about their own, their parents', or their grandparents' background growing up in the countryside and working on the land, and they often still had relatives living and working in rural regions. If they did not know any rural Russians, they might assume that all Russians came from an urban background. Furthermore, in many though not all republics, Russians occupied more blue-collar factory jobs than titulars who tended to work in nonindustrial settings. According to Soviet norms, industry was viewed as higher status than most other spheres of the economy. So even if titulars did not choose to work as an assembly line worker, for example, it is likely that they viewed such work as more prestigious than nonindustrial jobs requiring similar education and training. Second, ethnic entrepreneurs, many of whom were intellectuals, may have been predisposed to view the central state—i.e., Moscow and the Communist Party—in negative

---

45. I elaborate on this point in chapter 2 and describe various kinds of ethnic issues articulated by nationalists in subsequent chapters.

terms, like intellectuals living throughout the USSR in the late Soviet era. There-fore, ethnic entrepreneurs could not recognize or appreciate the beneficial effects of the state's economic policies, such as affirmative action and titular mobility. Finally, in most cases ethnic entrepreneurs came from the highly educated stra-tum of society. As professionals, they cared deeply about occupational status and achievement. It is not surprising that they considered issues of professional rep-resentation crucial to the current and future position of the ethnic group.

In fact, the nationalists' attention to issues of economic inequality reveals just how much they were products of the very Soviet state whose authority they were trying to undermine. Their focus on pragmatic issues of professional mobility, equal ethnic group representation, and individual advancement reproduced typ-ical late-Soviet-era ideals. They saw no contradiction in asserting the right to a nation-state in order to realize the goods of modernity as defined by the Soviet state. Like all nationalists, they drew on a range of extant beliefs and practices to construct an idea of national community deserving control of the state. They believed in the ideas that they articulated, understanding them to be accurate and fair descriptions of existing conditions. As sincere and committed actors, the nationalists did not necessarily understand what caused ordinary people to respond to their programs and thus did not strategically choose to focus on one issue frame rather than another. In short, the issues they chose to put forward reflected their worldview and thus involved a good deal of contingency.

Group grievances in Russia developed quickly as part of a contingent process of political mobilization. The longevity of a grievance among a population, often seen as an indication of intensity, is immaterial. What matters is how political en-trepreneurs infuse meaning into people's current experience of social conditions and connect that meaning to the pressing need to challenge political authority. Grievances were no less intensely held by ethnic groups in the republics because they emerged in the space of a few brief years.

My argument contributes to the current framework in political science that emphasizes a disconnect between structural conditions and people's perceptions of the economy. This insight—developed in recent work by Yoshiko Herrera and Rawi Abdelal, for example—shifts our focus away from explaining political outcomes using exogenous economic and other structural factors and toward examining how people's economic interests develop out of intersubjective un-derstandings in particular sociopolitical contexts.[46] My approach differs from

---

46. Herrera's book finds that regionalist movements developed in several Russian oblasts in the early 1990s when oblast residents developed certain understandings of their regions' economic interests—understandings that were not based in existing material conditions. In Abdelal's frame-work, national identity explains why Lithuania, Ukraine, and Belarus chose divergent foreign

Herrera's by emphasizing that in order for people to respond to elite programs, elite framings cannot be utterly divorced from actual conditions. By focusing on the particular way in which nationalists use ethnic frames to interpret economic conditions, I provide a mechanism that connects economic structures to group identity and the cohesion of ethnic group interests in support of nationalism.

How Nationalist Grievances Developed in Russia

In Russian republics with significant mass mobilization, nationalist entrepreneurs articulated issues in such a way as to draw boundaries between people with titular and Russian identities. Nationalists claimed that Moscow denied titular nationalities full participation in republican economies by blocking access to desirable jobs and resources. Titulars worked in low-status professions in rural economies, they argued, while Russians enjoyed unrestricted access to higher education and the best jobs. This argument characterized titulars as unjustly second-rate within their own republics. Nationalist entrepreneurs tried to stoke a sense of outrage among people with ethnic identities by articulating the ways in which economic inequalities had turned them into victims. They then placed blame for the titulars' inferior status on current economic conditions and existing political authorities. Only by replacing the current order with a new one in which titulars controlled the state, they argued, could this injustice be rectified. Thus nationalists linked titular group identity to their critical objective: achieving republican sovereignty. Sovereignty, a concept whose meaning was not self-evident, denoted a range of possibilities and in some cases changed over time from increased regional autonomy to outright secession. Nationalist leaders agreed, however, that they could not wait for Moscow to bestow sovereignty upon the republics; they would have to seize it themselves.

It is critical to note that the nationalists' message of titular economic subordination vis-à-vis Russians did not directly reflect the position of titular populations in republican economies. Although titulars began the twentieth century lagging behind Russians socioeconomically, they took advantage of *korenizatsiia* policies and made enormous strides in professional achievement, especially in the decades after World War II. By the end of the Soviet era, titulars worked beside Russians in factories, economic management, and government administration.

---

economic policies after 1991 despite their common economic dependence on Russia. See Herrera, *Imagined Economies: The Sources of Russian Regionalism* (New York: Cambridge University Press, 2005), and Abdelal, *National Purpose in the World Economy: Post-Soviet States in Comparative Perspective* (Ithaca: Cornell University Press, 2001).

An ethnic division of labor among Russians and titulars in the republics, to the degree that it had ever existed, was breaking down.

On the other hand, there was a kernel of reality in the nationalists' message: titulars *were* to some extent still underrepresented in white-collar jobs in republican urban economies by comparison with Russians. But the nationalists, by presenting a snapshot of socioeconomic conditions as of 1989 rather than describing gains made by titulars over time, could build a convincing case for ethnic inequality. So which view was accurate—titular subordination or titular opportunity and achievement? Both were. I argue that there were multiple legitimate interpretations of conditions in the republics in the late Soviet era. But nationalist leaders could not make a convincing case for state sovereignty by recognizing and thanking the Soviet state for advancing the socioeconomic position of their ethnic group. Instead, they described economic inequality in order to emphasize the victimization of titulars and to appeal for state sovereignty to eradicate that oppression.

The nationalist framing of issues of ethnic economic inequality resonated with the experiences that many people were having at that time. When nationalists described the economic subordination of titulars vis-à-vis Russians in republican economies, many titulars responded because it helped them to make sense of growing competition for jobs and their fears about social mobility in a deteriorating, state-controlled economy. In republics where nationalists articulated issues of ethnic economic inequality, popular support for nationalism developed. Ordinary people with ethnic affiliations responded to nationalist leaders not because their group was objectively socioeconomically subordinate to Russians and angry about it. Titular ethnic groups did not have preexisting economic grievances. They responded because the nationalists' claim of ethnic economic subordination provided people with an explanation for their experiences and anxieties at the time.

The macroeconomic decline that had begun in the Brezhnev era of the 1960s and 1970s accelerated under Gorbachev. Long-term trends in the Soviet Union including urbanization, industrialization, and public education produced growing numbers of people pursuing higher education and good jobs. Then, in the late 1980s, economic production began to contract sharply. People spent hours waiting in lines as food and consumer goods became increasingly scarce. At the same time, Gorbachev's glasnost policies were igniting rapid and transformative change. In 1991 when Yeltsin suddenly freed prices that had remained state-controlled and static for decades, the cost of goods skyrocketed. Amid great economic and political uncertainty, people deeply feared unemployment. They doubted that the state could continue to provide them and their families with educations, secure careers, and professional advancement. Since all people

were in the same listing boat, there is no reason why individuals with ethnic affiliations would necessarily have perceived these experiences as related to their
ethnicity rather than to a shortage of opportunity for everyone. But ethnic entrepreneurs, by describing ethnic economic inequality, channeled these fears in
an ethnic direction.

The nationalist issue frame of ethnic economic inequality seemed plausible to
people. Even if educated titulars did not personally occupy a subordinate position in the labor market, they could accept the veracity of an ethnic division of
labor by thinking about the current precariousness of their position, as well as
their family history in which parents or grandparents lived as uneducated man-
ual laborers in the countryside. The nationalists' description of ethnic economic
inequality was not a phenomenon dreamed up out of the blue but based on an
accurate description of past inequalities among rural and urban populations in
Russia, though not necessarily among titulars and Russians.

Nationalist entrepreneurs also offered a target of blame—current political
authority—as well as a solution to concerns about life chances: achieving sovereignty by capturing the state. Nationalist leaders, in other words, politicized
ethnicity by convincing people to connect personal material interests to one of
their social identities—ethnicity. They persuaded them that their personal life
chances depended on the political fate of their ethnic community.

Nevertheless, there were limits to the influence of nationalist leaders, even
when they employed an ethnic economic inequality frame. First, not all people
with titular identities in the republics were convinced by the nationalist message.
Even in those republics with high mass nationalist mobilization, large numbers
of titulars simply remained agnostic about nationalist sovereignty, and others opposed it. As research on preference formation in American politics has
found, elites do not have unqualified latitude in using frames to manipulate mass
opinion.[47]

Ultimately, in most republics, group grievances that produced a sense of nationhood did not endure. Dramatic changes in economic and political conditions
during the early years of the Russian Federation gave people new experiences. It
can be argued that these experiences reduced the plausibility of the nationalists'
claim that people's personal life chances were connected to the political status of
their ethnic group. Specifically, the end of the Soviet system of central economic
planning ended the state's monopoly over the distribution of jobs. Economic
liberalization began to transform the labor market. More and more people, es-

---

47. James N. Druckman and Arthur Lupia, "Preference Formation" *American Political Science
Review* 3 (2000): 1–24; James N. Druckman, "The Implications of Framing Effects for Citizen Competence," *Political Behavior* 23, no. 3 (September 2001): 225–56.

pecially those with higher education, found new paths to professional mobility outside the state sector. Moreover, the emerging private sector, for the most part, did not take people's ethnicity into account as the Soviet state had with its affirmative action policies. Thus, job allocation changed from an ethnicized process directed by the state to a decentralized process involving a variety of decision makers uninterested in using ethnicity as an allocative rule.[48]

Overall, these developments related to economic liberalization diminished the relevance of the nationalist message about the presence of, and need to remedy, ethnic economic inequality. The supposedly subordinate status of the ethnic group mattered less to people in an economy in which the state did not have the sole power to determine socioeconomic mobility. Thus, capturing the state in the name of the ethnic group—the raison d'être of nationalist movements—became less urgent. As a result, popular support for nationalism declined in most of Russia's republics as the 1990s progressed.

The case of Russia, with its fluctuating and ultimately failed mobilizations, illustrates the point that nationalist mobilization occurs less frequently than is generally thought. Nationalist leaders do not possess some kind of unqualified capacity to "convert" ordinary people into nationalists by channeling socioeconomic grievances that already exist among the masses. Nor do nationalists attract support by making people aware of socioeconomic inequities that structure their lives. As Breuilly argues, "Nationalist ideology matters, not so much because it directly motivates most supporters of a nationalist movement, but rather because it provides a conceptual map which enables people to relate their particular material and moral interests to a broader terrain of action."[49] The fact of nationalist demobilization and the ultimate demise of the nationalist movements in Russia points to the limits of the influence political entrepreneurs have in shaping people's perceptions and political behavior. Overall, my theoretical framework for understanding the relationship of ethnicity to politics joins a growing consensus among social scientists that views ethnic identities in constructivist terms and argues that ethnic affiliations do not easily translate into nationalist mobilization.[50]

48. Viktoria Koroteeva, Ekonomicheskie interesy i natsionalizm [Economic Interests and Nationalism](Moscow: Rossiiskii gosudarstvennyi gumanitarnyi universitet, 2000).

49. Breuilly, Nationalism and the State, 13.

50. For an excellent statement of this position see V. P. Gagnon Jr., The Myth of Ethnic War: Serbia and Croatia in the 1990s (Ithaca: Cornell University Press, 2004). David Laitin also emphasizes the challenges ethnic entrepreneurs face in mobilizing people in Nations, States, and Violence, as does Mark Beissinger in "Nationalisms That Bark and Nationalisms That Bite: Ernest Gellner and the Substantiation of Nations," in Hall, State of the Nation, 169–90. Also see Rogers Brubaker, Margit Feischmidt, Jon Fox, and Liana Grancea, Nationalist Politics and Everyday Ethnicity in a Transylvanian Town (Princeton: Princeton University Press, 2006), and Brubaker, Ethnicity without Groups.

Implications for Understanding Nationalism and Ethnic Politics

This book offers a comparative analysis of the rise of ethnonationalism across Russia's sixteen republics. The enormous variation among the republics despite their common history, political and economic institutions, and shared experience of turbulent change during the Soviet transition presents an interesting set of puzzles. The republics offer a set of conditions that allow us to hold many factors constant in examining these puzzles. Therefore, a systematic comparison of cases characterized by an absence of mass nationalist mobilization justifies a sustained focus on a set of substate regions that rarely make international headlines.[51] Examining the rise of ethnic nationalism also provides new information about how the transition from communist rule proceeded within each subfederal region. Greater insight into political processes within the regions can shed light on present-day politics in the Russian Federation, where relations between the center and region continue to be characterized by a very unstable equilibrium. Finally, the theoretical framework developed in this book has important implications for the broader issue of how identity influences political behavior. This issue is a critical one for policymakers working in multiethnic societies to understand in order to avoid promoting policies that view people with ethnic identities as automatic supporters of nationalist politicians.

The Russian Federation offers a fitting context in which to study nationalism because it has experienced relatively little violence by comparison with other cases such as Yugoslavia and the states of the Caucasus. Violence tends to reify ethnic groups as political actors and harden the boundaries between groups. People who do not perceive information or condition their behavior on ethnic distinctions will often begin to do so after being attacked by a perpetrator who justifies that attack on ethnic grounds.[52] A majority of scholarly studies have focused on multiethnic societies where violence has broken out and group identities have hardened. Yet by examining only these cases, analysts cannot make sense of why people who live in multiethnic societies where ethnicity is socially salient do not mobilize in support of nationalism.[53] By examining Russia, this book presents a corrective to bias in the cases usually selected for analysis and thus provides insight into the general phenomena of nationalism and ethnic politics.

---

51. Rogers Brubaker has called for research on the "weakness of nationalism in certain regions" of the former Soviet Union. "Myths and Misconceptions in the Study of Nationalism," 283.

52. For example, residents of Chechnya, who did not see themselves as part of a national community distinct from other Soviet citizens, began to do so after Moscow decided to bomb cities in Chechnya.

53. James Fearon and David Laitin argue that case selection bias in studies of violent ethnic conflict leads analysts to overpredict the likelihood of ethnic violence. See "Explaining Interethnic Cooperation," *American Political Science Review* 90 (December 1996): 715.

Finally, the findings of this book challenge the idea—put forward in several major political science studies and commonly found in the media—that states undergoing a transition to democracy produce ethnic mobilization and ethnic violence, especially when those states are multiethnic and postcolonial. Transitions from authoritarian rule, to be sure, weaken the central state and shatter existing institutions, thereby creating opportunities for counterelites and opposition figures to mobilize people. Yet there is no a priori reason why ethnicity will be the cleavage along which such mobilizations take place. The supposed incompatibility of democracy and ethnic pluralism is an assumption that results from the failure of many analysts to theorize why ethnic masses follow elites. For example, Jon Elster, Claus Offe, and Ulrich Preuss claim that democratic institutions—such as political parties, free media, and elections—allow polarized groups to introduce fear, distrust, and repression into plural societies and that these in turn engender ethnonationalism and ethnic violence.[54] Jack Snyder and Edward Mansfield maintain that the lack of institutions of democratic accountability in states transitioning from authoritarian rule creates electoral incentives for politicians to mobilize citizens using exclusivist nationalist appeals. Nationalism, Snyder states, is an "easy" and "effective" way to build popular support among a mass public.[55]

I demonstrate, on the contrary, that appeals to nationalism are actually a highly unreliable way for elites to attract popular support. Would-be nationalist leaders in Russia's republics faced significant difficulties in mobilizing ethnic populations despite the presence of conditions—at the international, state, and individual levels—that would seem to have inspired a demand for independent statehood. Individuals with ethnic identities neither automatically nor routinely become nationalist at the command of ethnic entrepreneurs. I find instead that it is possible for individuals to genuinely and intensely identify with a particular ethnicity but neither automatically support a nationalist program nor respond to nationalist elites' appeals for statehood or the subjugation of an ethnic other. The analysis of politics in Russia's sixteen republics demonstrates how difficult it is for nationalist leaders to attract popular support. Once we recognize that ethnic entrepreneurs cannot manipulate coethnics at will, the phenomena of nationalist mobilization and ethnic conflict will become more susceptible to policy solutions.

---

54. Jon Elster, Claus Offe, and Ulrich K. Preuss, *Institutional Design in Post-Communist Societies: Rebuilding the Ship at Sea* (Cambridge: Cambridge University Press, 1998), 250, 252, 254.

55. Edward D. Mansfield and Jack Snyder, *Electing to Fight: Why Emerging Democracies Go to War* (Cambridge. Mass.: MIT Press, 2005); Snyder, *From Voting to Violence;* and Jack Snyder, "Problems of Democratic Transition in Divided Societies," in *Domestic Perspectives on Contemporary Democracy,* ed. Peter F. Nardulli, 15 (Urbana: University of Illinois Press, 2008).

Plan of the Book

In chapter 2 I briefly describe the emergence of opposition nationalist movements in Russia's republics. Then I define the dependent variable of the study by coding Russia's sixteen republics in terms of the level of mass support for nationalism in each of them. This establishes the striking difference in levels of mass nationalism across the republics. The third section of the chapter critically evaluates explanations of nationalist mobilization in the literature on post-Soviet politics in terms of both their logic and their empirical predictions. I systematically evaluate these arguments against evidence from Russia and find that they do not offer sufficient explanations for the emergence of nationalist mobilization or its variance across republics.

In chapter 3, I consider whether adverse economic conditions in republican labor markets at the end of the Soviet era inspired popular support for nationalism. I evaluate the claims of nationalist leaders who maintained that titular minorities were socioeconomically subordinate to Russians within their republics. First, I outline socioeconomic mobility in each of the sixteen republics by presenting Soviet state statistical data on population growth, urbanization, linguistic Russification, education, and occupational representation and find that the data do not present a clear-cut picture. On the one hand titular populations in all republics demonstrated social mobility; on the other hand, they lagged behind Russians at the end of the Soviet era. This finding suggests that nationalist leaders and ordinary people interpreted economic conditions in various ways. I analyze the data to evaluate whether these conditions by themselves could have directly produced a group grievance that led to nationalist mobilization. I test whether two different economic structures—interethnic job competition and an ethnic division of labor—are correlated with nationalism in Russia's republics and find that they are not. These results suggest that structural economic variables alone cannot explain variation in nationalism across the republics.

Chapter 4 shifts to a microlevel investigation of processes that produced mass nationalism in one of Russia's most nationalist republics—Tatarstan. I demonstrate how Tatar nationalists constructed an ethnonational grievance that produced mass support for Tatar nationalism. First I show that social mobility for Tatars rose throughout the Soviet era, as did their representation in urban labor markets. Next I describe how Tatar ethnic entrepreneurs framed issues of Tatar occupational underrepresentation vis-à-vis Russians in order to characterize Tatars as socioeconomically subordinate and as victims within their own republic. This framing allowed nationalists to attract support to a program that called for replacing an inegalitarian status quo with state sovereignty.

In chapter 5 I analyze why Tatarstan's second largest city, Naberezhnye Chelny, experienced a greater level of nationalist mobilization than the capital city of Kazan. The majority of the residents of Naberezhnye Chelny were employed by a single state enterprise: the Kamskii Automobile Works, or KamAZ, where Russians held a greater percentage of white-collar jobs than Tatars did. Tatar nationalists in the city made much of this fact in the discourse they articulated during national revival.[56] However, data on the relative proportion of each ethnic group in the KamAZ workforce in 1989 obscures a trend that contradicts the nationalists' picture of blocked opportunity. Namely, significant preference policies were enacted in the city that moved large numbers of rural, uneducated Tatars into training programs and jobs and up the professional ladder at KamAZ. Tatar nationalists in the city again downplayed the social mobility of Tatars and emphasized instead blocked opportunity and ethnic economic underrepresentation at KamAZ. In so doing, they attracted popular support to the nationalist program.

Chapter 6 demonstrates that group grievances do not inevitably develop among people with ethnic minority identities. Even when structural economic conditions indicate that minorities are subordinate in some way to other groups in society, and even when ethnic politicians emerge to represent their interests, they do not necessarily respond. This was the case in the low-mobilization republic of Mari El, where Maris were underrepresented in high-status jobs. Although nationalist movements emerged during glasnost, Maris did not support them. I also show that people with minority identities do not necessarily respond to nationalist politicians when they enjoy a relatively strong socioeconomic position, as in the Republic of Komi. Ethnic groups, in other words, are not automatically motivated by the prospect of future wealth to mobilize behind a program of national sovereignty. Through a comparative case study analysis of all Russia's republics and a comparative discourse analysis of nationalist rhetoric in newspaper articles published there, I show that people supported nationalism only in those republics where nationalist leaders framed issues of ethnic economic inequality, as in Chechnya, Tatarstan, and Tuva. In republics where nationalists focused on other issues, as they did in Komi and Mari El, they failed to attract mass support.

Chapter 7 makes the argument that the level of mass support for opposition nationalist movements within Russia's republics is the critical variable determining the strength of republican secessionism vis-à-vis Moscow during the late

---

56. David Laitin defines national revival as "a political movement whose purpose is to wrest control of a territory from a regime that leaders of the movement consider to be 'foreign' to that territory." See "Language and Nationalism in the Post-Soviet Republics," *Post-Soviet Affairs* 12 (January–March 1996): 5.

1980s and early 1990s. I introduce a coding of republican secessionism based on actions initiated by the republics as well as their responses to policies initiated by Moscow. Next I analyze how, as the Soviet Union democratized, a shift in political accountability facing republican leaders allowed mass nationalist mobilization to exert a significant influence on republican separatist campaigns toward Moscow. Evidence for this argument consists of data showing correlations between secessionism on the one hand and ethnic demonstrations and ethnic violent events in the republics on the other. Finally, case studies of three republics demonstrate that mass nationalism in Tuva and Yakutia influenced republican demands on Moscow at key moments in their sovereignty campaigns, while little mass nationalism in Mari El resulted in low secessionism there.

In the concluding chapter, I summarize my findings and reiterate how they challenge common understandings of ethnicity's power to motivate political behavior. The findings suggest a reconceptualization of nationalism as a highly contingent and fragile political event. Thinking about nationalism as transient—while ethnic identities remain deeply felt—can help to reduce expectations that minority populations are on the verge of mobilizing behind nationalist programs. These insights may be applied to multiethnic societies outside the Soviet space, such as China and Iraq where minority populations and people with ethnic and sectarian identities are often viewed as discrete political blocs. Focusing on how economic structures, people's experiences of those structures, and the discourse of political entrepreneurs interact to shape people's political preferences may help to inform policies that avoid reifying ethnic groups as political actors.

2

VARIATION IN MASS NATIONALISM ACROSS RUSSIA'S REPUBLICS

The dramatic intervention by Mikhail Gorbachev into an ideologically, politically, and economically stagnant Soviet Union in the late 1980s triggered unanticipated political developments that weakened the system it was meant to rescue. The policies of glasnost and perestroika permitted people and organizations to articulate ideas challenging prevailing ideologies and the status quo itself. Risk-taking newspaper editors began to publish articles about ethnic relations and editorials written by intellectuals with minority ethnic identities. With press reports of popular protests taking place among Crimean Tatars, Armenians in Karabakh, and Latvians and Estonians, awareness of ethnic issues began to develop in Russia's republics.[1] Ethnic intellectuals there founded informal organizations devoted to ethnocultural issues. Groups such as the Club of Udmurt Culture in Udmurtia (Vseudmurtskaia Assotsiatsiia "Udmurt Kenesh," or VAUK) and the Society of Vep Culture in Karelia (Obshchestvo Vepsskoi Kul'tury, or OVK) sponsored national concerts, advocated naming streets after national poets, and held conferences on subjects like Lenin's nationalities policies.[2] Cultural

---

1. Mark Beissinger describes the beginnings of nationalist mobilization in the Soviet Union in *Nationalist Mobilization.*

2. G. A. Komarova, *Khronika mezhnatsional'nykh konfliktov v Rossii: 1991 god.* [Chronicle of interethnic conflicts in Russia: 1991.] (Moscow: Institute of Ethnography and Anthropology, 1994); Komarova, *Khronika zhizni natsional'nostei v SSSR: 1990 god.* [Chronicle of the life of nationalities in the USSR: 1990.] (Moscow: Institute of Ethnography and Anthropology, 1996). Komarova, *Khronika zhizni natsional'nostei nakanune raspada SSSR: 1989 god.* [Chronicle of the life of nationalities on the eve of the collapse of the USSR: 1989.] (Moscow: Institute of Ethnography and Anthropology, 1997).

organizations sometimes focused on restoring spiritual traditions shattered by the Soviet state's campaigns against religion, as when the All-Buryat Association for the Development of Culture (Vseburiatskaia Assotsiatsiia Razvitiia Kul'tury, or VARK) helped organize a visit to the republic by the Dalai Lama.[3] Most of this activity fell within the bounds of officially sanctioned behavior or was tolerated by local leaders in the spirit of glasnost.

Soon, however, ethnic activists began to raise overtly political issues and to establish formal nationalist organizations. In some republics, these organizations grew out of the cultural societies; in others, they were formed from scratch. In still other republics, nationalist organizations spun off from Popular Front movements that included prodemocracy and environmental groups. At first, all opposition groups cooperated with one another since prodemocracy and environmental activists shared the nationalists' commitment to ethnic minority rights and greater local autonomy. Over time, however, environmental activism declined, and the interests of the nationalist and democratic opposition diverged. Nationalist organizations emerged as the locus of opposition to communist rule in the republics. Republican officials, for the most part, opposed the nationalists, prompting some scholars to label the nationalists "counterelites."[4]

The founders of nationalist movements generally belonged to the creative intelligentsia and included academics and writers in particular.[5] In Chuvashia, for example, the Chuvash Party of National Rebirth (Chuvash Atalana Partii, or ChAP) was led by a locally prominent lawyer, Nikolai Lukiianov, and the philologist and writer Atner Khuzangai, the son of a famous Chuvash poet.[6] Ethnic elites who had devoted their careers to studying the titular nationality—writers, artists, ethnographers, historians, linguists, sociologists, and others—were personally and professionally committed to making sense of their own ethnic identity and the place of their ethnic community in Soviet society. At the same time, these individuals were among the most educated and professionalized of Soviet citizens; they were highly conscious of their own elevated status within society. Many of them, in addition to joining opposition groups, used their positions in official state institutions to advance demands for greater ethnic rights. For example, as early as 1989, the Writers' Union in Tatarstan, an official state

---

3. Timur Muzaev, *Etnicheskii separatizm v Rossii* [Ethnic Separatism in Russia] (Moscow: Panorama, 1999); Caroline Humphries, "Buryatia and the Buryats," in *The Nationalities Question in the Post-Soviet States,* ed. Graham Smith (New York: Longman, 1996), 113–25.

4. See, for example, Suny, *Revenge of the Past,* and Roeder, "Soviet Federalism" and *Where Nation-States Come From.*

5. There were some exceptions: nationalist leaders in Buryatia included doctors and government bureaucrats.

6. Muzaev, *Etnicheskii separatizm,* 203; Gorenburg, *Minority Ethnic Mobilization,* 61.

organization, appealed to the USSR Congress of People's Deputies to grant the republic union republic status—the highest rank in the Soviet Union's ethno-territorial administrative hierarchy—so that it could elect a larger number of deputies and obtain increased support for Tatar radio and television stations.[7]

Nationalist entrepreneurs raised new and varied issues. They criticized official Soviet histories of the republics and sought to write new ones. They lamented Russification and encouraged the study of national languages. They advocated reviving religious traditions associated with the ancestors of the titular group. Nationalists in some republics demanded a redrawing of republican borders to include territory inhabited by coethnics.[8] In others, they recognized threats to their nation's existence from declining birth rates or outmigration. They occasionally demanded greater ethnic representation in political institutions, advocated establishing republican presidencies, and called for privileges for titulars in local economies. Overall, nationalist groups sought greater recognition, rights, and resources—in short, autonomy—from Moscow. Thus before the Soviet collapse, they favored raising the administrative status of their republics from "autonomous" to "union." After 1991, as the realm of what was politically possible suddenly widened, some nationalist groups began to advocate secession, while others continued to seek autonomy within Russia.

In most republics, the nationalist movement was split between two formal organizations—a main, moderate group and a radical group that had either formed concurrently with the first group or splintered off from it as a result of ideological or personnel differences. Usually it was the radical group that advocated secession, often with the support of a nationalist youth organization. Some youth groups claimed to have formed national militias.[9] However, in certain places, it was the main group that backed secession; for example, the Karelian Movement (Karel'skoe Dvizhenie) advocated that Karelia join Finland.[10]

To build popular support, nationalist groups engaged in varied activities and transmitted their message to the public using a range of tactics. At first, activists met in small groups to exchange ideas and then held founding congresses where formal charters (*ustavy*) were adopted. These organizations established local branches throughout the cities and *raions* (administrative districts) of the

---

7. "The Congress of USSR Peoples' Deputies-Verbatim Report, *Izvestia,* June 8, 1989, 4–7 in *Current Digest of the Soviet Press (CDSP)* 51, no. 29 (1989): 20.

8. For example, the Buryat nationalist movement advocated redrawing Buryatia's pre-1937 borders to incorporate ethnic Buryats living in compact settlements in Ust'-Ordynskii and Aginskii autonomous okrugs and in Irkutsk and Chita oblasts. Muzaev, *Etnicheskii separatizm,* 73.

9. N. Morozov, "Tatarstan—A People's Militia Is Being Created," *Pravda,* October 16, 1991, 1, in *CDSP* 53, no. 42 (1991): 28.

10. Muzaev, *Etnicheskii separatizm,* 149.

republic, and in neighboring oblasts and republics. In some places, nationalist organizations served as umbrella associations for other groups associated with the titular population, such as religious and cultural associations and youth and women's groups. They made extensive use of the media, giving interviews and publishing editorials in state-run newspapers whose liberal editors were willing to provide a forum for alternative viewpoints. They spoke on radio and, less often, on television programs. They also published their ideas in academic monographs and books, as well as in newspapers and journals established by the organizations themselves.

In March 1990, nationalist groups sponsored candidates in the Soviet Union's first semi-free elections to both the Congress of People's Deputies in Moscow and republican supreme soviets, or local legislatures.[11] Elections to the supreme soviets were a defining moment in the politics of certain republics even though party members retained a majority of seats. For the first time, independent candidates—including nationalists—were elected to legislatures that up to that point had been filled by Communist Party appointees.[12] Within the supreme soviets, nationalist deputies formed voting blocs, sometimes in cooperation with the prodemocracy faction.[13] The presence of nationalists in republican parliaments expanded the movements' influence as some independents and communist nomenklatura came to support the nationalist position.

One of the most important activities for most, though not all, nationalist organizations was public activism. They employed grassroots tactics including mass demonstrations, factory strikes, rallies, pickets, and hunger strikes. Nationalist activists, however, had to tread carefully at first in order to avoid provoking Communist Party leaders in the republics. Officials in Tatarstan, for example, would not permit the nationalist Tatar Public Center access to a printing press, forcing the group to publish its material in Lithuania.[14] In Yakutia, after the radical nationalist Sakha Perspective (Sakha Keskile) supported Boris Yeltsin during the 1991 attempted coup d'etat against Gorbachev by hard-line communists, the republic's

---

11. Technically, the 1989 elections to the USSR Congress of People's Deputies were the first semi-competitive elections in the USSR. However, Gorbachev manipulated voting rules, which produced a congress dominated by conservatives. Darrell Slider, "The Soviet Union," *Electoral Studies* 9, no. 4 (1990): 295–301. For a discussion of electoral support for nationalists in four republics, see Gorenburg, *Minority Ethnic Mobilization,* 132–48.

12. Olga V. Kryshtanovskaia, "Transformation of the Old Nomenklatura into a New Russian Elite," *Russian Social Science Review* 37, no. 4 (July–August 1996): 18–40.

13. In Udmurtia, for example, deputies associated with the nationalist Udmurt Kenesh entered into formal cooperation with deputies from Democratic Russia, until the two blocs split over the issue of which candidate to nominate for president of the republic. Muzaev, *Etnicheskii separatizm,* 192–94.

14. Interview with Damir Iskhakov, TOTs member, November 1996.

Communist Party fired group members from their jobs in provincial republican cities to slow the group's growing influence.[15] Despite episodes of harassment from state officials, however, over time the nationalists became free to engage in public activism without the expectation of serious state repression.

Another initiative undertaken by nationalist organizations was the establishment of national congresses in an attempt to establish formal legislative institutions that would pressure or even supplant republican supreme soviets. The congresses billed themselves as "the highest representative assembly of the nation," invited coethnics from outside the republic to serve as delegates, and elected formal leaderships. They adopted resolutions on subjects such as republican sovereignty, language, and culture and took a stand on political developments at the federal level, such as whether to support Yeltsin's federation treaty delimiting the rights and status of Russia's regions.[16]

In certain republics, popular support for nationalism began to grow. Small meetings sponsored by nationalist organizations grew into large rallies and demonstrations as support spread from the urban intelligentsia to students, workers, shop clerks, Communist Party members, and government administrators. In some places, people living in rural areas also backed the movement, though this occurred less frequently since nationalist organizations were headquartered in the cities and conducted most of their activities in urban areas. In places where popular nationalism was growing, demonstrations took place often, becoming the subject of ongoing public discussion. Each day brought new headlines about the activities of nationalist groups. However, in other republics where support for nationalism was weak, life continued as usual. In these places, the support base of the nationalist movement never spread beyond a small layer of the urban intelligentsia.

Russia's nationalist movements fit Sidney Tarrow's definition of social movements as "collective challenges by people with common purposes and solidarity in sustained interaction with elites, opponents and authorities."[17] The nationalist movements, however, sought a more fundamental transformation of the status quo than most social movements because they were oriented toward taking over the state. According to Breuilly, nationalist movements seek state power "and justify this objective on nationalist grounds."[18] Before 1991, the movements in the republics challenged the sovereignty of the Soviet central state in Moscow;

---

15. Marjorie Mandelstam Balzer, "A State within a State: The Sakha Republic (Yakutia)," in *Rediscovering Russia in Asia*, ed. Stephen Kotkin and David Wolff (Armonk, NY: M.E. Sharpe, 1995).

16. By the mid-1990s, however, these congresses were co-opted by republican governments.

17. Sidney Tarrow, *Power in Movement: Social Movements, Collective Action and Politics* (Cambridge: Cambridge University Press, 1996) 3–4.

18. Breuilly, *Nationalism and the State*, 9.

after 1991 they challenged the sovereignty of the Russian federal government. In the nationalists' view, the center denied their ethnic group adequate recognition, in particular the right to political control of the territory they considered their historical homeland. However, because of the radical and rapid political transformations taking place at this time, the nationalists' relationship to the state, at both the federal (Moscow) and regional (republican) level, was more complicated than one of simple opposition.

Many accounts of separatism in Russia focus on the relationship between the republics and Moscow and gloss over politics within the republics. They fail to distinguish between opposition nationalist movements and official republican administrations and instead view the republics as unitary actors in their relations with Moscow. This approach assumes that the nationalist movements were mere instruments of powerful and autonomous republican leaders. In this book I distinguish nationalist movements from republican administrations and investigate the motivations and behavior of each in order to produce an empirically accurate understanding of variations in nationalist mobilization and republican separatism in Russia. Without investigating subfederal politics, it is impossible to answer the question of why people in some republics supported nationalism more than people in other republics and why some republics mounted aggressive separatist campaigns toward Moscow while others remained quiescent. Below, I code Russia's republics in terms of the highest and lowest levels of mass support for nationalism.

Levels of Mass Nationalism

Popular support for nationalism varied dramatically across Russia's republics. Though opposition nationalist movements led by vocal, committed leaders existed in every republic, the degree to which mass publics mobilized behind these movements differed. The republics with the greatest mass support for nationalism were Tatarstan, Tuva, and Chechnya, followed by Yakutia and Bashkortostan, which displayed moderately high mass nationalism. At the other end of the spectrum, popular nationalism was the lowest in Dagestan, Chuvashia, Udmurtia, Mari El, and Mordovia. Russia's other republics also displayed relatively low levels of mass nationalism, with negligible differences in the levels of support. For clarity, I separate the republics into two categories: those with high mass nationalism and those with low mass nationalism (table 2.1). My coding is based on several different kinds of indicators of popular support for nationalism, including (1) the number of ethnic demonstrations that occurred in each republic; (2) the incidence of ethnic violence in each republic; (3) public opinion data

Table 2.1   Mass nationalism in Russia's republics, 1989–94

HIGH NATIONALISM	LOW NATIONALISM
Tatarstan	Komi
Tuva	Kabardino-Balkaria
Chechnya	Dagestan
Yakutia	Chuvashia
Bashkortostan	Udmurtia
	Mordovia
	Mari El
	Kalmykia
	Karelia
	Buryatia
	North Ossetia

from the 1993 Colton/Hough survey on support for two key aspects of the nationalists' program—republican declarations of sovereignty and the right of the republics to secede from Russia—as well as survey data on whether people identified with their republic or with Russia; and (4) a systematic cross-case comparison of ethnic and nationalist politics in Russia's sixteen republics. I describe each indicator below.

Mass Demonstrations and Ethnic Violence

The number of ethnic demonstrations that occurred in each republic is a reliable indicator of popular support for nationalist movements. Participation in demonstrations indicates support for nationalism because it suggests people's willingness to engage in risky behavior to express dissatisfaction with state authority and the status quo. An individual's decision to step onto the streets represents a public assertion of community and national identity.[19] The number of participants at demonstrations varied across republics and over time. In some republics thousands of people took to the streets at key moments during the period of national revival. Based on data from Mark Beissinger's extensive data set of mobilization events in the USSR, figure 2.1 presents the number of ethnic demonstrations with one hundred or more participants held in each of Russia's republics from 1987 to 1992.[20] Tatarstan and Checheno-Ingushetia had the

---

19. Beissinger discusses the meaning of nationalist event in *Nationalist Mobilization*, 18–28.

20. I am grateful to Mark Beissinger for providing these data. Beissinger defines a demonstration as a "voluntary gathering of persons with the purpose of engaging in a collective display of sentiment for or against public policies." All demonstrations in the data set had a minimum of one hundred participants. Beissinger defines a mass violent event as "a mass political action whose primary purpose was to inflict violence, either in the form of an attack on people or on property." Violent events had a minimum of fifteen participants. See *Codebook for Disaggregated Event Data: "Mass Demonstrations and Mass Violent Events in the Former USSR, 1987–1992,"* available at:

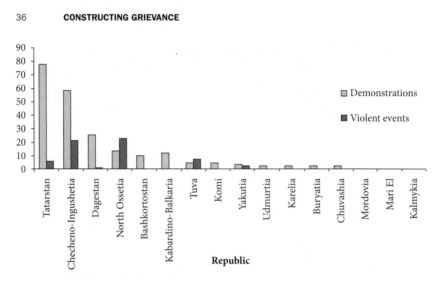

FIGURE 2.1   Ethnic demonstrations and violent events in Russia's autonomous repub-lics. *Source:* Mark Beissinger, *Codebook for Disaggregated Event Data: "Mass Demonstrations and Mass Violent Events in the Former USSR, 1987–1992,"* http://www.princeton.edu/~mbeissin/research.htm.

highest number of demonstrations of all of Russia's republics, seventy-seven and fifty-eight, respectively.[21] The nonnationalist republics of Mordovia and Mari El had no demonstrations. However, in other nationalist republics, few demonstrations were held: Bashkortostan(ten), Tuva (four), and Yakutia (three).[22]

The number of demonstrations in the republics may be slightly underrepresented here for several reasons.[23] First, because Beissinger's data set concludes in the year 1992, whereas republican campaigns for sovereignty continued until 1994, demonstrations that took place in 1993 and 1994 are not included in the

http://www.princeton.edu/~mbeissin/research.htm. 4, 6. For more on the procedures utilized in collecting the data, see Mark R. Beissinger, "Event Analysis in Transitional Societies: Protest Mobilization in the Former Soviet Union," in *Acts of Dissent: New Developments in the Study of Protest,* ed. Dieter Rucht, Ruud Koopmans, and Friedhelm Neidhardt, 284–316 (Berlin: Sigma Press, 1998); and Beissinger, *Nationalist Mobilization.*

21. Note that this data includes demonstrations and violent events only from the Soviet era, before Ingushetia split off from Chechnya.

22. According to Gorenburg, Bashkortostan had fewer demonstrations than other nationalist republics because nationalist groups there chose to focus on a strategy of sponsoring candidates in local elections instead. The demonstrations that did occur were usually in response to a specific crisis. See *Minority Ethnic Mobilization,* 126–28.

23. Note that the data set does not include hunger strikes or general strikes. I chose to rank the republics according to the number of *ethnic* demonstrations rather than the number of total demonstrations, since this period generated much popular protest by many groups concerning a diverse array of issues. However, the number of ethnic demonstrations is correlated with the total number of demonstrations.

data. Second, the coding of demonstrations as ethnic may not capture demonstrations sponsored by nationalist groups in conjunction with other organizations, such as environmentalist and democratic groups. Finally, Beissinger collected data from newspapers published in the center rather than in the republics. Central newspapers were likely to underreport instances of local demonstrations and violence that occurred in the republics.[24]

The three North Caucasian republics of Dagestan, Kabardino-Balkaria, and North Ossetia, it should be noted, hosted a large number of ethnic demonstrations. However, most of these concerned ethnic issues other than republican sovereignty. Major issues included the repatriation of ethnic groups deported by Stalin and the armed conflict between Georgia and the republics of Abkhazia and South Ossetia.[25] For example, in Kabardino-Balkaria, from which Stalin had deported ethnic Balkars to Kazakhstan in 1944, the Balkar nationalist movement wanted to restore the borders of the *raions* populated by ethnic Balkars to their pre-1944 borders, provoking opposition from the Kabard nationalist movement.[26] Ethnic demonstrations in these republics revolved around intraethnic conflicts and displays of sympathy with neighboring Abkhazia and South Ossetia and were not part of nationalist movement campaigns for sovereignty. This is not to say that these republics did not have nationalist movements that held demonstrations; they did. However, most of them did not concern nationalist challenges to state control.

Several republics also experienced ethnic violence during this period, though in general it occurred very infrequently. It was related to nationalist mobilization in some, though not all, republics. Those with the largest number of ethnic violent events were Checheno-Ingushetia (twenty-one), Tatarstan (six), Tuva (seven), and Yakutia (two). Also, North Ossetia experienced comparatively high ethnic violence because of the conflict that took place there between Ingush and Ossetians in fall 1992. This violence, however, was not related to a campaign for sovereignty.[27] Ethnic violence in Dagestan took place when the repatriated Akkintsy

---

24. See Mark Beissinger, *Codebook for Disaggregated Event Data: "Mass Demonstrations and Mass Violent Events in the Former USSR, 1987–1992,"* http://www.princeton.edu/~mbeissin/research.htm.

25. Concerning repatriation issues, Akkintsy clashed with neighboring ethnic groups in Dagestan, Balkars challenged Kabards in Kabardino-Balkaria, and Ingush made claims in the Prigorodnii region of North Ossetia. In terms of the regional armed conflicts, North Ossetia supported South Ossetia against Georgia by taking Ossetian refugees and sending aid and volunteer fighters, while Kabardino-Balkaria took the side of Abkhazia against Georgia. See Jane Omrod, "The North Caucasus: Confederation in Conflict," in *New States, New Politics,* ed. Ian Bremmer and Ray Taras (Cambridge: Cambridge University Press, 1997).

26. Muzaev, *Etnicheskii separatizm,* 118–29.

27. Tomila Lankina discusses ethnic conflict and mobilization in North Ossetia in *Governing the Locals: Local Self-Government and Ethnic Mobilization in Russia* (Lanham, Md.: Rowman & Littlefield, 2004).

fought over land ownership with various groups in that republic. In contrast, the other republics witnessed little to no ethnic violence during this period.

Overall, data on ethnic demonstrations and violent events reveal significant differences in the frequency of demonstrations and violence across Russia's republics. The data also suggest that Tatarstan and Checheno-Ingushetia, as the sites of the most demonstrations and violent events during the period 1987 to 1992, could be characterized as the most nationalist republics.

Mass Attitudes

Data from a 1993 survey of people in Russia's republics led by political scientists Timothy Colton and Jerry Hough provide information on the degree of popular support for two aspects of the nationalists' agenda: republican declarations of sovereignty and the right of the republics to secede from Russia.[28] In response to the question, "How do you feel about the declarations of sovereignty by the former ARs of the Russian Federation?" the largest percentages of people identifying with the following ethnic groups supported or partially supported the declarations: Yakuts, Ingush, Chechens, Tuvans, Bashkirs, Kalmyks, and Tatars. Between 56 percent and 94 percent of these nationalities supported republican sovereignty. Significantly lower levels of support for the sovereignty declarations were expressed by Mordvinians, Mari, Chuvash, and Dagestanis (figure 2.2).

Another question on the Colton/Hough survey concerned whether republics should have a right to secede from the Russian Federation. Results from the question "Should all republics have the right of self-determination, including the right of withdrawal from the federation?" indicate that most support was found among Ingush, Chechens, Tuvans, and Yakuts (figure 2.3). Bashkirs and Tatars, however, were in the middle of the group. Very few Mordvinians, Mari and Chuvash (fewer than 10 percent) supported secession. Support for secession represented the radical end of the spectrum among nationalist programs in the republics at this time. Only a few nationalist organizations—for example, radicals in Chechnya, Tuva, and Tatarstan—articulated a right to secession as a central part of their programs. It should also be noted that popular support for nationalism in many republics was already beginning to decline across Russia by 1993. Thus the percentage of titulars supporting republican sovereignty declarations and secession was probably slightly higher in the two years before this survey was conducted.

---

28. Colton/Hough NSF Pre-election Survey, 1993. The survey did not include a question about support for nationalist organizations.

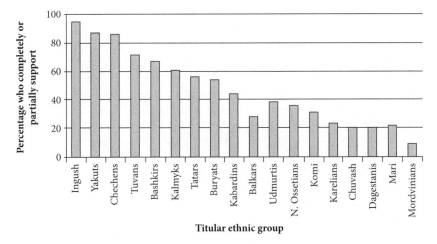

FIGURE 2.2   Titular support for AR declarations of sovereignty ("How do you feel about the declarations of sovereignty by the former autonomous republics of the Russian Federation?"). *Source:* Colton/Hough NSF Pre-election Survey, 1993.

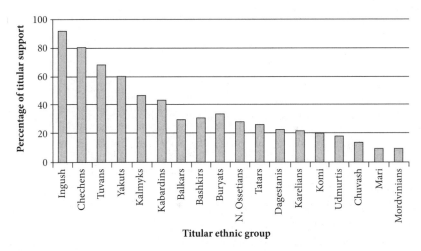

FIGURE 2.3   Titular support for secession ("Should all republics have the right of self-determination, including the right of withdrawal from the Russian Federation?"). *Source:* Colton/Hough NSF Pre-election Survey, 1993.

Another indicator of support for nationalist separatism could be the degree to which people identify with a substate region more than with the country as a whole. The Colton/Hough survey included a question asking respondents whether they considered themselves residents of their republic or residents of Russia. When asked, "Of what polity do you consider yourself a representative?"

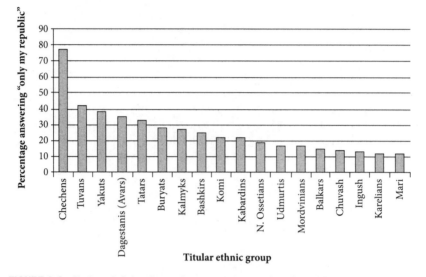

FIGURE 2.4 Titulars defining themselves as representative of republic rather than Russia ("Of what polity do you consider yourself a representative?"). *Source:* Colton/ Hough NSF Pre-election Survey, 1993.

respondents could answer "only my republic"; "more my republic than Russia"; "equally my republic and Russia"; "more Russia than my republic"; or "only Russia." The survey offered respondents a choice of membership in one of two civic polities, their republic or the Russian Federation, by employing the term *Rossiia* to denote the Russian Federation. Rossiia denotes the Russian state, a polity defined in terms of civic rather than ethnic membership.

I include the results here on the percentage of titulars who chose the first answer, "only my republic," since this is the most extreme expression of loyalty to a substate region and is likely to be related to support for nationalism (figure 2.4). Chechens comprised the largest percentage by far of all titulars claiming to be representative of only their republic, followed by Tuvans, Yakuts, Avars (a Dagestani nationality), Tatars, Buryats, Kalmyks, and Bashkirs. Survey results for the second answer—"more my republic than Russia"—revealed a similar ranking, with many titulars considering themselves equally representative of their republic and of Russia.[29] Overall, these results show that titulars in Chechnya, Tuva, and Yakutia supported certain elements of the nationalist program more than titulars in other republics. Tatars and Bashkirs also demonstrated support for these issues, though not to the same degree.

---

29. Valery Tishkov, *Ethnicity, Nationalism and Conflict in and after the Soviet Union* (Thousand Oaks, Calif.: Sage, 1997), 262.

Case Studies

In order to understand nationalist politics within Russia's republics, I completed case studies of each of the sixteen autonomous republics during the transitional period 1988–93. The studies compared information on the types and activities of nationalist organizations in each republic, whether their representatives received electoral support in the 1990 semicompetitive elections to republican supreme soviets,[30] the relationship between the nationalist movement and republican authorities, and the presence of mass support for nationalism. I compiled the studies using (1) documents published by nationalist organizations in each republic, (2) Russian-language articles and monographs published in both the republics and Moscow, (3) articles written by Western and Russian experts on each region, and (4) a systematic reading of news reports from *Radio Free Europe/Radio Liberty Research Reports* and *Current Digest of the Soviet Press* during 1988–93.

My case study analysis indicates a high degree of popular support for opposition nationalist movements in the republics of Tatarstan, Tuva, Bashkortostan, Yakutia, and Chechnya and weak mass nationalism in most other republics. Leading Russian experts on politics in Russia's republics also identify these republics as the most nationalist.[31] It is critical to note, however, that high popular support for nationalism in these republics does not mean that all people identifying with the titular nationality in these places were suddenly won over to the nationalist cause. On the contrary, support for nationalism varied greatly, and even within the most nationalist republics many people who identified with a particular ethnic group were indifferent or opposed to nationalism. Mass apathy and opposition are not unique to the Russian context. As Breuilly states, "nationalism is usually a minority movement pursued against the indifference and, frequently, the hostility of the majority of the members of the 'nation' in

---

30. Data on the 1990 Supreme Soviet elections in the ARs are sporadic: some local newspapers published the electoral results at the time the elections took place. However, because under Soviet law candidates in the elections were not permitted to affiliate with particular parties or movements, it is not possible to determine the political affiliation of a particular deputy from a list of those elected. Personal knowledge of the affiliations of individual deputies is therefore necessary in order to code him or her as a nationalist. In the absence of this local knowledge, I rely on the observations (albeit incomplete) of the Russian scholar Timur Muzaev in his book *Etnicheskii separatizm,* 1999.

31. Russian scholars Valery Tishkov, Leokadia Drobizheva, and Mikhail Guboglo headed ongoing, multiyear studies through the Institute of Ethnography and Anthropology of the Russian Academy of Sciences (IEA-RAN) in conjunction with American political scientists and funded by the National Science Foundation and the John D. and Catherine T. McArthur Foundation. See, in particular, Tishkov, *Ethnicity, Nationalism and Conflict;* and Leokadia M. Drobizheva, A. R. Aklaev, M. C. Kashuba, and V. V. Koroteeva, in *Natsional'noe samosoznanie i natsionalizm v Rossiiskoi Federatsii nachala 1990-kh godov* [National Consciousness and Nationalism in the Russian Federation in the early 1990s] (Moscow: IEA-RAN, 1994).

whose name the nationalists act."[32] Nevertheless, the fact remains that significant differences in levels of popular nationalism existed among Russia's republics. Though all republics faced similarly fluid and ambiguous conditions as a result of central state implosion, only some used the opportunity to support nationalist transformation.

Explanations for Republican Secessionism

The post–Soviet politics literature has put forward several kinds of arguments to explain nationalist mobilization and campaigns for sovereignty in the Soviet Union and Russia; these can be grouped into four categories: historical-institutional, ethnodemographic, cultural, and economic-structural. While some existing explanations have advanced our understanding, most share several shortcomings. They explain the emergence of nationalist separatism by focusing mainly on regional elites or on the presence of structural economic and political variables. They treat ethnic groups as bounded political actors, an approach that essentializes ethnic masses and overpredicts the politicization of ethnicity. As a result, most explanations cannot account for empirical variation in either the degree of mass mobilization within the republics or the intensity of sovereignty demands that republics made on Moscow.

Historical-Institutional Arguments

A series of early, important analyses by Ronald Suny, Philip Roeder, and Rogers Brubaker argue that nationalist separatism among the USSR's union republics developed as a result of the Soviet state's nationality policies and federal structure.[33] These studies have stimulated theorizing in ways that go beyond the authors' original insights and are equally relevant to Russia's republics. They emphasize how Soviet state policies served to nurture and institutionalize ethnicity within the republics, creating both national elites and masses who were prepared to support nationalism when the opportunity arose during glasnost.

To begin with, Lenin's initial decision to endow minority populations with territorial rather than cultural autonomy granted certain populations nominal "homelands" in the form of republics or autonomous regions and provided them with rights within those homelands. Titular groups developed an official, state-recognized language and culture, but Russians and other cultural groups could

---

32. Breuilly, *Nationalism and the State*, 405.
33. Roeder, "Soviet Federalism"; Suny, *Revenge of the Past*; Brubaker, *Nationalism Reframed*.

not. Second, the Soviet state instituted a system of passport identity in which citizens "inherited" nationality (ethnic affiliation) at birth, thereby instilling the idea that identity was something primordial and unalterable rather than based on place of residence or self-identification.[34] Soviet citizens had to report the identity listed in their passport in all official encounters with the state—e.g., when applying for training programs in factories, higher education, and jobs, as well as to the various institutions the Soviet regime established for educated titulars, such as ethnic research institutes, writers' and artists' unions, and publishing houses. The Soviet state also implemented a set of policies known as *korenizatsiia* (indigenization), which granted preferences to titular nationalities in higher education, enterprise management, job training, the Communist Party, and government administration. These privileges, which titulars could enjoy only within the boundaries of their republics, were designed to advance the position of titular populations vis-à-vis other nationalities living there. By the late Soviet era, titulars had made significant gains in education and professional achievement. They worked in the Communist Party, universities, trade unions, the Council of Ministers, writers' unions, local government administration, security organs, and the Academy of Sciences. Titular peasants became "proletarianized," taking jobs in newly industrialized republican cities.[35] State-defined incentives and quotas succeeded in moving titulars from farm to factory, from primary school to university, and into the highest reaches of management and government administration. Thus, korenizatsiia created an educated middle class and a local political leadership out of the titular population, and it simultaneously assimilated them into a Russified, Soviet social order.[36]

The Soviet policies of indigenization and passport identity within the context of industrializing, pseudostate republican territories ended up providing, according to Ronald Suny, "a social and cultural base" for republican counterelites to establish broad-based nationalist movements. As he states, "[A] state that had set out to overcome nationalism....had in fact created a set of institutions and initiated processes that fostered the development of conscious, secular, politically mobilizable nationalities."[37] Philip Roeder points to the consequences of ethnofederalist institutions to explain differences in the level of nationalist sepa-

---

34. Only children of mixed parentage were allowed to choose their nationality at age sixteen. See Victor Zaslavsky, *The Neo-Stalinist State: Class, Ethnicity, and Consensus in Soviet Society* (Armonk, NY: M.E. Sharpe, 1982).

35. Yuri Slezkine, "The USSR as Communal Apartment, or How a Socialist State Promoted Ethnic Particularism," *Slavic Review* 53, no. 2 (Summer 1994): 433.

36. Victor Zaslavsky, "Nationalism and Democratic Transition in Postcommunist Societies," *Daedalus* 121, no. 2 (Spring 1992): 102.

37. Suny, *Revenge of the Past,* 126.

ratism that existed among the union republics. Titular nationalities in Georgia, Armenia, and the Baltics, he argues, were so successful at building an indigenous cadre and intelligentsia inside their republics that Moscow redirected resources away from them and toward the underdeveloped Central Asian republics. Then, when the Soviet economy contracted at the end of the 1980s, titular elites in the advanced republics found their own social mobility and opportunities frustrated, a situation that inspired them to seek national autonomy from Moscow.[38]

These accounts provide clear arguments about the origins of elite identity and interests and why they promoted nationalist programs. They have less to say, however, about the general phenomenon of nationalism—that is, why masses follow elites. The fact that Soviet history and institutions helped create ethnonational identity at the mass level does not mean that those identities led logically to mass mobilization in support of nationalism. If identity led deterministically to nationalism, we would observe nationalism in all Soviet and Russian republics rather than in just some of them.

Dmitry Gorenburg provides an explanation for the variation in mass nationalism in Russia's republics by emphasizing different kinds of Soviet state institutions.[39] Instead of assuming that ethnic masses automatically follow nationalist leaders, Gorenburg argues that the institutions of native language education, academic institutes studying local culture, ethnic preferences in government employment, and cultural institutions explain the degree to which ethnic masses mobilized behind nationalist movements. These institutions strengthened ethnic identities and established dense social networks among titulars in high-mobilization republics such as Tatarstan and Bashkortostan, thereby facilitating mass mobilization. In republics where institutional penetration did not reach as deeply (e.g., Chuvashia), popular support for nationalism was correspondingly lower.

Historical-institutional explanations offer a thought-provoking analysis of the effects of central state policy and institutions on elites in the republics. However, aside from Gorenburg's account, they fail to address the question of why masses responded to elites. These accounts maintain that state institutions exert a powerful or even deterministic effect on people's identity. But the link between identity and interest is underspecified. The fact that people had ethnic identities does not mean that they necessarily desired national sovereignty or the particular policies promoted by nationalist elites. Why were national policies and institutions so powerful that they were able to crowd out the influence of other Soviet institutions and experiences so that ethnicity became people's primary and politically relevant identity? Though historical-institutional explanations provide

---

38. Roeder, "Soviet Federalism," 216–19.
39. Gorenburg, *Minority Ethnic Mobilization*, 24.

compelling explanations for the nationalist behavior of titular elites, they leave an open space for further theorizing on the link between individual identification and mass support for nationalism.

Demographic Arguments

Theories that emphasize the importance of demography maintain that nationalist separatism is more likely to develop when an ethnic group forms a numerical majority of a region's total population. In the words of Donald Horowitz, "The strength of a secessionist movement and the heterogeneity of its region are inversely related."[40] The fact that Russians rather than titular nationalities were a majority of the population in most of Russia's republics is frequently invoked to explain why the republics did not imitate the secessionist behavior of the Soviet Union's union republics. Gail Lapidus and Edward Walker, for example, write that sizable Russian populations in the republics "make Russia less vulnerable to fragmentation along ethnic lines than the former USSR, Yugoslavia, and Czechoslovakia."[41] James Hughes, noting that titulars constitute a simple plurality in only three of Russia's republics[42] and an absolute majority in only four,[43] concludes that separatism was impeded by the "spatial dispersion of Russians...throughout the...territory of the Federation."[44]

These analysts do not necessarily believe that demography alone accounts for the emergence of nationalist separatism, but they see relative ethnic percentages as an important background condition or as one of several key factors. This argument seems so commonsensical that analysts often provide no explanation as to why demography should matter. It is reasonable to expect that a critical mass of people identifying with a particular ethnic group is necessary for nationalist mobilization. Without it, there simply may not be enough people to administer an ethnonational state, such as in Karelia, where Karelians form only 10 percent of the population. Moreover, separatist regions with large ethnic populations are generally taken more seriously as potential states by the international community than are regions with tiny ethnic populations—and, as Mark Beissinger

---

40. Horowitz, *Ethnic Groups in Conflict*, 267.

41. Lapidus and Walker, "Nationalism, Regionalism, and Federalism," 87. Also see Lapidus, "Asymmetrical Federalism," and Monica Duffy Toft, *The Geography of Ethnic Violence: Identity, Interests and the Indivisibility of Territory* (Princeton: Princeton University Press, 2003).

42. Tatarstan, 48 percent; Kalmykia, 45 percent; Kabardino-Balkaria: Kabards, 48 percent and Balkars, 9 percent.

43. Tuva, 64 percent; North Ossetia, 53 percent; Chechnya, 58 percent; and Chuvashia, 68 percent.

44. Hughes, "From Federalism to Recentralization," 131, 134.

argues, international support is itself a resource that nationalist organizations can use to accomplish their goals.[45]

The primary way in which demography is thought to influence nationalist mobilization in a plural society, however, is through the logic of an ethnic census. In this view, a national election resembles an ethnic census insofar as the majority ethnic group will supposedly win more votes than the minority group and dominate all future electoral contests. But elections resemble censuses only if we believe that all people sharing a particular ethnic identity act as a political bloc with fixed interests that always oppose the interests of other ethnic groups. This logic is erroneous at both a theoretical and an empirical level. In using demographic structure as a proxy for political preferences, the logic essentializes the behavior of individuals with ethnic affiliations. Whether political preferences cohere among people with a common ethnic identity and whether the preferences of different ethnic groups coincide are empirical questions. By assuming that ethnic demography determines electoral outcomes, observers essentialize the relationship between ethnic identity and politics and therefore overpredict nationalist separatism in some places and fail to predict it in others.

The ethnic census logic as applied to Russia and the Soviet Union would predict that people with Russian identities and people with titular identities always disagree on the question of republican separatism. Yet this was not the case. First, a significant minority of Russians living in the republics supported titular nationalism. For example, 47 percent of Russians in Tatarstan voted in favor of sovereignty in a popular referendum held there in 1992, just as many Russians had voted for Ukrainian independence a year earlier.[46] To be sure, many ethnic Russians opposed titular nationalism, and Russian politicians emerged to form pro-Russian organizations and stage counterprotests. But the support they received from ordinary Russians never reached significant levels. Most Russians who participated in politics did so along ideological dimensions, joining, for example, democratic, agrarian, or communist parties.

Next, and again contrary to the prediction that demography is a critical variable, popular support for ethnonationalism *among* titular populations varied widely. Many titulars, in fact, opposed nationalist programs or remained indifferent to them. During the extremely volatile years of political transition, various alternatives to nationalism existed. The group Democratic Russia, for example, offered a democratic ideology and well-organized political movement.

---

45. Beissinger, *Nationalist Mobilization.*

46. Forty-six percent of Russians failed to vote in Tatarstan's sovereignty referendum, and only 7 percent voted against sovereignty. Also, in Estonia and Latvia many Russians supported nationalist campaigns prior to 1991.

Conservatives and others clung to the status quo. Other people with titular identities remained ideologically committed to the Communist Party.[47] Still others, unsure of what the future held, adopted an agnostic attitude about politics. So while fluid and ambiguous conditions during the period of political transition permitted the formation of new social identities such that many titulars began to understand their identity in a way that entailed supporting nationalism, other titulars embraced identities such as democrat, citizen of the Russian Federation, or businessman. Still others, apprehensive about the many changes each new day brought, clung to their identities as Soviet citizens. Thus we cannot assume that ethnicity will become the primary cleavage in politics during times of massive change.

The failure of ethnic demography to explain nationalist separatism in Russia is demonstrated by the fact that nationalism is not correlated with republics in which titulars formed either a majority, a plurality, or a minority (table 2.2). First, in two of the most nationalist republics—Yakutia and Bashkortostan— titulars were a distinct minority as of 1989: 33.4 percent and 22 percent, respectively. Next, popular nationalism failed to develop in two republics where titulars constituted a majority: Chuvashia (68.7 percent) and North Ossetia (53 percent). On the other hand, Chechnya and Tuva, where titulars formed 58 percent and 64 percent of each republic's population, did experience strong mass nationalist mobilization. Among the republics where titulars were a plurality of the population, Tatarstan (48.5 percent) was strongly nationalist. Yet two other republics with a plurality of titulars, Kabardino-Balkaria and Kalmykia, demonstrated moderate to low and very low nationalism. Overall, the data show an indeterminate relationship between ethnic demography and nationalist mobilization, undercutting the explanatory power of demography as a critical variable.

In sum, the logic of the demographic hypothesis predicts nationalist mobilization among titulars in republics where little or none occurred and fails to predict nationalism in several republics where it did develop. Moreover, the logic makes erroneous predictions about the behavior of ethnic Russians in some republics. By assuming that people with ethnic affiliations act as voting blocs, demographic hypotheses both over- and underpredict nationalism in Russia's republics and obscure our understanding of the reasons why some people choose to engage in nationalist activity.

---

47. See Geoffrey Hosking, Jonathan Aves, Peter J. S. Duncan, *The Road to Post-Communism: Independent Political Movements in the Soviet Union, 1985–1991* (New York: St. Martin's Press, 1992).

Table 2.2   Demography and nationalist mobilization in Russia's republics, 1989

	NATIONALIST REPUBLICS	NONNATIONALIST REPUBLICS
Titular majority	Checheno-Ingushetia (71%)* Tuva (64%)	Chuvashia (69%) North Ossetia (53%) Dagestan (90%)*
Titular plurality	Tatarstan (48%)	Kalmykia (45%) Kabardino-Balkaria (57%)*
Titular minority	Yakutia (33%) Bashkortostan (22%)	Karelia (10%) Buryatia (24%) Komi (23%) Udmurtia (31%) Mari El (43%) Mordovia (33%)

Source: Data compiled from the 1989 USSR All-Union census.

* *Note:* Chechens formed 58% and Ingush 13% of Checheno-Ingushetia; Kabards were 48% and Balkars 9% of Kabardino-Balkaria; and Dagestan was made up of multiple nationalities: Avars (28%); Dargins (16%); Kymyk (13%); Lezgin (11%); Lak (5%); Tabasaran (4%); Azeris (4%); Chechens (4%); Nogai (2%); and Jews (1%).

Cultural Arguments

In some accounts, culture plays an important role in motivating nationalist mobilization and ethnic conflict. Though very few observers today take a primordialist approach in which cultural difference is considered a sufficient condition for political mobilization,[48] the relevance of culture to political behavior is nevertheless often overstated. Some accounts assume first, that all people who have a particular ethnic identity share common cultural attributes and beliefs such as language, religion, livelihood, historical understandings, myths, and memories; and second, that ethnic identities, once they become established as social facts, engender intense emotional attachments.[49] These assumptions rely on Anthony Smith's definition of ethnic community in which the culture of a group endures over time and exists prior to political mobilization.[50] In this view, ethnic groups

48. Robert Kaplan, *Balkan Ghosts: A Journey through History* (New York: St. Martin's, 1993); Hélène Carrère d'Encausse, *The End of the Soviet Empire: The Triumph of the Nations* (New York: Basic Books, 1993); Clifford Geertz, *Old Societies and New States: The Quest for Modernity in Asia and Africa* (New York: Free Press, 1963).

49. Walker Connor states that "the national bond is subconscious and emotional rather than conscious and rational" in "Beyond Reason: The Nature of the Ethnonational Bond," *Ethnic and Racial Studies* 16, no. 3 (July 1993): 373–89. For Horowitz, the strong emotions associated with ethnicity are due to people's psychological need to belong to a kinlike community. See *Ethnic Groups in Conflict,* 55–64. Also see Anthony Smith, "The Ethnic Sources of Nationalism" in *Ethnic Conflict and International Security,* ed. Michael Brown (Princeton: Princeton University Press, 1993), 27–42.

50. Smith defines an ethnic community as sharing a common proper name, myths of common ancestry, historical memories, distinctive elements of culture, an association with a given territory, and a sense of social solidarity. *The Ethnic Origins of Nations* (Oxford, UK: Basil Blackwell, 1986), 32.

have beliefs and strong feelings about themselves and about other ethnic groups that are rooted in history, myth, and memory.[51] Nationalist mobilization and ethnic violence are caused, in part, by these static beliefs and feelings. Although many studies claim to have jettisoned primordialist assumptions, they make similar essentialist assumptions that reify ethnic groups and overpredict the incidence of mobilization and conflict.

In popular understanding, for example, nationalist mobilization is caused by intergroup cultural difference, especially when the culture of an ethnic minority differs from that of the group in control of the central state.[52] Evidence from the Soviet Union and Russia contradicts this claim. As has been observed, popular nationalism was weak in the Muslim, clan-based, "traditionalist" republics of Central Asia. Likewise, in Russia, Buddhist Buryatia and Kalmykia and Muslim North Ossetia, Dagestan, and Kabardino-Balkaria are all examples of rural, poor republics with distinct local cultural practices and low nationalist mobilization. The populations of two republics that did experience nationalist mobilization— Tatarstan and Bashkortostan—were nominally Muslim. Only in the nationalist republic of Chechnya did a significant portion of the population practice Islam. Thus there is almost no correlation between the cultural distinctiveness of republican populations and nationalist mobilization across Russia's republics.

Among political scientists, a significant part of the international relations literature assumes that ethnic groups maintain static cultural practices and beliefs that determine group interests. For example, several theories identify strategic conditions such as a weak central state and the security dilemma as fundamental causes of nationalism and ethnic conflict.[53] Under anarchic conditions, ethnic groups feel threatened by each other, evaluate each other's intentions based on past historical conflicts, and thus have incentives to attack preemptively. These

---

Stephen Van Evera relies on Smith's definition in "Hypotheses on Nationalism and War," *International Security,* 18, no. 4 (Spring 1994): 5–39, as does Michael Brown, "Causes and Implications of Ethnic Conflict," in Brown, *Ethnic Conflict and International Security,* 3–26.

51. Many scholars, of course, have moved beyond this static view of culture and theorize culture as a dynamic and changing arena of interaction. For example, see Laitin, *Nations, States and Violence.*

52. This hypothesis is largely discredited among scholars. For an exception, see Jerry Muller, "Us and Them: The Enduring Power of Ethnic Nationalism," *Foreign Affairs,* March/April, 2008, 425–52.

53. See Barry Posen, "The Security Dilemma and Ethnic Conflict," *Survival* 35, no. 1 (Spring 1993): 27–47; Michael Brown, "The Causes of Internal Conflict: An Overview," in *Nationalism and Ethnic Conflict,* ed. Michael Brown, Owen R. Cote, Jr., Sean M. Lynn-Jones, and Steven E. Miller (Cambridge, Mass.: MIT Press, 1997), 3–25; and David Lake and Donald Rothchild, "Containing Fear: The Origins and Management of Ethnic Conflict," in Brown et. al., *Nationalism and Ethnic Conflict,* 97–131; and David Lake and Donald Rothchild, "Spreading Fear: The Genesis of Transnational Ethnic Conflict," in *The International Spread of Ethnic Conflict: Fear, Diffusion, and Escalation,* ed. David A. Lake and Donald Rothchild (Princeton: Princeton University Press, 1998), 3–32.

accounts maintain first, that ethnic groups are distinct cultural entities[54] and second, that a history of oppression or conflict means that intense emotions and negative evaluations of other ethnic groups are present prior to political mobilization.[55] According to these and similar accounts,[56] when central states collapse or democratize, ethnic groups encounter each other with latent hostilities, prejudices, or hatreds that were established at some point in the past. While such intergroup hatreds may not be quite as ancient as those invoked by primordialists, they are assumed to be a constitutive part of ethnic groups. Thus the boundaries between people—i.e., who will mobilize and against whom—are fixed and exogenous to the politics of national revival. If ethnic groups are cohesive political blocs with static beliefs and feelings, then the right combination of structural conditions will easily trigger mobilization and violence. These accounts overpredict nationalist mobilization and ethnic violence. Michael Brown, for example, erroneously forecast ethnic conflict in Russia by assuming that the "dozens of ethnic groups" there had "spent centuries despising each other"—a situation that could "spark violent conflict" if irresponsible leaders were to emerge during the country's economic crisis.[57]

Other accounts hypothesize that historical events like colonization, oppression, and violence against a minority ethnic group encourage demands for independent nationhood.[58] History by itself, however, is rarely determinative. A traumatic historical episode is not understood in identical terms by all people who share an ethnic identity. Political entrepreneurs must frame and define past events in particular ways to persuade people in the present that an injustice has occurred. They must actively choose to interpret historical events as unjustly perpetrated on an innocent collective by a malicious and culpable state or ethnic other. Conversely, politicians may choose to define past events in a manner that integrates people and ties them to a common state. As Valerie Bunce states, a

---

54. As Posen states, "The 'groupness' of the ethnic, religious, cultural and linguistic collectivities that emerge from collapsed empires gives each of them an inherent offensive military power." "The Security Dilemma," 30.

55. For Brown, if antagonistic historical events have occurred, negative group perceptions and emotions are simply there. Lake and Rothchild agree but maintain that they must become magnified by structural conditions and self-interested entrepreneurs for mobilization to occur. See Brown, "Causes of Internal Conflict," 3–25; Lake and Rothchild, "Containing Fear," 97–131.

56. Stephen Van Evera, for example, emphasizes demographic intermingling of ethnic groups as well as other factors as possible sources of nationalist conflict in "Hypotheses on Nationalism and War," 26–60.

57. Brown, "Causes of Internal Conflict," 23.

58. Stuart Kaufman states that Moldova had a history of oppression by Russia in "Spiraling to Ethnic War: Elites, Masses, and Moscow in Moldova's Civil War," *International Security* 21, no. 2 (Fall 1996): 108–38. See also Van Evera, "Hypotheses on Nationalism and War," 44–46.

"painful past can serve as a pretext for cooperation, as in Spain, or conflict, as in Yugoslavia."[59]

The point that cultural entrepreneurs play a key role in defining the meaning of past events has been emphasized by many scholars of nationalism, including Jack Snyder, M. Crawford Young, and John Breuilly.[60] But it bears repeating with regard to the Soviet context. The historical fact that Stalin deported Chechens in 1944 suggests that this traumatic experience may have inspired nationalism among Chechens. Yet it is critical to keep in mind that some of the very Chechens who personally suffered or lost relatives in the deportation later joined the Communist Party and built successful careers as productive members of Soviet society. They understood the Soviet state as their homeland. The same is true of many Ukrainians and titular nationalities in the Baltics whose ancestors experienced deportation, murder, and famine.[61] Despite past traumatic experiences, titular nationalities in the USSR had good reasons to appreciate the Soviet system since they benefited from central state policies of education, urbanization, and employment, as well as from a rising standard of living in a state that became a superpower after World War II. In general, regardless of whether people have experienced historical injustice or historical advantage in the past, political entrepreneurs must define events in the present in particular ways in order to shape the shared social understandings necessary for mobilization.

A brief review of repressive historical events in Russia's other republics demonstrates this point. Like the Chechens, Balkars in Kabardino-Balkaria and Karachai in Karachaevo-Cherkessia were also deported but did not exhibit any significant level of nationalist mobilization. Other severely destructive historical events took place in the republics, including the destruction of religion and Stalin's murder and imprisonment of members of national intelligentsias. In Buryatia, for example, the intelligentsia was purged and Buddhist monasteries destroyed.[62] Although various events that harmed people identifying with titular nationalities occurred in all Russia's republics, mass support for nationalism developed in

---

59. See Valerie Bunce, "Subversive Institutions: The End of the Soviet State in Comparative Perspective," *Post-Soviet Affairs* 14, no. 4 (October 1998): 323–54. See 338–39.

60. Jack Snyder argues that historical legacies create a propensity for ethnic conflict, but he highlights the role of elite mythmaking among other factors in *From Voting to Violence*. See also Young, *Politics of Cultural Pluralism*, and "The National and Colonial Question and Marxism" in *Thinking Theoretically*, pp. 67–97; Breuilly, *Nationalism and the State*.

61. It is also true of many citizens in East European states who viewed communist rule after World War II as their own national system of government rather than as something imposed by a foreign oppressor.

62. Humphries, "Buryatiya and the Buryats"; Gail Fondahl, "Siberia: Assimilation and Its Discontents," in *New States New Politics: Building the Post-Soviet Nations,* ed. Ian Bremmer and Ray Taras (New York: Cambridge University Press, 1997), 190–232.

only a few of them. Moreover, republics with considerably less dramatic histories of Soviet oppression, such as Tuva and Tatarstan, did develop mass support for nationalism. Empirically, then, there is no correlation between the fact of historical oppression and nationalist mobilization across Russia's republics.

Interestingly, even scholars who view ethnic groups as having fixed cultures and histories recognize the key role that elites play in interpreting these events. For example, Stephen Van Evera argues that the size and severity of the crimes matter in determining whether violent nationalist conflict will occur, but he also states that people's interpretation of events is critical. Heinous past crimes are more likely to motivate violence, he argues, if the victim attaches responsibility to a group that still exists.[63] Barry Posen makes the structuralist argument that ethnic groups assess each other's military intentions on the basis of historical conflict, but then he undercuts his point in discussing the case of Ukraine. He attributes the absence of ethnic conflict there in part to the decision by Ukrainian president Leonid Kravchuk to blame the Great Famine of the 1930s that killed millions of Ukrainians on the Bolsheviks rather than the Russians. Thus Posen implicitly recognizes that ethnic Ukrainians did not enter 1991 with a shared view of the famine as crime perpetrated by Russians.[64] Overall, the mere fact of a traumatic historical event does not denote the presence of a group grievance that persists over time and produces ethnic mobilization when conditions permit.

Another hypothesis maintains that nationalist mobilization is more likely to occur when the state discriminates against a minority along cultural lines, e.g., by banning its religion, language, or economic livelihood. Some international relations scholars make this argument implicitly in assuming that entire ethnic populations support certain policies, such as minority language or religious revival.[65] The fact of discrimination may provoke a grievance among people with a shared ethnicity. But this outcome is not inevitable because people with the same identity do not all have common cultural attributes and intense feelings about those attributes, and, as discussed above, they do not necessarily interpret their experiences and interests in the same way.

This point may be illustrated by the example of religion in Russia's republics. The Soviet state essentially obliterated organized religion in Russia—a fact that could have produced a grievance among ethnic minorities who were associated

---

63. Elsewhere in the same article, Van Evera explicitly emphasizes the role of politicians, historians, and writers in making myths that glorify the nation, whitewash its wrongdoings, and malign ethnic others. "Hypotheses on Nationalism and War," 44–45 and 48–49.

64. Posen, "Security Dilemma," 3. Also see Jack Snyder's discussion of the lack of common attitudes among Ukrainians in *From Voting to Violence*, 257–59.

65. Brown, "Causes and Implications of Ethnic Conflict," 3–26; Kaufman, "Spiraling to Ethnic War," 108–38.

with a minority religion such as Islam or Buddhism. However, such a result was not inevitable. In Tatarstan, for example, Islam was as alien to most ethnic Tatars as Orthodoxy was to ethnic Russians. Throughout the decades of Soviet rule, many Tatar families had hidden the fact that a grandparent was a village mullah and had raised their children as secular in order to avoid punishment from Soviet authorities. Generations raised in this way did not know, value, or even associate Islam with their ethnicity. For example, Asilbilka Zakirovna, a middle-aged woman and government administrator, strongly identified as a Tatar. She stated that as a Tatar, she had a Muslim identity but that neither she nor her husband (who was a Russian and therefore a Christian) followed religious traditions or even knew what they were. She explained that she hadn't been raised that way and that it all seemed very strange to her. "Maybe," she said, "I'll have more time when I retire, although I know that I would find the time to go to mosque and pray if I wanted to."[66] Zakirovna's comments capture a common sensibility among many Tatars. But even Tatars who were practicing Muslims—religious revival during glasnost increased the numbers of converts to Islam—rarely linked their Islamic identity to the Tatar nationalist program or to politics in general.[67] Finally, many Tatars in Tatarstan were not Muslim: the Kriashen Tatars were Orthodox Christian, whereas other Tatars became Jehovah's Witnesses during Soviet rule.[68] Rather than preserve certain cultural practices associated with a particular ethnicity, many individuals choose to adapt, change, or assimilate in response to various conditions they face.

Rural populations are often assumed to support nationalism because they are supposedly committed to the continuation or reestablishment of cultural practices, customs, and traditional modes of living. But the end of Soviet rule did not witness the mass conversion of rural titular populations to Islam, Buddhism, or Christianity. Rural dwellers also might have been expected to back automatically the promotion of national languages, which the Soviet regime had subordinated to Russian, or to reestablish traditional livelihoods made obsolete by state-led industrialization and collectivization, such as nomadic pastoralism, sheep or reindeer herding, and cattle raising.[69]

Yet the reality of rural life was more complex. Soviet rule dramatically transformed rural life by suppressing religious practice, imposing collectivization

---

66. Interview with Asilbilka Zakirovna, Tatarstan GosSobranie (State Duma), Kazan, March 4, 1997.

67. Interview with Tatar informant, June 1, 1997 Naberezhnye Chelny; interview with Tatar student, March 25, 1997, Kazan; interview with Valyulya Yakup, imam, February 12, 1991, Kazan.

68. Field notes, Naberezhnye Chelny, May–June 1997.

69. These forms of discrimination were also experienced by ethnic Russians, including the grandparents of Boris Yeltsin. See Timothy Colton, *Yeltsin: A Life* (New York: Basic Books, 2008).

and industrialization, and promoting education and urbanization. Rural dwellers responded in various ways. Some adapted to the new conditions to avoid persecution; others genuinely committed to communist ideology; still others pragmatically learned Russian and migrated to the cities to work in industry. Traditional practices and beliefs were preserved in some places and fused with new Soviet institutions elsewhere.[70] In addition, the Soviet state labeled most rural practices backward and inferior—values that were absorbed not only by ethnic Russians but by minority populations as well. In fact, precisely *because* certain cultural practices signified a subordinate social status, many people abandoned them to assimilate to the dominant community. Thus people with ethnic identities whose ancestors engaged in cultural practices different from those of the dominant society do not automatically perceive those practices as either "theirs" or in need of political expression.

By the time national revival began in the late 1980s after decades of Soviet rule, many people with ethnic identities who had been living out their lives in modern Soviet society saw a return to traditional practices as quite irrelevant to their current concerns and beliefs. In the USSR, where national revival began *after* the period in which the state had banned minority cultural practices, many people had already discarded those practices and beliefs—if they ever had them in the first place—while preserving their ethnic identities. People with titular identities living in agrarian areas did not constitute a monolithic group in terms of their various social identities, cultural attributes, attitudes and beliefs, or behavior. Despite the particular ways in which rural and ethnic identities overlapped, it is incorrect to view the countryside as home to ethnic groups prepared to mobilize in support of nationalism when given the opportunity.

Economic-Structural Arguments

Another influential approach—which I label the "wealth hypothesis"—explains secessionism by focusing on macroeconomic conditions in Russia's republics. In this approach, economic resources are the critical variable motivating republican separatism: leaders of resource-rich, economically developed republics made separatist demands on Moscow while leaders of comparatively poor republics did not. Economic explanations build on a general logic developed by Ernest

---

70. In Chechnya, for example, collective farms existed next to "traditional Chechen farms and communal organizations." See Valery Tishkov, *Chechnya: Life in a War-Torn Society* (Berkeley: University of California Press, 2004), 24. In Kazakhstan, according to Martha Brill Olcott, traditional clanic and clerical leaders initially dominated local soviets and party cells. Cited in Suny, *Revenge of the Past*, 113–17.

Gellner, Peter Gourevitch, Michael Hechter, Donald Horowitz, and Tom Nairn in which economic conditions produced by modernization and industrialization induce actors to support secession when they expect to profit from it.[71] The wealth hypothesis has practically become conventional wisdom despite the fact that empirically it cannot account for separatism in Russia's poor republics nor its absence in the rich ones. Wealth is also poorly correlated with secessionism among the union republics of the USSR.[72] The inability of this approach to explain variance in outcomes is due to the fact that fixed structural or exogenous variables, divorced from intersubjective meanings shared by relevant political actors, tell us little about the actual interests and motivations of people on the ground. In addition, by focusing solely on elites, the wealth hypothesis overlooks the critical role played by mass publics. It fails to consider how the massive political transformations occurring at the time restructured incentives of republican leaders in ways that made them accountable to mass publics within the republics.

There are several variants of the wealth hypothesis.[73] The first maintains that the high level of separatism among certain Russian republics was a function of their natural resource endowments. Kathryn Stoner-Weiss, for example, writes that political intransigence and tax revolts in the republics of Tatarstan, Bashkortostan, and Yakutia "were part of a broader strategy to widen the economic control rights of these wealthy republics over the proceeds from the extraction and sale of oil, gas, and diamonds located on their territories."[74] A second set of hypotheses defines

---

71. Ernst Gellner famously argued that nation-states were created by the effect of uneven modernization on economically marginalized groups exhibiting genetic-somatic, linguistic, or religious traits distinct from those of the economically dominant or state-bearing population. Peter Gourevitch and Tom Nairn hypothesize that relatively economically advanced ethnic elites in politically peripheral regions advocated secession to develop their regions' economic potential. Hechter and Horowitz argue, by contrast, that relative economic backwardness inspires ethnic groups to increase their regions' prospects through greater autonomy or independent statehood. See Gellner, *Thought and Change* and *Nations and Nationalism;* Horowitz, "Patterns of Ethnic Separatism" and *Ethnic Groups in Conflict;* Hechter, *Internal Colonialism* and "Group Formation and the Cultural Division of Labor"; Gourevitch, *Paris and the Provinces: The Politics of Local Government Reform in France* (Berkeley: University of California Press, 1980); and Nairn, *The Break-up of Britain: Crisis and Neonationalism* (London: New Left Books, 1977).

72. Herrera, *Imagined Economies,* see chapter 1.

73. Philip Roeder's explanation for variation in separatism among the URs could be considered the original version of the wealth hypothesis insofar as he notes that the republics with the most socioeconomically advanced nationalities were the most secessionist. However, instead of focusing on fixed economic structures, Roeder emphasizes how political and institutional factors interact to motivate the identities and behavior of elites and counterelites within the republics. Conversely, most accounts based on the wealth hypothesis address how economic structures directly inform republican leaders' relations with Moscow. Roeder, "Soviet Federalism."

74. Stoner-Weiss, "Federalism and Regionalism," 239. Similarly, James Hughes notes that "the single most important common factor among the four most "'secessionist'...republics (Chechnya,

wealth more broadly to mean a republic's level of socioeconomic development. Henry Hale indicates economic development using the measure of retail commodity turnover per capita; Daniel Treisman uses a high industrial output and export, a high raw materials production, and a large population; and Kisangani Emizet and Vicki Hesli develop two indicators: a social development index (consisting of small family size, high urbanization, and the number of women workers) and a regional development index (including a high rate of consumer goods production and a high growth rate in its food industry). Each of these authors articulates a slightly different logic to explain the correlation between republican wealth and separatism.[75] Emizet and Hesli as well as Hale maintain that Moscow's status as a rapidly transforming, potentially hostile center inspired economically advanced republics to secede so they could protect privileges they had attained in the late Soviet era. If new elites hostile to regional autonomy were to win power in Moscow and recentralize the state, relatively rich republics had more to lose than did poor ones. Poor regions, on the other hand, depended on Moscow for the "goods of modernity."[76] Treisman argues that leaders of economically advanced republics understood that wealth, a large population, and bountiful resources increased their republics' economic potential as independent states and thus strengthened their bargaining position with the center. Conversely, republics with weaker economies made few autonomy demands because leaders there weighed the cost of seceding against the benefit of continuing to receive subsidies and transfers from Moscow.[77] According to Steve Solnick and others, economic wealth can also explain why the Russian Federation, unlike the Soviet Union, survived as an ethnofederal state. In response to separatism, the federal government granted the richer republics tax breaks, credits, subsidies, and political autonomy. In appeasing the wealthy republics at the expense of both the poorer ones and the nonethnic regions, Moscow created an asymmetric federation and avoided state collapse.[78]

Tatarstan, Bashkortostan, and Sakha) is that they all have significant economic resource endowments." "From Federalism to Recentralization," 134.

75. Emizet and Hesli, "The Disposition to Secede"; Treisman, "Russia's 'Ethnic Revival'"; Hale, "Parade of Sovereignties"; and Hale and Taagepera, "Russia: Consolidation or Collapse?"

76. Robert Bates delineates this logic in "Modernization, Ethnic Competition, and the Rationality of Politics in Contemporary Africa," in *State versus Ethnic Claims: African Policy Dilemmas,* ed. Donald Rothchild and Victor Olorunsola (Boulder: Westview, 1983), 159.

77. Treisman, "Russia's 'Ethnic Revival,'" 239. Treisman also finds that the variables of administrative status (republic vs. oblast or okrug), experienced leaders, strong ethnic movements, and institutionalized federal borders correlate with republican activism, and he argues that these factors strengthened the bargaining position of republican leaders as well. Ibid., and *After the Deluge*

78. Steven Solnick, "Will Russia Survive? Center and Periphery in the Russian Federation," in *Post-Soviet Political Order: Conflict and State-Building,* ed. Barnett R. Rubin and Jack Snyder (London: Routledge, 1998), 58–80; Mikhail Alexseev, "Decentralization versus State Collapse: Explaining Russia's Endurance," *Journal of Peace Research* 38, no. 1 (2002): 101–6; Hale and Taagepera, "Russia: Consolidation or Collapse?"; Daniel Treisman, *After the Deluge.*

These wealth hypotheses seem persuasive because they explain strong separatism in certain union republics—the Baltics—and weak separatism in the underdeveloped Central Asian republics. Yet there is little correlation between separatism and republican wealth among the other union republics or among Russia's republics. Moldova, for example, was not among the wealthiest of the URs, yet its separatist activity approached that of the Baltics; it hosted large mass nationalist demonstrations,[79] was one of the first republics to pass a language law and demand full independence, and was one of six republics to boycott the March 1991 referendum on preserving the USSR.[80] Armenia also was highly secessionist but not among the wealthiest republics.[81] The republic of Belarus, on the other hand, displayed very little separatism yet was one of the most economically developed of the union republics.[82] In Russia, the fact of separatism in Tuva—a tiny, poor republic whose economy centered on livestock herding—flatly contradicts the wealth hypothesis.[83] The same is true of Chechnya. Though Chechnya contained some crude oil and an oil pipeline connecting Russia with refineries in Baku, its reserves made up a minuscule 1 percent of Russia's total output in 1992, and its pipeline was threatened with redundancy by new pipeline projects already underway that bypassed the republic.[84]

The inconclusive relationship between republican wealth and separatism persists regardless of the way in which analysts measure republican wealth. Henry Hale and Rein Taagepera rank republican economic development based on retail commodity turnover as of 1988.[85] Of the wealthiest Russian republics according to this measure—Komi, Karelia, and Yakutia—only Yakutia was separatist. Chechnya, with the lowest retail commodity turnover, was arguably the most

---

79. Paul Goble, "Moscow's Nationality Problems in 1989," *RFE/RL Research Report,* January 12, 1990, 13–14.

80. The others were Latvia, Lithuania, Estonia, and Georgia.

81. Hale and Taagepera rank Armenia as the ninth-wealthiest of the fifteen URs. "Russia: Consolidation or Collapse?" 1108. Not only did Armenia's leaders refuse to hold the referendum, but they sponsored an alternative referendum on independence in which 99 percent of the population voted in favor. Ann Sheehy, "The All-Union and RSFSR Referendums of March 17," *RFE/RL Research Report,* March 29, 1991, 19–23.

82. Hale and Taagepera rank Belarus as the fourth-wealthiest of the URs. "Russia: Consolidation or Collapse?"1108.

83. Treisman's study develops a useful index of secessionism based on multiple indicators of republican activity but miscodes the critical case of Tuva as minimally secessionist. "Russia's 'Ethnic Revival,'" 224–25. He also reports a weak to nonexistent statistical relationship between the variables of wealth and separatism: his multivariate analysis shows only a fragile relationship between raw material output and industrial exports and high activism, and his bivariate analysis reveals no relationship between economically dependent republics and low activism. Ibid., 239n, 240.

84. Anatoly Khazanov, *After the USSR: Ethnicity, Nationalism and Politics in the Commonwealth of Independent States* (Madison: University of Wisconsin Press, 1995), 219.

85. Of the fifteen union republics, Hale and Taagepera rank Moldova, Armenia, and Georgia seventh, eighth, and ninth but label them (along with the Baltics) the leading separatist regions. "Russia: Consolidation or Collapse?" 1106–7.

nationalist of all Russian republics. In general, Chechnya and Tuva rank among Russia's poorest regions, whether measured in terms of raw materials, population size, standard of living, or industrial production—yet they were the most secessionist.[86] Moreover, an advanced economy did not spur separatism in Komi— a highly industrialized republic that contained enormous coal deposits and significant oil and gas fields.[87] Therefore, though we observe that the republics of Tatarstan, Yakutia, and Bashkortostan were relatively resource-rich and experienced significant separatism, the fact remains that the wealth hypothesis can explain neither separatism in the poor republics of Russia nor its absence in the rich ones.[88]

This is not to say that the presence of economic wealth in Russia's republics was inconsequential; it unquestionably informed the strategies of some republican leaders in their relations with Moscow. Republican leaders and other elites debated and considered local economic conditions during the course of campaigns for sovereignty and in negotiations with Moscow. But the mere presence or absence of wealth was not determinative; it did not influence the strategies of all nationalist and republican leaders, and it did not determine why ethnic populations in only certain republics responded to those leaders. Wealth hypotheses have little to say about where the masses fit into the story and cannot account for variation in mass response to nationalist leaders. These accounts assume that republican leaders acted autonomously within republican politics, conceiving of and making separatist demands on Moscow.[89] Though it is clear that republican leaders strategically took advantage of nationalist mobilization within the republics to strengthen their negotiating position with the center, there is no evidence

---

86. Oksana Genrikhovna Dmitrieva, *Regional'naia ekonomicheskaia diagnostika* [Regional Economic Diagnostics] (Saint Petersburg: Izdatel'stvo Sankt-Peterburgskogo Universiteta Ekonomiki i Finansov, 1992), 128–32.

87. Similarly, Russia's wealthiest ethnic regions—the autonomous okrugs of Khanty-Mansisk and Yamal-Nenets—also failed to make separatist demands. Though as okrugs, these regions had fewer institutions, rights, and privileges than republics, they were far richer, producing 80 percent of Russia's oil and gas. Roy Bahl and Christine I. Wallich, "Intergovernmental Fiscal Relations in the Russian Federation," in *Decentralization of the Socialist State,* ed. Richard M. Bird, Robert D. Ebel, and Christine I. Wallich (Washington D.C.: World Bank, 1995), 326. After federal relations had stabilized in the late 1990s, okrug leaders demanded administrative independence from Tyumen oblast to retain more control over natural resources. See "Khanty-Mansi Avtonomnyi Okrug" in *Regiony Rossii: Statisticheskii sbornik* [Regions of Russia: Statistical Handbook] (Moscow: Goskomstat, 1999).

88. Dmitry Gorenburg's study also challenges the wealth hypothesis. He finds that nationalism was lower in the republic of Khakassia than in Chuvashia, despite the fact that the former was more economically developed than the latter. *Minority Ethnic Mobilization,* 165–66.

89. Henry Hale's account is a partial exception insofar as he recognizes that support for nationalism may differ among republican leaders and other subrepublican actors. Hale maintains, however, that the same macroeconomic factors will motivate all republican actors. Hale, "The Parade of Sovereignties."

that republican populations reflexively mobilized when republican leaders told them to.

Characterizing ethnic populations as passive tools of politicians overestimates the power of ethnicity as a basis for political behavior. It assumes that ethnic populations are naturally or automatically nationalist or will become nationalist upon the command of politicians. This view treats elites as strategic actors but mass populations as passive instruments who were either (1) "genuine" nationalists, patiently waiting for their chance at statehood or (2) Soviet subjects, dutifully obeying their leaders' commands. Such a distinction between crafty leaders and credulous masses rings false and is also empirically inaccurate insofar as local populations and nationalist movements did not allow republican leaders to direct their political behavior. This approach essentializes Russia's ethnic populations and overestimates the power of ethnicity as a basis of political action. Instead, republican residents, like citizens living in Russia's nonethnic regions, behaved rationally, backing one or another politician and occasionally shifting or withdrawing their support. Thus, although economic-structural hypotheses clearly delineate economic and structural influences on elite strategies, they make the invalid assumption that the ethnic masses are either perpetually nationalist or easily become so at the will of nationalist politicians.

In conclusion, the hypotheses found in the post–Soviet politics literature on secessionism that emphasize variables of ethnic group demography, cultural difference, economic resources, and strategic elites do not, in and of themselves, provide sufficient explanations for either the emergence of nationalist mobilization in Russia's republics or the variance in mobilization across republics. Such approaches naturalize the existence of bounded ethnocultural groups and view them as easily triggered into political action along ethnic lines. This cancels out the very difficult question of why ethnicity matters politically in the first place and why people mobilize along ethnic lines to achieve particular political goals. The next chapter addresses this question.

DOES STRUCTURE MATTER?
Local Labor Markets and Social Mobility

Did adverse economic conditions at the end of the Soviet era in Russia's republics inspire people to support republican nationalism? This chapter addresses this question by analyzing socioeconomic stratification among ethnic groups. This theme has received wide attention in the general literature on ethnic politics, perhaps most famously in Gellner's model in which Ruritanian workers seek national independence from Megalomania after being shut out of desirable jobs in the core state.[1] In this chapter I investigate social mobility and the labor market position of Russians and titulars in Russia's sixteen republics to understand how these variables relate to the emergence of, and variation in, mass nationalist mobilization across republics.[2] The argument of this book is that mass nationalism developed when people had certain experiences in local economies that allowed entrepreneurs' issue framings of ethnic economic inequality to resonate. I describe those experiences in the first part of this chapter by presenting data on social mobility and discussing the macroeconomic contraction of the Soviet economy during perestroika. Then I examine whether socioeconomic structural

---

1. Gellner, *Nations and Nationalism.* Also see Horowitz, *Ethnic Groups in Conflict,* 108–31; Leo Despres, ed. *Ethnicity and Resource Competition in Plural Societies* (The Hague: Mouton, 1975); Edna Bonacich, "A Theory of Ethnic Antagonism: The Split Labor Market," *American Sociological Review* 37 (October 1971): 547–59.

2. Several studies of nationalism in the USSR examine these variables, though not at the mass level. See Roeder, "Soviet Federalism"; David Laitin, "The Nationalist Uprisings in the Soviet Union," *World Politics* 44 (1991): 139–77. An exception is Robert Kaiser's "Nationalizing the Work Force: Ethnic Restratification in the Newly Independent States," *Post-Soviet Geography* 36, no. 2 (February 1995): 87–111.

conditions motivated people to support nationalist transformation once economic crisis set in. Specifically, I test whether the variables of interethnic job competition and an ethnic division of labor (EDL) are associated with nationalism across Russia's republics.[3] I find no clear relationship between either of these variables and nationalist mobilization. Therefore, adverse socioeconomic structural conditions by themselves cannot explain mass nationalist mobilization in Russia.

Socioconomic Stratification and Ethnic Mobilization

At the beginning of the Soviet era, a division of labor existed in which titular ethnic groups in Russia's republics worked in the countryside while Russians occupied more highly skilled jobs in republican cities. This division was not structured entirely along ethnic lines since almost all citizens at that time, including ethnic Russians, lived and worked in rural regions. However, cities in the republics were dominated by Russians who held highly desired jobs. By the end of the Soviet era the situation had changed dramatically. Large numbers of titulars had moved to the cities, had assumed jobs alongside Russians, spoke Russian, and lived their lives in a Soviet cultural milieu. The acculturation of non-Russians to a homogenized, Soviet standard progressed further in most of the ARs than in the URs, but it also varied across Russia's republics.[4] Some residents of the republics with titular identities continued to speak non-Russian languages, maintain traditional livelihoods such as farming or herding, and live in rural areas. But even in the poorest, least industrialized republics, titulars had made substantial socioeconomic gains.

The Soviet citizenry as a whole underwent enormous social change as a result of general development programs instituted by the Soviet state, including urbanization, public education, and industrialization. As Moshe Lewin has argued, these programs so transformed the Soviet population following World War II that by the late 1980s, a new urban constituency consisting of a managerial, technical, educational, and political elite had emerged to challenge the Soviet system.[5] Titular populations also experienced massive social change, in large part because the Soviet state implemented nationality policies designed to advance

3. I adapt Michael Hechter's concept of a cultural division of labor, discussed below.

4. See Suny's discussion of acculturation in *Revenge of the Past,* 125.

5. Moshe Lewin, *The Gorbachev Phenomenon: A Historical Interpretation* (Berkeley: University of California Press, 1988).

their socioeconomic position within the republics.[6] These policies included Russian language education, the use of internal passports listing ethnic affiliation, and korenizatsiia, or affirmative action policies in higher education and the occupational sphere. This chapter examines social change in the republics and rising social mobility among titulars by presenting data on population growth, urbanization, linguistic Russification, education, and occupational representation from the USSR State Statistical Committee, or Goskomstat.

By the end of the Soviet era, socioeconomic mobility led people to anticipate that the state would continue to provide educations, jobs, occupational advancement, and in many cases, social status. Yet the Soviet economy's stagnating rates of growth that had begun during the Brezhnev era accelerated under Gorbachev. A deteriorating economic situation led to a general increase in competition for education and jobs and also raised people's fears about job loss. I will discuss how macrolevel change brought about by the Soviet state's production crisis and economic reforms affected employment in the country.

I then consider whether socioeconomic structural conditions induced people to support nationalism as the country's economic crisis deepened. Did the fact of rising social mobility and job competition in a centrally planned economy motivate demands for nationalist transformation in the republics? Or were titular nationalities driven to support nationalism by other forms of economic adversity such as an ethnic division of labor, in which they lagged behind Russians socioeconomically?

To address these questions, I compare Russia's republics by constructing two indexes of socioeconomic stratification: one using data showing change in socioeconomic processes over time in the republics (index of trends in socioeconomic stratification) and one using cross-sectional data from a fixed point in time—the end of the Soviet era (index of socioeconomic stratification as of 1989). The indexes rank Russia's republics according to population growth, urbanization, linguistic Russification, education, and occupational representation. Each of these processes is an indicator of the position of titulars and Russians on a scale of socioeconomic stratification. For each indicator, I assign the republics a score of 1, 2, or 3. Republics that fall at the high end of the scale have titular and Russian populations that are more separated or socioeconomically stratified than other republics and are thus more likely to display an ethnic division of labor. Republics at the low end of the scale have titular and Russian populations that are more integrated or socioeconomically equivalent than other republics and

6. Suny, *Revenge of the Past*, 109. Also see Graham Smith, "The Soviet State and Nationalities Policy" in Graham Smith ed., *The Nationalities Question in the Post-Soviet States* (New York: Longman, 1996), 2–22.

are therefore more likely to experience competition for jobs. In order to summarize the descriptive statistics, I add the scores of all indicators and compute an average rank of socioeconomic stratification for each republic. I treat the indicators as if they are categorical variables that can be compared with each other, although they are not. Examining the average scores of the republics on the two indexes provides a quick numerical depiction of two compelling points.

First, the socioeconomic position of Russians and titulars in most republics was not clear-cut. Contrary to expectations about minority populations in the Soviet Union and to observations made by some Western and Russian analysts,[7] a pronounced ethnic division of labor did *not* exist in any of Russia's republics. Titular populations in *all* republics demonstrated social mobility, even in places like Checheno-Ingushetia and Tuva, where Russians continued to hold a majority of white-collar jobs at the end of the Soviet era. However, while the fact of titular mobility suggests a homogeneity across republics, in fact, the picture of titular-Russian socioeconomic stratification detected in a republic depends on the particular indicator we observe. Examining a particular indicator may show that titulars lagged behind Russians on that indicator—i.e., that an ethnic division of labor was present—whereas examining another indicator may show that titulars were in a position to compete with Russians for educations and jobs. This means that it is not possible to state that either an EDL or ethnic competition objectively existed in Russia's republics during the period of national revival. This is precisely the reason why multiple interpretations of economic conditions were possible at the time. Ethnic entrepreneurs, nationalist leaders, and ordinary people could observe and understand local socioeconomic conditions in different ways. In certain republics, nationalists focused their message on specific conditions in order to make a case for inequality and discrimination facing titular ethnic groups.

Second, comparative analysis of Russia's sixteen republics reveals no correlation between mass nationalism and the variables of socioeconomic stratification. In other words, neither the republics that might be characterized as having an EDL according to certain indicators nor those that might be characterized as displaying ethnic competition are associated with nationalist mobilization. This suggests that structural conditions—the socioeconomic exclusion of titulars or competition between titulars and Russians—did not generate a group grievance among people with titular identities.

A cultural division of labor (CDL) forms, according to Michael Hechter, when members of an economically subordinate group become aware of their

---

7. For example, see Andrew Jack's characterization of Chechens as subordinate to Russians in Chechnya in *Inside Putin's Russia* (Oxford: Oxford University Press, 2004)

exclusion from desirable occupations and when objective cultural differences among groups—in language, religion, and lifestyle—overlap with occupational exclusion.[8] In a situation of internal colonialism, a dominant group from the state core exploits a minority living in an economically subordinate periphery. Once members of a minority group become aware of the exploitation, they establish social and political organizations to express a grievance and mobilize politically to augment their rights or secede from the state.[9] Observers might characterize Russia's republics as internal colonies with an ethnic division of labor since titular nationalities lived in economically underdeveloped and politically peripheral areas of the country, whereas Russians controlled the core state and dominated advanced economic sectors. If an EDL had been present in Russia's republics, we would have observed titular populations concentrated in republican rural regions, speaking titular languages instead of Russian, poorly represented in higher education, and underrepresented in white-collar jobs by comparison with Russians. According to Hechter's model, titulars would have become conscious of these inequalities and resentful of the central state and would have mobilized behind nationalism.

Alternatively, Russia's republics could be described as having experienced interethnic labor competition at the end of the Soviet era. According to competition theory, industrialization and modernization bring "culturally heterogeneous populations" into competition for rewards and resources such as jobs. As people compete, solidarity within societal groups increases, stimulating mass mobilization.[10] For example, Susan Olzak shows that workers born in the United

---

8. Michael Hechter, *Containing Nationalism* (New York: Oxford University Press, 2000); *Internal Colonialism;* and "Group Formation and the Cultural Division of Labor." Hechter's argument belongs to the "reactive ethnicity" category of explanation. See Charles Ragin, "Class, Status, and 'Reactive Ethnic Cleavages': The Social Bases of Political Regionalism," *American Sociological Review* 42 (June 1979): 438–50.

9. Note that for Hechter, a CDL does not invariably produce ethnic mobilization. People must also have a general awareness of the situation as "unjust and illegitimate," which, he argues, develops through communication among members of the "oppressed community" at schools, the workplace, neighborhoods, churches, social clubs, and voluntary organizations. Thus residential and occupational segregation of the oppressed community critically contributes to the formation of ethnic group consciousness. Hechter also argues that the more pronounced and visible the cultural differences between the subordinate and core groups are, the more solidary the subordinate group will become and the more likely it will be to mobilize for separatism. Hechter, *Internal Colonialism,* 40, 42, 43; Hechter, "Group Formation," 297, 300. Also see Hechter, "Nationalism as Group Solidarity," *Ethnic and Racial Studies* 10 (October 1987): 415–26.

10. Competition theorists build on the pathbreaking work of anthropologist Frederik Barth, who observed that conflict among ethnic groups results not from differences over cultural attributes or practices but from competition over common resources after people move into one another's ecological niche. Barth notes, however, that resource competition can also produce intergroup stability. See Barth, ed., *Ethnic Groups and Boundaries. The Social Organization of Culture Difference* (Boston: Little, Brown, 1969); Francois Nielsen, "Toward a Theory of Ethnic Solidarity," and "The Flemish

States mobilized against European immigrant and black workers from the U.S. south when they began to compete for jobs in American labor markets at the turn of the century.[11] She finds that exogenous shocks to labor markets—such as a sudden contraction of the economy, a surge in immigration, and the desegregation of the markets—increased competition for jobs, and this in turn raised group consciousness, increased the salience of group boundaries, and produced ethnic conflict. If interethnic competition had driven ethnic mobilization in the ARs, we would have observed an increase in competition between Russians and titulars brought about by rising titular urbanization, linguistic Russification, expanding titular access to education, and increasing representation of titulars in white-collar occupations. Macroeconomic contraction during late perestroika could have intensified that competition, inspiring titular nationalities to mobilize for sovereign statehood.

The next section describes how populations in Russian's republics underwent major social transformation during the twentieth century and compares the republics by ranking each according to the degree to which the socioeconomic position of Russians and titulars could be described as indicating either an ethnic division of labor or interethnic competition.

Social Transformation in Russia's Republics

Population Growth

After the Second World War, the size of the population in Russia's republics swelled as a result of both natural rate of increase (birthrate) and in-migration. In the thirty-year period from 1959 to 1989, the rate of population growth in the republics exceeded that of the RSFSR (35.3 percent vs. 25.1 percent) and was comparable to the rate of growth in the USSR overall.[12] During the same period, the size of the Russian population in the republics also expanded. Russians

---

Movement in Belgium." Conversely, Horowitz argues that job competition rarely leads to interethnic conflict. See chapter 4 in *Ethnic Groups in Conflict*.

11. Susan Olzak, *The Dynamics of Ethnic Competition and Conflict* (Stanford: Stanford University Press, 1992).

12. This can be partly explained by a birthrate that was nearly twice as high among titular populations as among ethnic Russians living in the republics. Within this general trend of population growth some titular populations expanded faster than others: Chechens and Ingush tripled, and Tuvans and Kalmyks more than doubled. All other titular populations increased at a lower but positive rate except those in Mordovia and Karelia. M. N. Guboglo, *Razvitie etnogdemografcheskoi situatsii v stolitsakh avtonomnykh respublik v 1959–1989 gg (po materialam perepisei naseleniia SSSR)*, document no. 33 (Moscow: IEA-RAN, 1992), 2–4. Guboglo notes that the state published fewer statistics about the ARs than about the URs.

Table 3.1 Demographic and socioeconomic trends in Russia's republics

| | PERCENTAGE CHANGE IN RUSSIAN POPULATION, 1926–89 | URBAN PERCENTAGE OF TITULARS, 1989 | INCREASE IN TITULAR SHARE OF URBAN POPULATION, 1959–89 | TITULAR SHARE OF URBAN POPULATION, 1989 | PERCENTAGE OF TITULARS SPEAKING RUSSIAN, 1989 | PERCENTAGE CHANGE IN TITULAR VUZY STUDENTS, 1974–89 | TITULAR STUDENTS IN VUZY, 1989 |
	RPOP	URB1	URB2	URB3	LANG	EDU1	EDU2
Tatarstan	0.2	69	8.9	42.1	80.6	8	171
Tuva	12	31.9	25.9	41.2	59.3	70	195
Checheno-	20.5	28	37	46	73.6 Ch	64	151
Ingushetia					80 Ing	89	212
Yakutia	39.7	27.9	-2.4	12.8	69.9	22	234
Bashkortostan	-0.5	51.2	6.6	14.5	78.5	38	170
Kalmykia	27	49.4	14.8	49.4	93.6	36	304
Karelia	16.5	62.6	1.1	7.6	97.5	-28	106
Buryatia	17.2	42.3	9.2	17.3	84.2	-42	354
N. Ossetia	23.3	65.6	20.5	49.3	88.7	19	272
Komi	51.1	46.7	0.8	14.4	90.9	-11	119
Kabardino-	24.4	44.6	26.3	43	79.6	13	206
Balkaria					83.8	-7	279
Udmurtia	15.6	48.8	5	19.8	91.9	9	115
Chuvashia	6.7	50.8	18.8	54.7	84.1	29	139
Dagestan	-3.3	38.4	31.6	67.2	69	27	173
Mordovia	1.6	54.1	10.3	22.1	91.8	16	118
Mari El	3.9	41.7	14.7	26.1	86.9	16	116

Table 3.2 Index of trends in socioeconomic stratification

	TATARSTAN	TUVA	CHECHENO-INGUSHETIA	YAKUTIA	BASHKORTOSTAN	KALMYKIA	KARELIA	BURYATIA	N. OSSETIA	KOMI	KABARDINO-BALKARIA	CHUVASHIA	UDMURTIA	DAGESTAN	MARI EL	MORDOVIA
POP	3	2	1	1	3	1	2	2	1	1	1	3	2	3	3	3
URB2	2	1	1	3	2	2	3	2	1	3	1	2	3	1	2	2
EDU1	2	1	1	2	2	2	3	3	2	3	3	2	2	2	2	2
SUM	7	4	3	6	7	5	8	7	4	7	5	7	7	6	7	7
AVG. RANK	2.3	1.3	1	2	2.3	1.6	2.6	2.3	1.3	2.3	1.6	2.3	2.3	2	2.3	2.3

Note: 1 = ethnic competition (EC); 3 = ethnic division of labor (EDL).

POP: 1 = Size of Russian population increased by 20% or more, 1926–89; 2 = Size of Russian population remained relatively same (10% to 20% increase), 1926–89; 3 = Size of Russian population decreased or grew by less than 10%, 1926–89.

URB2: 1 = Titular share of urban population grew by 20 percentage points or more, 1959–89; 2 = Titular share of urban population grew by 6 to 19 percentage points, 1959–89; 3 = Titular share of urban population grew by 5 percentage points or less, 1959–89.

EDU1: 1 = Percentage change in titular VUZy students, 64% or more, 1974–89; 2 = Percentage change in titular VUZy students, 8%–38%, 1974–89; 3 = Percentage change in titular VUZy students, –7% or more, 1974–89.

from throughout the Soviet Union moved to the republics to take jobs at new industrial production and natural resource extraction sites, and this movement caused the proportion of Russians relative to titulars to rise in all but five republics.[13] For example, the discovery of gold in the 1920s in Yakutia caused the Russian portion of the population there to increase from 11 to 50 percent by the end of the Soviet era. The percentage point change in the size of Russian populations in all republics from 1926 to 1989 (RPOP) is shown in table 3.1.

A growing population and a rising Russian population in particular brought more people in the republics into contact with one another. Because most Russians migrating to the republics did so to work in cities and at industrial sites, an increase in the size of the Russian population in a particular republic bolstered the possibility that competition for resources could develop between titulars and Russians. Therefore, I include this indicator in the index of trends in socioeconomic stratification (table 3.2) and assign a score of 1 to those republics with the largest increase in the Russian population: Checheno-Ingushetia, Yakutia, Kalmykia, N. Ossetia, Komi, and Kabardino-Balkaria.[14] Conversely, the size of

---

13. Russians also moved to work in industrial sites in Latvia, Estonia, Kazakhstan, Kyrgyzstan, and Ukraine. For a comparison of the UR and ARs, see Alastair McAuley, ed., *Soviet Federalism: Nationalism and Decentralisation* (New York: St. Martin's, 1991), 68.

14. See Guboglo, *Razvitie*, 127–28. In these places, there was a corresponding decline in titulars' share of republican populations. Although some nationalist leaders lamented this drop, it was not correlated with mass nationalist mobilization.

Table 3.3   Index of socioeconomic stratification as of 1989

	TATARSTAN	TUVA	CHECHENO-INGUSHETIA	YAKUTIA	BASHKORTOSTAN	KALMYKIA	KARELIA	BURYATIA	N. OSSETIA	KOMI	KABARDINO-BALKARIA	CHUVASHIA	UDMURTIA	DAGESTAN	MARI EL	MORDOVIA
URB1	1	3	3	3	2	2	1	2	1	2	2	2	2	3	2	2
URB3	1	1	1	3	3	1	3	3	1	3	1	1	3	1	3	3
LANG	2	3	2	3	2	1	1	2	2	1	2	2	1	3	2	1
EDU2	2	2	2	1	2	1	3	1	1	3	1	2	3	2	3	3
JOB	2	2	3	2	2	1	2	1	1	1	2	2	2	2	3	2
SUM	8	11	11	12	11	6	10	9	6	10	8	9	11	11	13	11
AVG RANK	1.6	2.2	2.2	2.4	2.2	1.2	2	1.8	1.2	2	1.6	1.8	2.2	2.2	2.6	2.2

Note: 1 = ethnic competition (EC); 3 = ethnic division of labor (EDL).

URB1: 1 = Titular populations with largest percentage of urban dwellers (>62%); 2 = Titular populations with middle percentage of urban dwellers (41%–55%); 3 = Titular populations with smallest percentage of urban dwellers (28–38%).

URB3: 1 = Republics in which titular share of urban population. is greater than or equal to that of Russians (40% or more); 3 = Republics in which titular share of urban population is 26% or less.

LANG: 1 = Republics in which more than 90% of titulars speak Russian; 2 = Republics in which 70–90% of titulars speak Russian; 3 = Republics in which fewer than 70% of titulars speak Russian.

EDU2: 1 = Titulars with largest number of students in VUZy (>200 students per 10,000 people); 2 = Titulars with between 120 and 200 students in VUZy; 3 = Titular nationalities with fewest students in VUZy (<120 students per 10,000 people).

JOB: 1 = Titulars are overrepresented or nearly proportionally represented in white-collar jobs (titular/Russian ratio is greater than or equal to .9); 2 = Titulars are somewhat underrepresented in white-collar jobs (range of titular/Russian ratio = .64–.86); 3 = Titulars are underrepresented in white-collar jobs by comparison with Russians (range of titular/Russian ratio = .52–.54).

the Russian population fell or grew by less than 10 percent in other republics: Tatarstan, Bashkortostan, Chuvashia, Dagestan, Mordovia, and Mari El.[15] I assign a score of 3 to these republics to indicate the lower likelihood of ethnic job competition and the higher likelihood of an EDL or separation of Russians and titulars. Republics in the middle range, where the Russian population grew by 10 to 20 percent—Tuva, Karelia, Buryatia, and Udmurtia—receive a score of 2.

Urbanization

The move from countryside to city is a critical aspect of social mobility because it multiplies opportunities for contact among people from different backgrounds

---

15. Note that these figures do not capture fluctuations in the relative size of the Russian population during the 1950s and 1960s. For example, the relative proportion of Chechens and Russians in Checheno-Ingushetia changed radically after the deportation and subsequent resettlement of Chechens.

and increases access to education and employment for people formerly living in rural areas. Republics in which titular nationalities underwent significant urbanization, therefore, were more likely to display higher job competition and a low ethnic division of labor. Conversely, republics in which titulars experienced lower urbanization were likely to have had an EDL to some degree.

I examine three indicators of titular urbanization in each republic: (1) the percentage of titular populations that had become urban as of 1989 (URB1); (2) the change in the share of titulars in the populations of republican cities over time, from 1959 to 1989 (URB2); and (3) the share of titulars in the populations of the cities in 1989 (URB3). Below, I describe urbanization in the Soviet Union in greater detail and then report the coding for each republic on each of these three indicators.

Throughout the Soviet era, economic development and industrialization induced rural dwellers in all parts of the country to leave the countryside. In Russia's republics, urbanization occurred at a faster rate than in the RSFSR as a whole, partly because of the behavior of titular nationalities. Whereas in the 1920s very few titulars lived in the cities, they urbanized at twice the rate of Russians from 1959 to 1989. The share of urban dwellers among almost all titular groups increased by 20 to 30 percentage points during these years.[16]

The fact that significant portions of titular populations had become urban by 1989—between 28 and 69 percent—shows that titular social mobility had occurred in all Russian republics. Comparing the republics, we observe that titular populations with the smallest share of urban dwellers as of 1989 were Tuvans, Chechens, Yakuts, and Avars and Lezgins in Dagestan (URB1) (see table 3.1). These republics received a score of 3 in the index of socioeconomic stratification as of 1989 to indicate the possibility of an EDL (table 3.3). In contrast, the titular nationalities with the largest percentage of urban dwellers were Tatars, Karelians, and North Ossetians. These republics received a score of 1 to suggest the greater possibility of ethnic competition than in the former set of republics. The nationalities in between the two ends of the urbanization scale (with a score of 2) were Bashkir, Kalmyks, Buryats, Komi, Kabards and Balkars, Udmurts, Chuvash, Mordvinians, and Mari.[17]

Another trend showing titular mobility was the transformation of republican cities from what geographer Ralph Clem described as "islands of Russian people,

16. The rate of titular urbanization peaked during the 1960s at 85.2 percent. The urbanization rate of Russians in the republics during this decade was 35 percent. See Guboglo, *Razvitie,* 10–11.

17. Robert J. Kaiser, *The Geography of Nationalism in Russia and the USSR* (Princeton: Princeton University Press, 1994), 203–4.

language and culture" into multiethnic spaces.[18] From 1959 to 1989, the share of titulars among urban populations in almost every republic rose, on average from 18 to 30 percent, while the share of Russians declined from 66 to 54 percent. In republican capital cities, the proportion of each titular group was slightly higher. To get a sense of how the ethnic composition of cities in the sixteen republics varied, it is useful to examine two different kinds of data: the change over time in the share of titular populations in cities (URB2) and the share of titular populations in the cities at the end of the Soviet era, in 1989 (URB3) (see table 3.1). In terms of the former, the titular percentage of the urban populations grew the most—by 20 percent or more—in Tuva, Checheno-Ingushetia, North Ossetia, Kabardino-Balkaria, and Dagestan. In the index of trends in socioeconomic stratification (table 3.2), these republics were coded as 1 to signify the probability that ethnic competition took place in the cities.[19] The republics where titulars' share of the urban population grew very little (5 percent or less)—Yakutia, Karelia, Komi, and Udmurtia—were coded as 3 to indicate the probability of an ethnic division of labor. Seven republics fell into the middle range on this indicator (Bashkortostan, Tatarstan, Buryatia, Mordovia, Mari El, Kalmykia, and Chuvashia) and were coded as 2.

When we examine the ethnic composition of republican cities at the close of the Soviet era (URB3), we see that the proportion of titulars in the urban population was approximately greater than or equal to that of Russians (40 percent) in eight republics: Tatarstan, Tuva, Checheno-Ingushetia, Kalmykia, North Ossetia, Kabardino-Balkaria, Chuvashia, and Dagestan. (see table 3.1).[20] I coded these republics as 1 in table 3.3 to indicate the possibility of ethnic competition. In all other republics, titulars were outnumbered by Russians, forming 20 percent or less of the urban population in Yakutia, Bashkortostan, Karelia, Buryatia, Komi, and Udmurtia. I coded these republics as 3, indicating the higher likelihood of an EDL. This disparity is only partly attributable to the fact that Russians outnumbered titulars overall in the populations of these republics. The share of titulars in the urban populations of these republics ranged from seven to twenty points lower than their share of the republic's general population. Nevertheless, despite the differences among republics in the relative share of Russians and titulars in

---

18. Ralph Clem, "The Ethnic Dimension, Part II," in *Contemporary Soviet Society,* ed. Jerry G. Pankhurst and Michael Paul Sacks (New York: Praeger, 1980), 33–60. See p. 45.

19. Compiled from data in Guboglo, *Razvitie,* 5, 12. Also see Kaiser, *Geography of Nationalism,* 220–21.

20. The ethnic composition of republican capital cities—where most of the nationalist activity took place—was essentially the same as that of the urban population more generally. Most of the republics in which titulars formed a majority of the urban population also had capital cities dominated by titulars. See Guboglo, *Razvitie.*

the cities, titulars and Russians eventually narrowed the urban-rural gap that had separated them at the start of the Soviet era.

Nationality Policies

The Soviet state instituted nationality policies that pulled more and more people into republican urban and industrial centers. The 1977 Soviet constitution as well as statements made several years later by General Secretary Yuri Andropov articulated the concept of *sblizhenie,* or merging of ethnic groups, which held that if the socioeconomic gap between different nationalities could be narrowed, social homogeneity and political harmony would follow. To achieve these goals, ethnic minorities were encouraged to learn Russian, become highly educated, and work in the urban industrial and white-collar sectors of the economy.

Moscow used korenizatsiia policies in the republics to help titular nationalities catch up to the socioeconomic position of ethnic Russians. Legal regulations and quotas were established for titulars in higher education and training programs, and specific positions were set aside for them in the Communist Party, government administrations, and enterprise management. A key principle anchoring korenizatsiia was that of proportional representation. Soviet planners believed that the ethnic composition of a particular educational institution or workplace should "reflect the ethnic distribution of the region in which it is located."[21] Initially, korenizatsiia was a top-down set of rules instituted by Moscow, but over time both minority nationalities and Russians came to view proportional representation as natural, fair, and just. By the 1970s, ethnic leaders in the republics insisted on the continuation of quotas and preference policies initially put in place by Moscow.[22]

Nationality policies achieved their intended goals. An analysis of Soviet census data by Ellen Jones and Fred W. Grupp indicates that by the mid-1980s, a majority of titulars in Russia's republics had learned to speak Russian, and many of them worked in skilled jobs in industry and high-status professions.[23] The authors show that titular group representation relative to Russians rose in (1) higher education, (2) specialized secondary school (required for technical and lower-level specialist jobs), and (3) Communist Party membership—each of

---

21. Ellen Jones and Fred W. Grupp, "Modernisation and Ethnic Equalisation in the USSR," *Soviet Studies* 36, no. 2 (April 1984): 159–84. See p. 160.

22. Interview with Raman Yurevich Belyakov, official in the president's administration, Kazan, February 15, 1997. Also see Kaiser, *Geography of Nationalism,* 135–38.

23. Jones and Grupp, "Modernisation and Ethnic Equalisation." Their analysis does not include data from the 1989 all-union census. However, 1989 census data reveal that these trends continued. See Guboglo, *Razvitie.*

which represented a path to professional mobility. Disparity in the occupational structure was declining. Other analysts such as Victor Zaslavsky concur, arguing that titulars were coming to resemble urbanized ethnic Russians living in the republics by the end of the Soviet era.[24]

Linguistic Russification of Titular Nationalities

A central way in which the Soviet state sought to equalize ethnic nationalities was through linguistic Russification. Titular populations in Russia's republics became increasingly bilingual and fluent in Russian in the decades after World War II.[25] However, this was not a straightforward story of Russian replacing native languages spoken by indigenous language communities. The Bolsheviks, soon after taking power, began to standardize vernaculars and introduce mass education in what they called "native languages" (*rodnoi iazyki*) as part of the process of ethnoterritorial federalism. Consequently, communities of people developed that became literate in titular republican languages, especially from the 1920s through World War II.[26]

Then, beginning in the late Stalin period, the state started to encourage linguistic Russification. Over time, Russian "became the language of upward mobility throughout the USSR."[27] Starting in 1959, the regime promoted bilingualism more explicitly by introducing a law giving parents the right to choose the language of instruction for their children. Children could study in schools in which the medium of instruction was either the titular language or Russian. In Russian-language schools, they could opt to study titular languages as a separate subject. Most parents in the ARs moved their children into Russian-language schools. As a result, instruction in titular-language schools declined precipitously and virtually disappeared in urban areas.[28] However, many students continued to study

---

24. Victor Zaslavsky, "Ethnic Group Divided: Social Stratification and Nationality Policy in the Soviet Union," in *The Soviet Union: Party and Society,* ed. Peter J. Potichnyj (New York: Cambridge University Press, 1988), 226.

25. Barbara A. Anderson and Brian D. Silver, "Some Factors in the Linguistic and Ethnic Russification of Soviet Nationalities: Is Everyone Becoming Russian?" in *The Nationalities Factor in Soviet Politics and Society,* ed. Lubomyr Hajda and Mark Beissinger (Boulder: Westview, 1990), 95–130.

26. Kaiser, *Geography of Nationalism,* 253; Terry Martin, *The Affirmative Action Empire: Nations and Nationalism in the Soviet Union, 1923–1939* (Ithaca: Cornell University Press, 2001). Brubaker, *Nationalism Reframed,* 37–40.

27. Kaiser, "Nationalizing the Work Force," 89.

28. By contrast, native-language education was offered through the tenth grade on average in the URs. Of the ARs, only Tatarstan and Bashkortostan continued to have titular language instruction up to the tenth grade, and this occurred mainly in rural areas. See Gorenburg, *Minority Ethnic Mobilization,* 38.

titular languages as a separate subject and were able to do so at even higher grade levels than before.[29]

Another way in which the state promoted linguistic Russification was through the media. The state decided whether newspapers, magazines, journals, books, and television would be made available in non-Russian languages in the republics. The fact that ARs were assigned fewer forms of titular-language media than the URs increased people's use of Russian in everyday communication.[30]

Overall, the Soviet state's efforts to promote Russian fluency and bilingualism among ethnic minorities were very successful. The number of titulars speaking Russian rose in all republics. From the 1960s onward, more titulars reported Russian as their native language, especially in republican capital cities and among those in interethnic marriages.[31] In fact, according to Brian Silver, Russian fluency among ethnic minorities was probably higher than indicated by census data because the wording of the question led many non-Russians to report their nationality when asked about native language.[32] By 1989, therefore, the percentage of titulars who spoke Russian was very high, ranging from 59 to 97.5 percent.

Comparing the republics on the dimension of titulars' Russian language ability (LANG), the largest percentages of Russian-speaking titulars—more than 90 percent—were found in Kalmykia, Karelia, Komi, Udmurtia, and Mordovia (see table 3.1). Since the ability to speak Russian indicates upward mobility, I code these republics as 1—likely to display ethnic competition—in table 3.3. The republics with the lowest proportions of Russian-speaking titulars—which ranged from a still very significant 59 to 70 percent—were Tuva, Yakutia, and Dagestan (among Avars, Dargins, Kumyks and Lezgins).[33] Although this relatively high degree of Russian language knowledge does not indicate the presence of an ethnic

29. Kaiser, *Geography of Nationalism*, 257–58. Anderson and Silver found that when titular languages were offered as a separate subject at higher grade levels, non-Russians were more likely to identify them as their "native language" and to consider Russian their "second language" in the census. "Some Factors," 105–7.

30. Clem, "Ethnic Dimension, Part II," 49.

31. Guboglo cautions, however, that this did not mean that these respondents stopped speaking titular languages. *Razvitie*, 27. Also see Michael Paul Sacks, "Ethnic and Gender Divisions in the Work Force of Russia," *Post-Soviet Geography* 36, no. 1 (January 1995): 1–12.

32. Brian Silver, "The Ethnic and Language Dimensions in Russian and Soviet Censuses," in *Research Guide to the Russian and Soviet Censuses*, ed. Ralph Clem (Ithaca: Cornell University Press, 1986), 70–97; M. N. Guboglo, *Sovremennye etnoiazykovye protsessy v SSSR* (Moscow: Nauka, 1984). Also see Gorenburg, "Soviet Nationalities Policy and Assimilation," in *Rebounding Identities: The Politics of Identity in Russia and Ukraine*, ed. Dominique Arel and Blair Ruble (Baltimore: Johns Hopkins University Press, 2006), 273–303.

33. Soviet census data include titulars who report speaking Russian as a second language (*vtoroi iazyk*) and those speaking it as a "native language." *Analiz i prognoz mezhnatsional'nik konfliktov v Rossii i SNG Ezhegodnik 1994* [Analysis and Prognosis of Interethnic conflict in Russia and the CIS: Handbook 1994] (Moscow: Rossiiskii nezavisimyi institut sotsial'nykh problem tsentr sotsiolog-

division of labor, I code these republics as 3 because they are clustered at the opposite end of the range of Russian-language knowledge by comparison with the other republics. The republics in the middle range with a score of 2 are Tatarstan, Checheno-Ingushetia, Bashkortostan, Buryatia, N. Ossetia, Kabardino-Balkaria, Chuvashia, and Mari El, where 70 to 90 percent of titulars knew Russian.

Education

Education, a key route to occupational achievement, was a priority for the Soviet regime. The state invested sufficient resources that by World War II, non-Russians had overcome illiteracy and were receiving a basic education. After the war, minority access to secondary, specialized secondary, and higher education was expanded in order to develop qualified "indigenous cadres" to work in republican government and industry.[34] The state implemented two kinds of korenizatsiia policies to achieve this goal—policies, it should be emphasized, that were concealed from the general public. First, the USSR ministry of higher education assigned quotas to various universities for titular groups in the republics—a practice that began in the 1920s. Within the republics, local officials assigned quotas to institutes of higher education (Vysshee uchebnoe zavedenie, or VUZy) that were under the authority of either republican education ministries or the ministries of various economic sectors and also informally gave preferences to titulars in the admissions process. Second, beginning in 1969, preparatory departments were established at VUZy to provide remedial education to working-class and rural youth. Students in preparatory departments received exemptions from compulsory entrance exams, a practice that gave a distinct advantage in higher education to many working-class and rural youth of non-Russian nationality.[35]

Korenizatsiia produced impressive results. In the twenty-year span from 1959 to 1979, the number of titulars receiving secondary and higher educations rose in all republics, doubling in most cases and even quadrupling among Kalmyks, Tuvans, and Chechens. The average increase among titulars during this time was 31.1 percent, compared with Russians' 28.3 percent.[36] This trend continued during the last fifteen years of Soviet rule, when the rate of higher education among

---

icheskogo analiza mezhnatsional'nikh konfliktov, 1994), 71–72. Kaiser reports the same data but separated into the categories of "native" and "second language." *Geography of Nationalism*, 290–91.

34. See Kaiser, *Geography of Nationalism*, 128, 225.

35. See Rasma Karklins's excellent discussion in "Ethnic Politics and Access to Higher Education: The Soviet Case," *Comparative Politics* 16, no. 3 (April 1984): 277–94. These policies seem to have been the most widespread in Central Asia.

36. This average is based on Goskomstat data published in Kaiser, *Geography of Nationalism*, 227. Goskomstat did not publish comparable data for 1989. The number of Russians here includes all Russians in the RSFSR, not just those living in the republics.

titulars outpaced that of Russians in all but four republics. The nationalities with the highest percentage point change in the number of students enrolled in higher education from 1974 to 1989 were Tuvans, Chechens, and Ingush (EDU1) (see table 3.1). I assigned these two republics (Tuva and Checheno-Ingushetia) a score of 1 since a rise in titular education can lead to ethnic competition (table 3.2).[37] Conversely, the nationalities with the lowest percentage point change during this period were Karelians, Buryats, Komi, and Balkars. Note that a low percentage point change does not mean that titular students lagged behind Russians; in absolute terms there were still large numbers of titulars enrolled in higher education.[38] But a drop in the number of titulars receiving educations among these nationalities could be understood as a constriction of access and opportunity for titulars in higher education—a situation that can be likened to the inequality found in an EDL. Therefore, these four republics are coded as 3. The republics in the middle range on this indicator (score of 2) are Tatarstan, Yakutia, Bashkortostan, Kalmykia, N. Ossetia, Udmurtia, Chuvashia, Dagestan, Mordovia, and Mari El.

Examining higher education at the end of the Soviet era, we observe remarkable titular advancement, despite the fact that in absolute terms Russians still outnumbered comparably educated titulars.[39] The republics varied in terms of the number of titular students enrolled in institutes of higher education as of 1989 (EDU2). The nationalities with the most students enrolled in VUZy were Yakuts, Kalmyks, Buryats, N. Ossetians, Kabards, and Balkars,[40] while the nationalities with the fewest students enrolled were Karelians, Komi, Udmurt, Mordovians and Mari(see table 3.1).[41] This suggests that ethnic competition was more likely in the former set of republics (coded as 1 in table 3.3) and an ethnic division of labor more likely in the latter set (coded as 3). Titular nationalities in six republics fell in the middle range of the scale and are coded as 2: Tatars, Tuvans, Chechens, Bashkir, Chuvash, and Dagestan.

Part of the reason that the data show titulars making such rapid educational gains is the relative youthfulness of titular populations by comparison with Russians. Goskomstat did not publish data on the age structure of each nationality enrolled in higher education, but demographers report that there were more college-age titulars (18–30) than college-age Russians. Consequently, titulars appear

---

37. Kaiser, *Geography of Nationalism*, 232.

38. For example, more Buryats received higher educations at this time than any other nationality, including Russians.

39. The highly educated Ossetians and Buryats are exceptions.

40. The Ingush also had the most students enrolled in VUZy.

41. Kaiser, *Geography of Nationalism*, 232.

to be better represented among students than they probably were.[42] However, Jones and Grupp estimated the age-specific rate of education and found that the higher proportion of college-age titulars alone cannot account for their extremely rapid rate of educational attainment. They conclude that the presence of titulars in higher education increased so quickly because of Soviet state policies that facilitated their access to higher education.[43] In the sphere of education, we again observe state-led affirmative action helping titulars catch up to Russians.

Professional Mobility

During much of the Soviet era, ethnic Russians dominated the urban industrial workforce in Russia's republics. Starting in the 1930s, however, titular nationalities also began to work in urban industrial occupations—a trend that accelerated during the final decades of Soviet rule. In the nearly thirty-year period from 1960 to 1987, titulars entered the urban industrial workforce in the republics at rising rates, in some cases even surpassing those of Russians. The proportion of each titular group working as white-collar "specialists" grew by an average of 8 percentage points during this period.[44] In blue-collar occupations as well, the share of titulars relative to Russians increased over time.[45] According to the Russian expert Leokadia Drobizheva, the gap between Russians and titulars narrowed significantly as the educational levels and professional skills of all nationalities grew considerably.[46]

Social mobility in the USSR was not necessarily a gradual process occurring over several generations. While some children of collective farm workers became assembly-line workers in factories or store clerks in the cities, many others jumped directly into high-status positions in government administration, the Communist Party, and academia. For example, many government officials in Tatarstan—including the republic's president—grew up in the countryside, attended agricultural institutes, and went on to obtain prestigious leadership

---

42. Karklins makes this point with regard to the URs. "Ethnic Politics," 281–83.

43. Kaiser, *Geography of Nationalism*, 227–28.

44. The Soviet category of "specialist" refers to people with either a specialized secondary education or higher education. Kaiser calls titulars in this category the "national intelligentsia." Ibid., 239–40. Jones and Grupp find that the proportion of titular specialists in the ARs had already risen significantly by the mid-1970s. "Modernisation and Ethnic Equalisation," 170–71.

45. The data on blue-collar workers are less clear-cut than that of white-collar workers because the Soviet category of blue-collar worker included state farm workers (*sovkhozy*) as well as industrial workers. Jones and Grupp, "Modernisation and Ethnic Equalization," 170.

46. Leokadia Drobizheva, "Processes of Disintegration in the Russian Federation and the Problem of Russians," in *The New Russian Diaspora: Russian Minorities in the Former Soviet Republics*, ed.Vladimir Shlapentokh, Munir Sendich, and Emil Payin (Armonk, NY: M.E. Sharpe, 1994), 44–55.

posts.[47] By the late 1970s, as would be expected, titulars occupied a majority of white-collar jobs in republican rural areas, where they lived in higher concentrations than Russians. More surprisingly, they also could be found in the upper echelon of urban economies.

What were the relative proportions of titulars and Russians in republican workforces when national revival began? As part of the 1989 Soviet census, Goskomstat collected information on the ethnic affiliations of workers in various professions and divided the data into the categories of intellectual labor (*intellektualnii trud*), which I will refer to as white-collar labor, and physical labor (*fizicheskii trud*), or blue-collar labor. Goskomstat deemed this information too sensitive to publish. However, I obtained the unpublished raw data[48] and created a ratio of titular to Russian representation in the white-collar workforce of each republic by determining a ratio value for, first, the titular percentage of the white-collar workforce compared with titulars' share of the overall republican workforce and second, the Russian percentage of the white-collar workforce compared with Russians' share of the overall republican workforce. I then compared these two values to obtain a ratio of titular to Russian representation in the white-collar workforce. A ratio of 1 indicates that both titulars and Russians were equally represented in white-collar jobs in proportion to their percentage of the total workforce, and a ratio greater than 1 means that titulars occupied white-collar jobs in numbers greater than their percentage of the workforce. A ratio less than 1 indicates that as a proportion of each group's overall representation in the workforce, titulars were underrepresented (see Figure 3.1).

The data in Figure 3.1 show that in most republics, titulars and Russians worked in white-collar jobs in almost equal proportion to their share of the total workforce in each republic, though Russians were still somewhat proportionately overrepresented. The average ratio for the republics was 0.814, and most republics were close to this average as of 1989. Titulars were actually proportionately *over*represented in white-collar jobs compared with Russians in two republics—Buryatia and Kalmykia—as indicated by a ratio value greater than 1.0. In two other republics—North Ossetia (0.95) and Komi (0.9)—Ossetians and Komi held white-collar jobs in numbers nearly proportional to their share

47. Biographical sketches of government officials and other elites published in the republics describe these individual career histories. See, for example, *Kto est' Kto v Respublike Tatarstan* [Who's Who in the Republic of Tatarstan] (Kazan: Izdatel' Star, 1996).

48. Dmitri Gorenburg kindly provided me with these data after obtaining it directly from a Goskomstat employee in Moscow. *Professional'no-otraslevoi sostav intelligentsia naseleniia titul'noi i russkoi natsional'nostei absoliutnye znacheniia.* [Titular and Russian ethnic group composition of white-collar economic sectors]. Unpublished Goskomstat data from 1989 All-Union census.

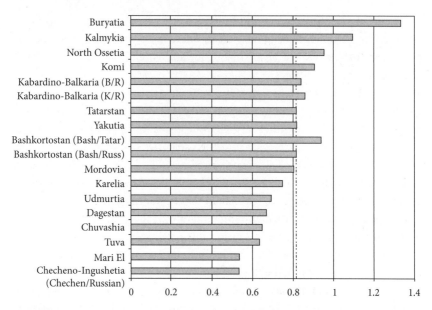

FIGURE 3.1   Ratio of titular/Russian representation in white-collar workforce, 1989. *Source: Professional'no-otraslevoi sostav intelligentsia naseleniia titul'noi i russkoi natsional'nostei absoliutnye znacheniia* [Titular and Russian ethnic group composition of white-collar economic sectors]. Unpublished Goskomstat data from 1989 All-Union census.

of the workforce. I assign these four republics a score of 1 in table 3.3 (JOB) to indicate the likelihood of Russian-titular job competition.[49]

Conversely, titulars were proportionately underrepresented in white-collar jobs by comparison with Russians in only two republics—Checheno-Ingushetia and Mari El, where the ratio of Chechen to Russian representation was .52, and Mari to Russian representation was .54. These data suggest an ethnic division of labor with many Chechens and Maris working in agriculture, while many Russians held urban, industrial jobs. Note that these republics did not have an absolute ethnic division of labor (a ratio value approaching zero), which would mean that virtually no titulars worked in white-collar professions.

Russia's other republics encompass a range of ratio values; I assign them a score of 2 in table 3.3. In Tuva, Chuvashia, Dagestan, Udmurtia, and Karelia, the ratio of titular populations to Russians ranged from 0.64 (Tuva) to 0.75 (Karelia), figures suggesting that titulars were somewhat underrepresented in white-collar jobs. The higher ratios in Kabardino-Balkaria (0.84 Balkar/Russians and 0.86 Kabards/Russians), Tatarstan (0.82), Yakutia (0.82), Bashkortostan (Bashkir/Russian 0.82),

---

49. Bashkirs in Bashkortostan were overrepresented by comparison with ethnic Tatars there: Bashkir/Tatar = 0.94.

and Mordovia (0.81) indicate that titulars and Russians were almost equally represented in white-collar positions in proportion to each group's percentage of the republican workforce.

Although these ratios provide information about the ethnic affiliations of workers in republican labor markets, they obscure two important points. First, the ratios portray ethnic representation in the labor market as of 1989 but do not show the growing professionalization of titular populations over time. Second, they do not capture what was taking place *within* the white-collar sector—i.e., the fact that Russians held a majority of white-collar positions in industrial production and scientific-technical fields, whereas titulars dominated government administration and the creative intelligentsia.[50] This occupational divide, however, began to change in the 1970s and 1980s, as titular nationalities "expand[ed] beyond the traditional sectors, of agriculture, healthcare, education, trade, and culture and the arts, into industry, construction, science, and transportation and communication."[51] Some republics had more titulars working in industry than others did; for example, in Tatarstan, Yakutia, and Bashkortostan, they served as engineers, economists, and agronomists in numbers greater than their overall percentage of the republic's workforce.[52] Goskomstat reports that in almost all republics titulars worked as directors of enterprises in numbers equal to or greater than their share of the total population.[53] Again, certain nationalities were overrepresented among enterprise directors (Avars, Kumyks, Lezgins, Balkars, Kabards, Kalmyks, Ossetians, Adygey, Karachay, and Cherkess), while others (Chechens) were underrepresented.[54] Overall, the data on ethnic representation presented here demonstrate that though titulars were still underrepresented in white-collar jobs in most republics (albeit to varying degrees) by the end of the Soviet era, they had made astounding socioeconomic strides over time in all republics.

---

50. Drobizheva, "Processes of Disintegration," 47, 52. This was also the case for most of the URs. See Iuryi Arutiunian and Iuryi Bromlei, eds., *Sotsial'no-kul'turnyi oblik Sovetskikh natsii* (Moscow: Nauka, 1986), cited in Paul A. Goble, "Gorbachev and the Soviet Nationality Problem," in *Soviet Society under Gorbachev: Current Trends and the Prospects for Reform,* Ed. Maurice Friedberg and Heyward Isham (Armonk, NY: M.E. Sharpe, 1987), 76–100.

51. Kaiser, "Nationalizing the Work Force," 94.

52. Drobizheva, "Processes of Disintegration," 47, 52.

53. *Narodnoe Khoziaistvo Rossiiskoi Federatsii* [The Economy of the Russian Federation] (Moscow: Goskomstat, 1990), 118. This fact would be more meaningful if Goskomstat had provided the number of titular enterprise directors relative to titulars' share of the working-age population in each republic, but it is clear that titulars were working in coveted management positions. These data are reported as percentages rather than raw numbers.

54. Kaiser, "Nationalizing the Work Force," 99.

Analysis of Socioeconomic Stratification

This examination of socioeconomic stratification in Russia's republics indicates that it is impossible to characterize them as having either an EDL or ethnic competition. In almost every republic, titulars both lagged behind Russians according to some indicators and were in a position to compete with them for educations and jobs according to other indicators. The average rankings of the republics underline this point: most republics cluster toward the middle of the scale of socioeconomic stratification on both indexes, as tables 3.4 and 3.5 demonstrate. Also, the two indexes show that almost no republics have consistent scores of either all 3s or all 1s across the indicators, suggesting again that no republic can be described as having either an unambiguous ethnic division of labor[55] or very low socioeconomic stratification as a result of ethnic mobility. Only two republics in fact—Kalmykia and North Ossetia—have relatively consistent scores across all indicators (1s and 2s) as well as a consistent average rank in the two indexes (a difference of .2 or less).[56] (See table 3.6) They have the lowest socioeconomic stratification or highest titular mobility compared to other republics.

Because all republics began the century with titular populations that lagged behind Russians but made astounding socioeconomic advances over the course of Soviet rule, by 1989 they all had elements of both titular inequality and titular parity vis-à-vis Russians. This is why they appear to be homogeneous when different indicators are added together. Depending on which individual indicator we examine in a given republic, we obtain different pictures of the socioeconomic position of titulars and Russians in that republic. For example, examining education and urbanization in Yakutia, it is clear that a very high percentage of Yakuts attended college by comparison with other republics (EDU2=1) but conversely that a low percentage of Yakuts had become urban (URB1=3) and that they formed a small share of the republic's urban population (URB3=3) as of 1989. Were Yakuts equivalent or subordinate to Russians?

In other republics, if we observe the socioeconomic situation as of 1989, a picture of titular subordination appears, whereas if we examine indicators of trends over time, a more promising picture of titular opportunity emerges. In the case of Tuva, for example, Tuvans spoke Russian to a lesser degree than in other republics as of 1989, a fact suggesting that they were less socioeconomically

---

55. Also, because the index is a comparative metric, a score of 3 does not signify that an absolute division of labor exists but only that in comparison with other republics, there is more separation or stratification between titulars and Russians.

56. Several other republics also have a relatively consistent average rank in the two indexes (a difference of .3 or less): Bashkortostan, Kabardino-Balkaria, Udmurtia, Dagestan, Mordovia, and Komi. However, with scores close to the middle of the scale, these republics cannot be categorized as having either an EDL or ethnic competition.

Table 3.4   Average rank of republics: Index of socioeconomic stratification, 1989

AVG. RANK	REPUBLIC
1	
1.2	North Ossetia
1.4	Kalmykia
1.6	Tatarstan/Kabardino-Balkaria
1.8	Buryatia/Chuvashia
2	Komi/Karelia
2.2	Tuva/Checheno-Ingushetia/Bashkortostan/Udmurtia/Dagestan/Mordovia
2.4	Yakutia
2.6	Mari El
2.8	
3	

Table 3.5   Average rank of republics: Index of trends in socioeconomic stratification

AVG. RANK	REPUBLIC
1	Checheno-Ingushetia
1.3	Tuva/North Ossetia
1.6	Kalmykia/Kabardino-Balkaria
2	Yakutia/Dagestan
2.3	Tatarstan/Bashkortostan/Buryatia/Komi/Chuvashia/Udmurtia/Mari El/Mordovia
2.6	Karelia
3	

Table 3.6   Average rank of Russia's republics on indexes of socioeconomic stratification

REPUBLIC	AVG. RANK 1989	AVG. RANK TRENDS
Tatarstan	1.6	2.3
Tuva	2.2	1.3
Checheno-Ingushetia	2.2	1
Yakutia	2.4	2
Bashkortostan	2.2	2.3
Kalmykia	1.4	1.6
Karelia	2	2.6
Buryatia	1.8	2.3
North Ossetia	1.2	1.3
Komi	2	2.3
Kabardino-Balkaria	1.6	1.6
Chuvashia	1.8	2.3
Udmurtia	2.2	2.3
Dagestan	2.2	2
Mari El	2.6	2.3
Mordovia	2.2	2.3

advantaged than Russians (LANG=3). On the other hand, examining trends in urbanization or education, we see that, instead of facing economic exclusion, Tuvans were undergoing socio-economic mobility (URB2=1 and EDU1=1). These examples may be multiplied.

The fact that pulling different indicators out of the index changes the picture of socioeconomic stratification means that ethnic entrepreneurs can choose to focus on particular indicators—or particular socioeconomic processes—to construct a story about an EDL and discrimination against titulars in republican economies.[57] Why do these stories gain traction with people if they rest on economic data that can be interpreted in multiple and contradictory ways? Part of the reason is the macroeconomic environment in the country at the time—a period of serious economic crisis and growing job insecurity.

Macroeconomic Change and Employment

The Soviet state exerted control over people's professional lives through various administrative means. First, according to the system of *raspredelniya,* or job distribution, graduates of higher education were assigned their first job by distribution commissions located inside VUZy, in secondary specialized education institutes (Srednee spetsialnoe uchebnoe zavedenie, SSUZy), and after 1980, in vocational-technical institutes. The state expected graduates to remain in their first job for three or four years, or ideally, for the rest of their lives.[58] The role of the state in job allocation did not necessarily end once people obtained their initial work assignments since senior positions were also allocated administratively via the nomenklatura system. The Communist Party maintained nomenklatura lists of people eligible for appointment to elite positions in management and administration. In addition, the state allocated jobs through the administrative system of *orgnabor,* or organized recruitment, in which rural-dwellers who did not have the right to move out of their home villages were sent to work in industry and construction at specific sites throughout the Union. Nevertheless, despite the state's considerable use of administrative methods to allocate jobs, labor mobility existed.[59] Some people changed jobs, for example, to advance their careers or for higher salaries, bigger apartments, and improved access to

---

57. I develop this point in subsequent chapters.

58. Top students with reliable political backgrounds enjoyed greater control than other students in selecting their first work assignment and in leaving it for a new one. Simon Clarke, *The Formation of a Labour Market in Russia* (Cheltenham, U.K.: Edward Elgar, 1999), 13–15.

59. Though limited by the *propiska* (residence permit) system Soviet citizens engaged in "inter-enterprise job hopping" in search of better benefits, especially larger apartments. Guy Standing, *Rus-*

goods and services, while others were ideologically motivated to join large new construction projects in order to build the socialist future. Overall, the Soviet state played a central role in assigning jobs to people based on their educational background, political reliability, and career experience and in shaping individual career trajectories. Yet precisely during the years when demand for jobs—and white-collar jobs in particular—was rising, the Soviet economy had stopped growing.

Soviet macroeconomic decline began during Brezhnev's "era of stagnation." In the late 1970s and the 1980s in the ethnic republics, the state's ability to meet demand for white-collar positions was shrinking.[60] The Soviet scholars Iurii Arutiunian and Iurii Bromlei maintain that as university enrollments expanded, graduates could not always find jobs commensurate with their educational level and were forced to accept lesser positions.[61] By the end of the decade, the Soviet Union was in the midst of a deepening economic crisis. As production declined and the central state lost revenue, it became increasingly difficult for the state to create new positions in industrial production, the bloated state sector, and academia, culture, and the arts. A stagnating economy could not, according to Philip Roeder, continue to "accommodate new aspirants to [the ethnic] elite."[62]

Officially, the Soviet state maintained that unemployment did not exist,[63] yet economists have shown that underemployment characterized the labor market.[64] In the Soviet command economy, enterprises, collective farms, and government organizations had many posts that were filled on paper only. They employed what economist Guy Standing calls "dead souls" because there were incentives for managers to report large workforces in order to secure greater resources from central ministries and to enhance their personal status and income. Many of these posts were "filled" by people of retirement age (sixty years old for men, fifty-five for women) who preferred to continue drawing a salary rather than subsist on a meager pension. Some came to work occasionally to visit with

---

sian Unemployment and Enterprise Restructuring: Reviving Dead Souls (New York: St. Martin's, 1996), 3. Also see Clarke, The Formation of a Labour Market in Russia, chapter 1.

60. Robert Kaiser reports that this was also the case in the union republics. Geography of Nationalism, 96.

61. The gap between supply and demand for white-collar positions was especially notable in the Baltics. See Arutiunian and Bromlei, Sotsial'no-kul'turnyi oblik, and Goble, Soviet Society under Gorbachev, 87–88.

62. Roeder, "Soviet Federalism," 1991, 214.

63. Therefore, there are no unemployment data until after 1991. See Valery Yakubovich and Irina Kozina, "The Changing Significance of Ties: An Exploration of the Hiring Channels in the Russian Transitional Labor Market," International Sociology 15, no. 3 (September 2000): 479–500.

64. There were two kinds of underemployed workers: people who held jobs officially but did little actual work and people who didn't work at all and simply weren't counted.

friends or take advantage of services, while many of the younger "pensioners" continued to work.[65]

During perestroika, Moscow attempted to improve economic efficiency by doing away with these dead soul posts. Older workers who had not been coming to work were let go, and many younger workers of pension age were forced to retire, eliminating the empty posts by 1991. More generally, enterprises in all sectors began reducing employment in 1990.[66] Thus, even before the Soviet Union collapsed, job security for some people was disappearing. Then Yeltsin passed the Employment Act in 1991, which allowed employers to fire workers, legalizing unemployment. It also granted workers more discretion in deciding for themselves where to work. As a result, people began to leave state employment and the level of unemployment started to rise, though it did not explode, as people had expected.

The problems faced by the Soviet state in satisfying growing demand for employment by its citizens at this time is suggested by figure 3.2. The figure indicates tightening competition for jobs by showing a rise in the number of working-age people who were not employed each year from 1985 to 1995. In the absence of data on unemployment or job allocation, I subtracted the average number of people employed each year (*srednegodovaia chislennost' zanyatykh v ekonomike*) from the number of working-age people (*naselenia v trudosposobnom vozraste*) in the population of each republic. The greater the gap in these two categories, the greater the number of people in each republic who made up the working-age population but who were not working. A rise in this number in almost all republics is observed beginning in 1990. The figure shows the populations of all republics added together.

By 1991 the expectation of mass unemployment had become pervasive.[67] According to economists Vladimir Gimpelson and Douglas Lippoldt, "the general public saw unemployment as a major threat," and once reforms began in the late 1980s, "perceived unemployment to be higher than it was."[68] People who expected their lives and those of their children to progress along familiar, state-established trajectories—secondary school followed by higher education or technical training and then by secure jobs and advancement up the career ladder—became

---

65. Standing, *Russian Unemployment,* xxv, 1–3.

66. Vladimir Gimpelson and Douglas Lippoldt, *The Russian Labour Market: Between Transition and Turmoil* (Lanham, Md.: Rowman & Littlefield, 2001), 30. Also, Standing cites the results of the first Russian Labor Flexibility Survey (RLFS) conducted in late 1991 as evidence. The first round of the RLFS, however, was not intended to be a representative sample and surveyed only enterprises in Moscow, St. Petersburg, and Moscow oblast. *Russian Unemployment,* 64–65 and chapter 3.

67. Standing, *Russian Unemployment,* 11.

68. Gimpelson and Lippoldt, *Russian Labour Market,* 7.

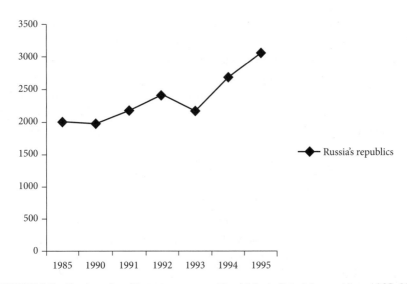

FIGURE 3.2   Number of working-age persons without jobs in Russia's republics, 1985–95 (in thousands). *Source: Regiony Rossii, statisticheskii sbornik* [Russia's Regions, A Statistical Handbook], vol. 1 (Moscow: Goskomstat, 1998).

uncertain that the state would continue to provide them and their children with educations and jobs. When food shortages and long lines for all kinds of consumer goods appeared in 1990 and 1991, they contributed further to people's falling confidence in their future prospects. After 1991, when Yeltsin freed prices, growing unemployment followed by runaway inflation profoundly destabilized the daily lives of Soviet citizens. The shock of the economic production crisis in the late Soviet era was exacerbated by the rapid and momentous political transformations occurring at the time, which contributed to further insecurity. Given this shift in the macroeconomic context, we might expect people to have become more aware of adverse labor conditions such as an ethnic division of labor or job competition. Did either of these economic structures inspire them to support nationalist programs demanding radical change?

Testing Structuralist Economic Theories

Proponents of structuralist models of mobilization would expect mass nationalism to develop in those republics with either an ethnic division of labor or ethnic job competition. Yet the indexes presented above reveal that almost none of Russia's republics had clear-cut high social stratification. Therefore, it is not possible to code them as having either an EDL or ethnic competition. The two republics that came closest to displaying an EDL, Karelia and Mari El—which both had an average rank of 2.6 but on two different indexes—did not have significant levels of popular support for nationalism. The republics with the greatest degree of mass nationalism were Tatarstan, Tuva, and Chechnya, followed by Yakutia and Bashkortostan. None of these can be considered republics with an EDL according to their average rank on the indexes.[69] Thus there is no correlation between nationalist mobilization and an ethnic division of labor in Russia's republics. See table 3.7.

Is there a relationship between nationalist mobilization and an EDL if we look only at the most direct indicator of socioeconomic stratification in the republics: ethnic representation in the white-collar workforce? Two republics in particular, Tuva and Chechnya, have been commonly described as places where Russians predominated in white-collar jobs. The low ratio values of the two republics in figure 3.1 support this point. The ratio of Chechen to Russian representation is 0.52 and that of Tuvan to Russian 0.64 indicating that, compared to other republics, titulars in Checheno-Ingushetia and Tuva were proportionately underrepresented in white-collar jobs by comparison with Russians. What was the socioeconomic situation inside each republic at the end of the Soviet era? I discuss each republic briefly below.

Both Checheno-Ingushetia and Tuva had a higher proportion of titulars working in rural agriculture and Russians working in urban industry as of 1989. In Tuva, Tuvans formed only 20 percent of the urban population but 80 percent of the rural population.[70] Tuvans lagged behind Russians in urbanization, education, and white-collar occupational achievement, prompting one Tuvan scholar to describe the republic's labor market as an EDL. Yet Tuvans made significant progress during the last decade of Soviet rule. Whereas in the early 1980s, there were twice as many Russian as Tuvan "specialists with higher education," by the end of the decade, equal numbers of Russians and Tuvans were about to graduate with higher degrees. Likewise, the percentage of Tuvans among white-collar workers rose faster (by seven points) than that of Russians (by four points) from 1979 to 1989.[71] Ethnic Tuvans were very well represented among academics and also could be found in the white-collar spheres of culture, science, communication, and education, as well as in the

---

69. Each one of these republics has at least one socioeconomic indicator with a score of 3, suggesting an EDL. This is true of every republic except North Ossetia and Kalmykia, which are the only two republics with consistently low scores of social stratification.

70. Zoia Anaiban, *Respublika Tuva: Model' etnologicheskogo monitoringa* [The Republic of Tuva: Model of Ethnographical Monitoring] (Moscow: Institute of Ethnography and Anthropology, Russian Academy of Sciences, 1996).

71. Drobizheva, "Processes of Disintegration," 49.

Table 3.7 Nationalism and socioeconomic stratification

	NATIONALIST REPUBLICS	NONNATIONALIST REPUBLICS
Ethnic division of labor	Tuva	Mari El
	Chechnya	Chuvashia
		Dagestan
		Udmurtia
Low ethnic division of labor / moderate to high ethnic job competition	Tatarstan	Buryatia
	Yakutia	Karelia
	Bashkortostan	Komi
		Mordovia
		Kabardino-Balkaria
		Kalmykia
		North Ossetia

most prestigious spheres of economic management and government, albeit in fewer numbers than Russians.[72]

Similarly, in Checheno-Ingushetia, there were more Russians than Chechens in high-status jobs in 1989. They dominated the spheres of oil extraction and engineering, whereas large numbers of Chechens worked in agriculture. Only 27 percent of Chechens were urban as of 1989, and their educational levels were lower than those of Russians. Several scholars in fact have argued that an ethnic division of labor caused nationalist separatism there.[73] Other scholars point to general poor economic conditions and low living standards as the source of nationalist grievances.[74] Yet this picture of Chechen disadvantage is tempered by dynamic trends in the republic's economy as the data on education (EDU1=1) and urbanization (URB2=1) in the index of trends in socioeconomic stratification (table 3.2) suggest. The Russian scholar Valery Tishkov describes the years 1960–80 as "a period of intense socio-cultural development.... Urbanization accelerated, and a significant part of the population acquired industrial skills, primarily in oil extraction and processing, and in the lumber and textile

---

72. Anaibin, *Respublika Tuva,* 47–51. Also see G. F. Balakina, Z V. Anaiban, *Sovremennaia Tuva: Sotsiokul'turnye i etnicheskie protsessy.* [Modern Tuva: Social and Ethnic Processes] (Novosibirsk: Nauka, 1995), 43–50.

73. Kaiser cites the fact that there were fewer Chechens than Russians among enterprise directors as a possible explanation for nationalism. "Nationalizing the Work Force," 99. Also see Victor Kogan Iasnyi and Diana Zisserman-Brodsky, "Chechen Separatism," in *Separatism: Democracy and Disintegration,* ed. Metta Spencer (Lanham, Md.: Rowman & Littlefield, 1998), 205–26.

74. John Dunlop, *Russia Confronts Chechnya: Roots of a Separatist Conflict* (Cambridge: Cambridge University Press, 1998), 87–88. Also Georgi M. Derlugian, who offers an otherwise sophisticated interpretation of the causes of Chechen separatism, also emphasizes how the republic's underdeveloped economy and Russian dominance of the industrial sector kept Chechens occupationally subordinate to Russians. See "Ethnofederalism and Ethnonationalism in the Separatist Politics of Chechnya and Tatarstan: Sources or Resources?" *International Journal of Public Administration* 22 (September/October 1999): 1387–1428.

industries."[75] Although Chechens were outnumbered by Russians in most white-collar economic sectors, they were not excluded from any sphere of the economy. In fact, Chechens were either overrepresented or equally represented by comparison with Russians in important, high-status spheres—the Communist Party and government administration, and science, the arts, and education.[76] Moreover, Chechens had been displacing Russian office workers in the cities for the last three decades of Soviet rule because Chechens tended not to take jobs in industrial production.[77] Overall, the labor market in Checheno-Ingushetia and Tuva at the end of the Soviet era can be characterized as having both elements of an EDL and opportunities for social mobility.

Since Chechnya and Tuva were two of the most nationalist republics, does the fact that Russians there dominated the white-collar labor market to a greater degree than in other republics mean that an EDL could be associated with nationalism? Examining the rest of the republics, we observe no relationship. First, the republic of Mari El, like Checheno-Ingushetia, had a white-collar sector dominated by Russians: the ratio value of Mari to Russian representation is .54 in figure 3.1. Yet Mari El had one of the lowest levels of mass nationalism in all the republics. Several other republics that had some degree of titular underrepresentation among white-collar workers vis-à-vis Russians—Chuvashia, Dagestan, and Udmurtia—also had low levels of nationalism. Thus a structural ethnic division of labor cannot account for variation in nationalism across Russia's republics.

Interethnic Competition

Theories of ethnic competition predict that an exogenous economic shock may spur mobilization as ethnic groups begin competing for scarce resources in a common economic niche. Did growing competition for state-distributed resources sharpen the boundary between ethnic groups and induce titulars to mobilize in support of republican nationalism? If so, we should observe mass nationalism in the republics with a high degree of titular urbanization, linguistic Russification, higher education, and relatively equal proportions of titulars and Russians in white-collar occupations. Do the average ranks of the republics in the two indexes indicate that this was the case? There were only two republics—North

75. Tishkov, *Ethnicity, Nationalism and Conflict*, 197.

76. Ibid.

77. The number of Russian office employees fell by more than half from 1959 to 1989. Galina U. Soldatova, "The Former Checheno-Ingushetia: Interethnic Relations and Ethnic Conflicts," *Anthropology and Archeology of Eurasia* 31, no. 4 (Spring 1993): 79.

Ossetia and Kalmykia—that came close to approximating ethnic competition according to their low average ranks (≤ 1.5) on the scale of socioeconomic stratification in both indexes. Neither of these republics experienced mass nationalist mobilization.

The two nationalist republics of Checheno-Ingushetia and Tuva also have low average ranks of stratification (1 and 1.3), but only on the index of trends in socioeconomic stratification (table 3.2). This indicates that titulars there experienced high mobility over time, which could have produced the job competition that inspired people to mobilize for nationalist change. Yet as described above, titulars there continued to lag behind Russians in white-collar jobs, which is an important element of an EDL. We may say, then, that Chechnya and Tuva had elements of both ethnic competition and an EDL. Since people are motivated to mobilize according to different logics in the two theories of EDL and ethnic competition, the relationship between these economic structures and the outcome of mass mobilization is indeterminate.

If we again examine just the indicator of ethnic representation in the white-collar workforce, do we find that ethnic competition is associated with mass nationalism? Competition theory would predict nationalist mobilization in republics in which titulars were either overrepresented in white-collar positions by comparison with their group's percentage of the total workforce or relatively equally represented with Russians. Both situations would reflect titulars' growing demand for, and ability to compete over, a limited supply of jobs. If we first consider the four republics in which titulars were proportionately overrepresented or nearly proportionately represented in white-collar jobs—Buryatia, Kalmykia, North Ossetia, and Komi, with a ratio value greater than or equal to .9 in figure 3.1—we find that none of these were the nationalist republics. The picture does not change if we expand the set of republics to include those where titular representation in white-collar jobs almost matched that of Russians (a ratio of .8 or greater): Kabardino-Balkaria, Tatarstan, Yakutia, Bashkortostan, and Mordovia. Of these republics, nationalist mobilization took place to a significant degree in three (Tatarstan, Yakutia, Bashkortostan) but did not occur in two (Kabardino-Balkaria, Mordovia). Therefore, the structural variable of job competition is not correlated with the presence of nationalist mobilization in certain Russian republics (see table 3.3). Overall, this analysis has demonstrated that there is no correlation between adverse conditions in the labor markets of Russia's republics at the end of the Soviet era and the emergence of or variation in mass nationalism in the republics, as shown in table 3.7.

This chapter demonstrates that both Russians and titular nationalities experienced significant geographic and social mobility throughout the decades of

Soviet rule and in particular in the postwar decades. Rising population growth, urbanization, and industrialization combined with Russification and indigeni-zation of titular nationalities to bring larger and larger numbers of people into industrial sites and urban areas within Russia's republics. In all republics, people who had relied on stable and secure jobs with opportunities for advancement suddenly faced a real threat concerning their prospects for the future when a crisis in economic production developed during the late 1980s. This experience and the feelings of fear of job loss were shared by all Soviet citizens accustomed to state provision of jobs, resources, and stability. Yet these adverse economic conditions by themselves did not inspire ethnonationalist mobilization. Nor did the production crisis in the Soviet economy suddenly cause people to realize that they lived in a society with structural inequities such as an ethnic division of labor or interethnic job competition. Neither of these factors inspired popular support for nationalism in Russia's republics.

The theories of a cultural division of labor and ethnic competition advance opposing hypotheses about whether a stratified labor market or the breakdown of that market causes ethnic mobilization. Both theories identify how an experi-ence central to people's lives—their jobs and social mobility—can shape material interests. Socioeconomic mobility is important insofar as it critically structures people's experiences and shapes their identities, interests, and feelings. However, a connection between social mobility on the one hand and ethnic group iden-tity or national consciousness on the other does not automatically exist. In sum, structural economic factors did not generate a grievance among titular popula-tions in the republics that inspired them to mobilize against the status quo and in favor of national renewal. We are left, then, with the question of how ethnic group affiliations came to matter politically in certain republics. The answer con-cerns the way in which nationalists framed issues of ethnic inequality.

4

SUPPORTING NATIONAL SOVEREIGNTY IN TATARSTAN

In the Kazan of my childhood, there were four of us friends. Kharis and Damir were Tatars, and Boris and I were Russians. Only none of us ever thought about that. Until today.

—Yevgenii Skukin, "Ordinary Ittifak Fascism?"

In 1991, Yeltsin came here [to Kazan] and said, "Take as much sovereignty as you can swallow." After four hundred years of oppression, it really seemed as if we would achieve everything we wanted in two or three months.

—Zaki Zainuillin, cochairman of Tatar Public Center

This chapter provides an in-depth study of the rise of mass support for nationalism by focusing on one of Russia's most nationalist republics—Tatarstan. This case is particularly revealing because people in Tatarstan supported the opposition nationalist movement to a greater degree than in other republics. The case also suggests, however, the ephemeral nature of nationalism: popular support for nationalism in Tatarstan peaked in 1991 and early 1992 and then began to decline. By the mid-1990s, the republican government led by former communist Mintimir Shaimiev had consolidated power. Tatar nationalist organizations faded into political irrelevance as much of the public lost interest in them by the mid- to late 1990s.[1]

Scholars and locals give much of the credit for both the rise and the decline of nationalism in Tatarstan to the communist leader turned republican president Mintimir Shaimiev. He has been lauded for successfully winning greater autonomy from Moscow, for keeping nationalist demands moderate, for avoiding the kind of nationalist escalation witnessed in Chechnya, and for maintaining interethnic peace in the republic.[2] Though he deserves recognition for his political

---

1. Field notes, Kazan, Tatarstan, 1996–97.
2. See Derlugian, "Ethnofederalism and Ethnonationalism"; Edward Walker, "The Dog That Didn't Bark: Tatarstan and Asymmetrical Federalism in Russia," *Harriman Review* 9 (Winter 1996): 1–35; Gulnaz Sharaftutdinova, "Chechnya versus Tatarstan: Understanding Ethnopolitics in Post-Communist Russia," *Problems of Post-Communism* 47, no. 2 (2 March/April 2000): 13–22; Jeffrey

moderation, focusing on Shaimiev tells us little about mass mobilization, and overlooks the fact that his administration was largely reactive to the initiatives of the Tatar nationalist movement and mass behavior during the early critical years of national revival.[3]

Other explanations for the high degree of nationalism in Tatarstan focus on the relative wealth of the republic. Tatarstan had the largest population among Russia's republics and was the most economically developed.[4] Situated at the confluence of the Volga and Kama rivers, it was a strategic crossroads for trade and transportation.[5] Its territory contained significant reserves of crude oil, coal, and gas, and by the 1980s it boasted an industrial output larger than that of the three Baltic republics combined.[6] These factors have been cited as motivating the republic's assertive secessionist campaign. Though many elites within the republic believed that they could maximize Tatarstan's wealth by winning greater autonomy from Moscow, mass nationalism cannot be reduced to this factor. Residents of the republic did not automatically understand structural economic conditions there in a uniform, ethnicized way. It took ethnic entrepreneurs to interpret these conditions by infusing them with particular ethnic meanings.

Tatar nationalist entrepreneurs viewed the socioeconomic position of Tatars relative to Russians as a serious injustice. Although Tatars had experienced significant social mobility, the nationalists emphasized their putative disadvantage and oppression in order to paint a picture of victimization. They attempted to connect Tatar identity to a sense of personal infringement as well as to the idea that a continuation of the status quo would limit the future development of the Tatar nation. To avoid this fate, Tatars had a responsibility to challenge current political authority and support national sovereignty.

The nationalist articulation of Tatar socioeconomic subordination resonated with many people, not because it perfectly described local conditions but because

Kahn, *Federalism, Democratization, and the Rule of Law in Russia* (Oxford: Oxford University Press, 2002); Treisman, "Russia's 'Ethnic Revival'"; Stoner-Weiss, "Federalism and Regionalism"; as well as studies by local scholars in Tatarstan.

3. The discussion of Tatarstan in books by Matthew Evangelista and Mark Beissinger makes this point very effectively. See Evangelista, *The Chechen Wars* (Washington, D.C.: Brookings Institution Press, 2002), and Beissinger, *Nationalist Mobilization*.

4. After shrinking slightly during the famine in the 1920s and World War II, Tatarstan's population grew from 2.85 million people in 1959 to 3.64 million in 1989—larger than five of the union republics.

5. Ronald Wixman, "The Middle Volga: Ethnic Archipelago in a Russian Sea," in *Nations and Politics in the Soviet Successor States,* ed. Ian Bremmer and Ray Taras (Cambridge: Cambridge University Press, 1993), 421–447.

6. Since oil was discovered in 1944, 2.6 billion tons have been extracted from the republic. "The Republic of Tatarstan: A Path-Breaker in Political and Economic Reform," prospectus, Chamber of Commerce and Industry of Tatarstan (Kazan, 1996), 18. This prospectus is based on a study conducted by the U.S. consulting firm, Monitor Company, Cambridge, Massachusetts.

it offered them a plausible interpretation of rising job insecurity and fear of un-employment in a tightening economy. Many Tatars became convinced by the nationalist claim that a gap in Tatar-Russian professional achievement unjustly hindered the Tatar nation. They were persuaded by the nationalist message that Soviet authorities and the current political order were to blame and that the only proper solution was to equalize Tatar opportunity and achievement through the realization of state sovereignty.

This chapter and the next focus on the interaction between people's lived experiences in local labor markets and elites' framing of issues of Tatar economic inequality. In this chapter I present data demonstrating Tatar social mobility and the educational, linguistic, and occupational position of Tatars relative to Russians in Tatarstan at the end of the Soviet era. I illustrate how entrepreneurs framed issues of Tatar underrepresentation in the republic's economy and how the Tatar nationalist movement took up this issue framing in order to construct a grievance among ethnic Tatars. To show how members of Tatarstan's population reacted to this issue framing, I first examine attitudes among Tatars and Russians using evidence from public opinion surveys, local newspapers, and interviews. I then show mass support for nationalism by describing the chronology of national revival in Tatarstan, emphasizing high mass participation at nationalist demonstrations and survey data on support for nationalist organizations and the goal of republican sovereignty.

Ethnicity and Professional Competition in Tatarstan

The Bolsheviks created the Tatar Autonomous Soviet Socialist Republic (Tatar ASSR) in 1920 after a complex series of debates in which local and Moscow elites considered establishing various forms of autonomy and administrative territories for the people of the Middle Volga. Some Volga Muslims and Tatar communists wanted to unite the region's Muslims by creating a territorially autonomous "Idel-Ural" (Volga-Ural) republic. Others supported the Bolsheviks' initial idea of establishing a Tatar-Bashkir Soviet republic. Ultimately, the Bolsheviks settled on a Tatar republic[7] and set about promoting a specific version of history in which the origins of the Tatar nation were to be found somewhere

---

7. According to Tatar and Western scholars, the Bolsheviks perceived a threat from Tatar nationalism, pan-Turkism, and pan-Islamism and so engaged in "divide and rule" by drawing the boundaries of the Tatar and Bashkir republics so that a large number of ethnic Tatars were assigned to the neighboring Bashkir republic. See Azade-Ayse Rorlich, *The Volga Tatars: A Profile in National Resilience* (Stanford: Hoover Institution Press, 1986).

within the boundaries of the republic.[8] Many of the people living on the land now defined as Tatarstan were peasants who continued to refer to themselves as Muslim, Turk, Turco-Tatar, or Bulgar. All would now become members of the Tatar nationality.

At the beginning of the Soviet era, the socioeconomic status of the republic's two major nationalities—Tatars and Russians—was similar: they were rural-dwelling peasants. Only about 8 percent of the republic's population lived in cities. Tatars and Russians formed relatively equal portions of the population—a pattern that would continue throughout the Soviet era. The main differences between the two groups consisted of a lower level of urbanization and education among Tatars. Five percent of the Tatar population was urban in 1926, compared with 18 percent of Russians,[9] and a mere 630 Tatars, or slightly more than 10 percent of the republic's entire student population, had completed higher education (table 4.1).[10] Bolshevik leaders considered the urban and educated Tatars to be somewhat of an elite compared with other Soviet national minorities and made use of their Turkic-language skills and relatively weak Islamic belief by sending them to Central Asia to campaign against Islam and proselytize for Bolshevism.

By the time national revival began in the late 1980s, the republic's ethnic demography had changed considerably. First, the share of Tatars in the republican population had increased from 44.9 percent in 1926 to 48.5 percent in 1989, while the percentage of Russians remained virtually constant.[11] More dramatically, Tatars urbanized at a remarkable rate: whereas only 5 percent of Tatars were urban in 1926, 63 percent had become urban by 1989. Russians also urbanized in large numbers, so the percentage of urban Russians (85.7 percent) still exceeded that of urban Tatars at the end of the Soviet era.[12] These changes occurred as part

---

8. The official version of Tatar history adopted in the 1940s traced the genesis of the Tatar people exclusively to the Finno-Ugric and Bulgar communities of the Middle Volga. Two protostates were identified as the precursor states to Tatarstan: the Khanate of Kazan and the Great Bulgar state. Victor A. Shnirelman, *Who Gets the Past? Competition for Ancestors among Non-Russian Intellectuals in Russia* (Baltimore: Johns Hopkins University Press, 1996).

9. D. Iskhakov, "Etnodemograficheskie protsessy v Respublike Tatarstan 1920–1989gg" [Ethnodemographic Processes in Tatarstan 1920–1989], in *Mnogonatsional'nyi Tatarstan* [Multiethnic Tatarstan] eds., I.V. Terent'eva and A.S. Alishev (Kazan: Tatarstan Presidential Apparat, 1993), 10. The data cited in the article are from Goskomstat.

10. I. V. Terent'eva and A. S. Alishev, eds., "Sotsial'no-professional'nye gruppy i obrazovanie osnovnikh natsional'nostei" [Socioprofessional Groups and the Education of Major Nationalities], in *Mnogonatsional'nyi Tatarstan*, 25.

11. Russians formed 43.1 percent of the population in 1926 and 43.3 percent in 1989. Tatarstan's third- and fourth-largest minority nationalities were Chuvash and Ukrainian. "Etnodemograficheskie protsessy," 9–10.

12. However, the urban population did not surpass the rural population until the end of the 1960s.

Table 4.1 The urbanization of ethnic groups in Tatarstan (%)

	1926	1939	1959	1970	1979	1989
Tatars	5.2	12.4	29.4	38.6	49.8	63.4
Russians	18.3	32.8	58.0	70.3	80.3	85.7

Source: D. Iskhakov, "Etnodemograficheskie protsessy v Respublike Tatarstan 1920–1989gg."
[Ethnodemographic Processes in Tatarstan], in *Mnogonatsional'nyi Tatarstan* [Multiethnic Tatarstan], ed. I. V.
Terent'eva and A. S. Alishev (Kazan: Tatarstan Presidential Apparat, 1993), 12.

Table 4.2 Level of education of Tatarstan's employed population, 15 years and older (%)

	1979		1989	
	TATARS	RUSSIANS	TATARS	RUSSIANS
Higher education/Incomplete higher education/ Specialized secondary	18.6	27.6	31.4	38.7
General secondary	30.4	28.6	43	38
Incomplete secondary	31.4	26.9	17.5	16
Elementary school	17.2	14.8	7.2	6.5

Source: I.V. Terent'eva and A.S. Alishev eds., "Sotsial'no-professional'nye gruppy i obrazovanie osnovnykh
natsional'nostie" [Socioprofessional Groups and the Education of Major Nationalities], in *Mnogonatsional'nyi
Tatarstan* [Multiethnic Tatarstan], ed. I. V. Terent'eva and A. S. Alishev (Kazan: Tatarstan Presidential Apparat,
1993), 26.

of a general urbanization trend in which 72 percent of the republic's population lived in the cities as of 1989.

For the Tatar population, as with other nationalities, social transformation accompanied the move to the cities. Tatars achieved mass literacy after World War II and attended secondary school in steadily rising numbers. Over time, the percentage of Tatars in higher education grew to equal that of Russians. Among the employed population, the number of Tatars with secondary or higher education degrees soared in the final decades of Soviet rule. In 1979, almost one out of every five employed Tatars had some form of higher education. By 1989 this number increased dramatically to nearly one out of every three. Comparing Tatars and Russians, it is clear that among both groups, many more people were entering the workforce with secondary or higher degrees in 1989 than in 1979 and that overall, the portion of the population with only an elementary or incomplete secondary education had declined (table 4.2).[13]

---

13. I. V. Terent'eva and A. S. Alishev eds., "Sotsial'no-professional'nye gruppy," 25, 26.

Most important, Tatars in Tatarstan were catching up to Russians profession-ally: more than 65 percent of them had achieved a higher social status than their parents during the period 1972–89.[14] As described in chapter 3, Tatars moved forward professionally because of the Soviet regime's commitment to rapid economic development and the occupational advancement of titular nationali-ties. Taking advantage of korenizatsiia policies, Tatars used their ethnic identity, listed on their domestic passports, to obtain desirable, white-collar positions. As a former party worker in charge of job quotas at the Kamskii Automobile Works (Kamskii Avtomobilnii zavod, or KamAZ) explained:

> In the last several decades, Soviet policies always controlled these things [job quotas]. Starting from the issue of acceptance into the party and continuing with the selection of cadres.... There was proportional rep-resentation in certain spheres.... There were fewer quotas in the pro-duction sphere because competency and ability played a bigger role. For example, in the 1960s there were no Tatars skilled in car production when KamAZ was built so they brought in people from the outside, especially from Russian cities that had experience making cars, such as Gorkii [Nizhnii Novgorod]. During World War II workers came here from regions that had experience manufacturing goods such as cars, watches, and airplanes.... But slowly, as Tatars became educated, Tatar specialists began appearing and they took on these positions in pro-duction.[15]

Tatars achieved their positions not only because they had been born Tatar but because they consented to play by the rules of the game: to learn Russian and speak it at work. They recognized that Russian, the "language of intereth-nic [mezh-natsional'nogo] communication," was necessary if they wanted to get ahead, and they generally accepted the view that Tatar language was second-class compared with Russian.[16] Moscow had succeeded in building a Russian-speaking Tatar middle class, dependent on the Soviet regime for jobs, privileges, and social status.

Many Tatars had made a decision to speak Russian as their first, and often only, language when they moved out of rural areas for the cities. In the capi-tal city of Kazan, Tatar professionals identified themselves as second-generation

---

14. Drobizheva, "Processes of Disintegration," 47.

15. Interview with Rashid Zakirov, KamAZ specialist, Naberezhnye Chelny, May 19, 1997.

16. Many called Tatar "unscientific" and "unnecessary" and maintained that it was not sophisti-cated enough to convey the complexity of concepts required in twentieth-century industrial society. Field notes, Kazan, Tatarstan, 1996–1997.

or third-generation—that is, Tatars whose parents or grandparents had moved from countryside to city. Other urban Tatars had made the move more recently, in the 1970s or 1980s. Most of the leaders of the Tatar nationalist movement were so-called second-, third-, or fourth-generation; their families had learned Russian and become educated and urban earlier in the Soviet era. Such people grew up, in the words of one local sociologist, "isolated from traditional [Tatar] culture and language...; the native language was for them simply a symbol."[17]

The founders of the first nationalist organization, the Tatar Public Center (Tatarskii Obshchestvennyi Tsentr, or TOTs), were urban Tatar intelligentsia and second-, third-, or fourth-generation city dwellers. Many were scholars in the Institute of Language, Literature, and History of the Tatarstan branch of the Russian Academy of Sciences (IIaLI-RAN) and at the University of Kazan (KGU) who had achieved their professional positions by virtue of both their ethnic identity and their ability and agreement to speak Russian. With some exceptions—notably the Ittifak (Alliance) leader Fauzia Bairamova—the leaders of the nationalist organizations in Kazan were highly Sovietized, as the following statement by a TOTs leader reveals: "Many of the members of our organization didn't speak Tatar. Some of the creative intelligentsia did know the language but very few. Many of the workers didn't know anything about Tatar culture, and many of the technical intelligentsia also had very weak knowledge of Tatar."[18]

With regard to socioeconomic achievement, Tatars and Russians worked in occupations with relatively similar social status at the time national revival began. At the same time, however, Tatars continued to occupy a larger portion of low-status jobs than did Russians. For example, both nationalities were well represented in the blue-collar workforce, but Tatars occupied slightly more blue-collar occupations than Russians (70 percent vs. 64 percent). This was due in part to the fact that Tatars outnumbered Russians in the agricultural sector, since more of them lived in the countryside, even as late as 1989, when the rural population was 65.5 percent Tatar and 22.9 percent Russian.[19] More Tatars than Russians worked in the sphere of trade and food preparation, since they often took jobs as store clerks and cafeteria workers after migrating to the cities. The prevalence of Tatars in blue-collar and lower-status occupations suggests that, as a group, they still lagged slightly behind Russians in socioeconomic status at the end of the Soviet era (table 4.3).

17. R. M. Akhmetov, "Elita tatar" [The Tatar Elite], in *Sovremennye natsional'nye protsessy v Respublike Tatarstan,* [Contemporary Nationality Processes in Tatarstan Vol. I] ed. D. M. Iskhakov and R. N. Musina (Kazan: Russian Academy of Sciences, Kazan Scientific Center, 1992), 119–27.

18. Interview with Damir Iskhakov, historian and TOTs cofounder, Institute for the Study of Language, History and Literature, Tatarstan Academy of Sciences, Kazan, June 10, 1997.

19. Thus Tatars held most of the white-collar managerial jobs in agriculture as well.

Table 4.3   Ethnic composition of the workforce in Tatarstan

	TOTAL WORKFORCE	WHITE-COLLAR WORKFORCE	BLUE-COLLAR WORKFORCE
Tatars	909,313	270,400 (29.7%)	638,913 (70.3%)
Russians	807,646	293,378 (36.3%)	514,268 (63.7%)
Chuvash	68,273	16,088 (23.6%)	52,185 (76.4%)
Other	96,352	31,051 (32.2%)	65,301 (67.8%)

Source: I.V. Terent'eva and A. S. Alishev, eds., "Sotsial'no-professional'nye gruppy," 22, 23.

Yet large numbers of Tatars had entered the white-collar urban sector of the economy alongside Russians. In absolute numbers, Tatars and Russians held a roughly equivalent number of white-collar jobs. There were, however, slightly more Russians in this workforce (36 percent) than Tatars (30 percent) (table 4.4).[20] This occupational equality between Tatars and Russians persists, for the most part, when the white- and blue-collar spheres are disaggregated by occupation.[21] The percentage of Tatars who worked in desirable white-collar positions as enterprise managers, economic planners, creative artists, doctors and health-care workers, and academics and teachers matched, almost matched, or slightly surpassed the percentage of Russians in these positions. For example, a study by the Tatarstan Academy of Sciences found that Tatars and Russians formed approximately equal proportions of scholars in most academic disciplines.[22]

However, Tatarstan followed the pattern established in most republics by the 1970s, in which Russians were proportionately overrepresented in white-collar engineering and technical occupations, and titular nationalities were proportionately overrepresented in high-status positions in the Communist Party and state administration.[23] The presence of more Russians than titular specialists in technical jobs was due to the way in which central economic planners in Moscow administered all-union enterprises considered crucial to the Soviet

20. The larger number of Tatars than Russians in the republican labor force reflects the fact that Tatars formed a slightly larger percentage of the total population than Russians did.

21. The same finding of ethnic job equality was reported by Moscow researchers relying on 1989 census data. See L. M. Drobizheva, A. R. Aklaev, M. C. Kashuba, and V. V. Koroteeva, *Natsional'noe samosoznanie i natsionalizm v Rossiiskoi Federatsii nachala 1990-x godov* (Moscow: IEA-RAN, 1994), 241.

22. M. N. Ganiev, "Sotsial'no-etnicheskaia struktura nauchnykh kadrov respubliki Tatarstan i nekotorye problemy ee optimizatsii" [Socioethnic Structure of Scientific Cadres in the Republic of Tatarstan and Several Problems of Its Optimization], in *Sovremennye natsional'nye protsessy v Respublike Tatarstan*, Vol. I, ed. D. M. Iskhakov and R. N. Musina (Kazan: Russian Academy of Sciences, Kazan Scientific Center, 1992), 91–99.

23. Roeder discusses this phenomenon in the union republics in "Soviet Federalism." Also see Kaiser, "Nationalizing the Work Force"; and Pal Kolstø, *Russians in the Former Soviet Republics* (Bloomington: Indiana University Press, 1995), 95–96.

Table 4.4 Percentage of Tatars and Russians employed in various economic sectors, 1989

	TATARS	RUSSIANS
White-collar labor	29.7	36.3
Directors of state administration	0.2	0.1
Directors of Communist Party and public organizations	0.4	0.1
Enterprise managers	2.1	2.9
Engineering-technical specialists	7.3	13
Agronomists, veterinarians, zoologists	0.7	0.2
Medical workers	3.0	2.8
Academics, teachers, educators	5.5	6.1
Literature and publishing	0.1	0.1
Cultural education workers	0.7	0.6
Artistic workers	0.3	0.4
Legal personnel	0.2	0.2
Security and social order personnel	0.7	0.8
Business and office workers	0.9	1.3
Housing and public service workers	0.1	0.2
Trade, catering and food preparation	1.6	1.3
Economic planning and accounting	4.9	4.9
Other	1	1.1
Blue-collar labor	70.3	63.7
Chemical workers	1.4	1.3
Power plant workers	1.4	1.4
Mechanical engineering and metal-working	15.3	21
Construction	4.8	3.9
Agriculture	14.1	4.6
Housing and public service	2.9	2.8
Trade and food preparation	4.2	2.7
Total	909,313	807,646

Source: I. V. Terent'eva and A. S. Alishev eds., "Sotsial'no-professional'nye gruppy," 22, 23.

Note: These data were compiled and analyzed by researchers in Tatarstan based on the 1989 All-Union census. The original table lists 48 sectors. I include all white-collar occupations and a representative sample of blue-collar occupations.

economy. Central planners preferred to staff these enterprises, such as military production and industrial engineering factories, with ethnic Russians and to assign management positions to Russians from outside the ethnic republics. Enterprises of lower economic and strategic importance, such as consumer goods factories, were administered by local authorities and considered republican enterprises. Although Tatars worked as white-collar specialists at both kinds of enterprises, their numbers still lagged behind those of Russians in all-union jobs.

Conversely, with regard to government administration and party leadership positions in the republics, Moscow used ethnic affirmative action policies to promote titular nationalities. As a result, a higher proportion of Tatars than Russians worked in these institutions. During the 1960s and 1970s, Tatar leaders turned ethnic quotas to their further advantage by "indigenizing" these positions themselves. Leaders handed out nomenklatura appointments to ethnic "kin," or to people from their region of birth in an informal process known as *zemlyachestvo*, which can be loosely translated as "gathering people from your home region [*zemlyaki*] around you." The practice was sufficiently entrenched that by the time quotas officially disappeared along with the Soviet state in 1991, *zemlyak* networks practically ensured the continuation of Tatar hegemony in local government administration.[24]

Despite Russians' slight overrepresentation in white-collar industrial enterprises and Tatars' slight overrepresentation in blue-collar positions, during the decades of Soviet rule, Tatars moved off the farm and into the republic's urban economy. Rustem Akhmetov, a Tatar scholar from Kazan, summarized the process as follows:

> Social mobility happened quickly for Tatars; they did it in one generation. What Russians did in two or three generations Tatars did in one. Their striving for careers in the 1960s through 1980s I would say was greater than Russians; they wanted to become engineers, administrators....Before 1990 there weren't many Tatars in engineering-technical fields. They formed the majority in government administration and in literature, art, and publishing—the cultural intelligentsia. But this [division] is natural because this is Tatarstan. In Russia, Russians are the majority. So there were and are differences in the types of labor [performed by Tatars and Russians], but there was never a rude polarization here between the ethnic groups.[25]

Social mobility among Tatars contributed to a growing demand for education and jobs. When the Soviet economy began to contract in the 1980s, Moscow suspended many of Tatarstan's subsidies and dispensations and cut the number of defense contracts awarded to military-industrial production facilities in Kazan. These developments contributed to people's shrinking sense of occupational

---

24. Akhmetov, "Elita tatar." Ron Suny discusses the tension between official korenizatsiia and local takeovers of party and republican administration based on traditional ethnic networks. See *Revenge of the Past*, 112–20.

25. Interview with Rustem Akhmetov, scholar at Tatarstan Academy of Sciences, Kazan, February 27, 1997.

Table 4.5 Distribution of employees in Tatarstan by economic sector, 1990–93 (in thousands)

ECONOMIC SECTORS	1990	1991	1992	1993
Industry	611.5	604.6	580.8	592.6
Agriculture	257.6	253.8	260	265.1
Transportation and communication	136.1	134.2	128.7	127.2
Construction	253.8	238.7	237.2	244
Government administration	27.1	35.8	26.6	26.9
Information-computer services	4.5	3.5	3.2	1.9
Social services and housing	77.6	76.2	70.9	71.9
Education, culture, art, science, and academics	249.6	254.8	245.1	238.2
Total	1878.4	1858.3	1839.7	1898.7

Source: "Raspredelenie zaniatogo naseleniia po otrasliam ekonomiki" [Distribution of Employed Population by Economic Sector], Statisticheskii ezhegodnik Respublika Tatarstana 1995 [Statistical Handbook of the Republic of Tatarstan] (Kazan: Goskomstat, 1996), 26.

opportunity. In fact, as Goskomstat data indicate, the number of employees fell between 1990 and 1993 in several key sectors of the economy while the absolute number of people of working age was rising.[26] Using this Goskomstat data as a proxy for unemployment data (which the Soviet state did not collect since unemployment officially did not exist), we observe a decline in the number of people working in the state sectors of industry, transportation and communication, social services, and construction (table 4.5). Thus, at a time when increasing numbers of highly educated Tatars and Russians had come to anticipate expanding opportunity and wide professional horizons, the Soviet Union's macroeconomic production crisis was frustrating those expectations.

Tatar Scholars and Ethnic Representation in the Local Economy

Tatar nationalists drew on the findings of Tatar academics—they were often one and the same—in order to construct a grievance of ethnic economic inequality. The nationalists "ethnicized" issues of occupational achievement and proportional representation in the labor market, framing them as unfairly impacting ethnic Tatars. Rather than blaming a contracting economy for creating conditions where rising numbers of applicants were chasing a limited number of jobs, the nationalists saw themselves as competing with Russians for education

---

26. The sectors of agriculture and government are partial exceptions insofar as they show movement in both directions during these years.

and jobs. This view permitted them to paint a picture of Tatars as victims and to place blame on the Soviet system. The nationalists could then identify solutions to rectify the injustice facing their group. Their message drew a boundary between Tatars and Russians in order to establish a sense of Tatar nationhood. The nationalists created a general sense of grievance among Tatars by defining a current, grave problem in their society that could be solved only through the acquisition of national sovereignty.

During glasnost, Tatar intellectuals began to produce a steady stream of monographs detailing Tatar representation in higher education and the professions. They were not isolated dissidents but employees of the Soviet state who had devoted their careers to studying the Tatar nation and republic. In fact, they were members of the titular communities whom Moscow had tried to tie to the Soviet regime with good jobs, status, and the knowledge that independence would end subsidies to the national culture.[27] Yet it was precisely these supposedly co-opted individuals who became the first leaders of the Tatar nationalist movement. In fact, nine of the eleven founders of the movement were scholars from the Institute of Language, Literature, and History or Kazan State University. These institutions were also the professional home of most of the two hundred attendees at the first TOTs meeting in 1988—a core group who would go on to anchor the organization. Gorenburg argues that a common identity and worldview, dense social ties and physical proximity, and access to resources among these scholars were key factors in the formation of the nationalist movement.[28]

Tatar professional scholars helped to define many of the issues that would figure centrally in national revival in the republic. Academic monographs and articles helped to establish the topic of Tatars' occupational status as an issue of injustice facing the ethnic group rather than as an indicator of their success in taking advantage of the Soviet state's affirmative action policies. These studies reported data on Tatar representation, identified the problem of Tatar underachievement, and explicitly linked it to the survival of the Tatar nation as well as to the possibility of interethnic conflict.[29] One such example is found in a report entitled "Tatarstan—A Country of Cities." The authors explained that

---

27. Zaslavsky, *Neo-Stalinist State,* 113, 118.

28. Gorenburg, *Minority Ethnic Mobilization,* 54–55.

29. For example, see Akhmetov, "Elita Tatar," and M. N. Ganiev, "Sotsial'no-etnicheskaia struktura"; and R. M. Akhmetov, "O problemakh kompleksnogo issledovaniia sotsial'nykh struktur russkikh i Tatar Tatarstan" [Research on the Social Structure of Russians and Tatars in Tatarstan], in *Sovremennye natsional'nye protsessy v Respublike Tatarstan* [Contemporary Nationality Processes in Tatarstan, Vol. I], ed. D. M. Iskhakov and R. N. Musina (Kazan: Tatarstan Academy of Sciences, 1994), 88–95.

Tatar professional achievement trailed that of the Russians, concluding that this situation could lead to conflictual interethnic relations.

> Tatars lag behind Russians in terms of qualifications....According to data from 1985, at KamAZ, there were almost two times fewer Tatar highly qualified workers than Russians....Russians occupy higher positions on the social hierarchy, they have a higher educational level than Tatars. And there are twice as many Russians among managers of work collectives. This social situation is typical for many of Tatarstan's young cities....Not only do these cities have the potential to be a source of social and interethnic conflict, but the conditions of multiethnic social inequality may be transferred to the sphere of interethnic relations.[30]

Another scholar, Rustem Akhmetov, understood that a contraction of high-status professional opportunities was taking place, and he considered rising competition for desirable posts an issue of ethnic inequality. Akhmetov argued that both Tatars and Russians were educated and qualified but that Tatars were being shut out of good opportunities: "For Tatars with higher education one out of twelve couldn't find work corresponding to their educational status and had to accept jobs corresponding to secondary educational status. For Russians, this only happened to one out of twenty."[31]

Sometimes scholars found themselves caught between acknowledging the significant rise in Tatar professional achievement and their desire to change what they perceived to be the unfair status quo. A solution to this tension was to acknowledge some Tatar achievement but label it artificial and forced, thereby delegitimizing it. By virtually wiping the slate clean of Tatar achievement or by emphasizing particular spheres of supposed Tatar inequality, the intellectuals could appeal for change of the current oppressive situation. For example, the Tatar researcher M. N. Ganiev, in a study on the ethnic composition of Tatarstan's intelligentsia, claimed that the relatively high number of Tatars among top directors (*pervye rukovoditeli*) "fulfill a certain 'compensatory' function during...current...conditions." Ganiev questioned the legitimacy of Tatar directors, which allowed him to focus on the scientific-technical fields in which Russians slightly outnumbered Tatars so that he could advocate increased Tatar representation in those fields.[32] Other scholars delegitimized Tatar achievement by

---

30. D. M. Iskhakov, Ia Z. Garipov, and Iu. V. Platonov, "Urbanizatsiia v Tatarstane v XX v: Osobennostii posledstviia" [Urbanization in Tatarstan in the 20th Century: Particularities and Consequences], in *Tatarstan—Strana gorodov* [Tatarstan—A Country of Cities] ed. D. M. Iskhakov (Naberezhnye Chelny: Krona, 1993), 6–15.

31. Akhmetov interview, February 27, 1997.

32. Ganiev, "Sotsial'no-etnicheskaia struktura," 97.

pointing out that it was the product of Soviet policy. Yagfar Garipov, another IIaLI researcher, told me,

> People always say that Tatars have achieved as much as the Russians and they point to particular Tatars, saying "he's the minister of such and such; he's the director of some high department at KamAZ." Or they say, "the mayor of Naberezhnye Chelny is a Tatar." But these are just the highest positions....If you look at the middle layer, there are very few Tatars compared with Russians. The middle layer (or class) of Tatars has to be built up *naturally, not artificially* [italics added].[33]

In one fell swoop, Garipov criticized Soviet quota policies, emphasized current barriers to Tatar advancement, and called for change. One former academic who became a government official criticized the Soviet quota policies more explicitly and pointed out that they served to provoke Russian resentment:

> Under the USSR there was the ideology that we created an ASSR and therefore all the Tatars' problems are solved. The Tatar cadres were very careful that their quotas were observed in universities and for leadership positions. The Supreme Soviet kept an eye on this conscientiously. But it was all artificial; not natural. It was deformed in actuality. There were internal problems. Then Russians believed that there was a distortion of cadres, too many Tatars in the government.[34]

Some nationalist leaders seemed to recognize that Soviet quotas helped Tatars to get ahead, yet they also blamed the state for not doing enough for Tatars, for blocking their access, and for offering them individual advancement at the expense of studying in a Tatar-language environment. As Raman Zaglidyuyuvich Yuldashev, the leader of the nationalist youth organization Azatlyk (Freedom), stated, "In the 1970s, during the era of stagnation, Tatars were allowed access to higher education, but it was limited. Tatars were hindered. Tatars were allowed in artificially. The Soviet system of education was very good and Tatars received a good secondary and higher education. But it was a system of Russification."[35]

Tatar scholars were not fabricating data, but they were interpreting it in a particular manner. They could have presented a different story describing the educational and professional gains that Tatars had made during the course of the twentieth century. Their studies could have included longitudinal data

---

33. Interview with Yagfar Garipov, Tatarstan Academy of Sciences, Kazan, April 27, 1997.
34. Interview with Raman Yurevich Belyakov, official in the president's administration. Kazan, February 15, 1997.
35. Interview with Raman Zaglidyuyuvich Yuldashev, Azatlyk, Kazan, February 16, 1997.

indicating upward trends in urbanization, education, and occupational achievement. Instead, they presented data as of the present time—the late 1980s—in order to convey Tatar disadvantage vis-à-vis Russians. In this way, the scholars could explicitly link the fact of an educational and professional imbalance between Russians and Tatars to the injustice of the current social system. Alternatively, they could have noted that Tatars were competing with other Tatars as well as Russians and that members of *both* groups could expect to lose more jobs as a result of the Soviet Union's economic decline. They chose, however, to emphasize interethnic competition instead of a generalized competition for resources.

However, it should be noted that not all Tatar scholars and intellectuals understood economic conditions in this way. Many did not read interethnic competition into the statistical data that they analyzed. The presence of a diversity of opinion among Tatar scholars underscores the fact that a person's ethnicity does not definitively determine his or her understandings of social and economic conditions. Nonetheless, in Tatarstan during the transition from Soviet rule, many Tatar academics conceptualized their society as composed of two separate ethnic groups that occupied unequal socioeconomic positions. The ideas they expressed on the subject informed the founding programs and platforms of nationalist groups as well as the thinking of nationalist leaders, as described in the following section.

Issue Framing by Tatar Nationalist Organizations

The opposition Tatar nationalist movement had its formal beginning with the founding of the Tatar Public Center in 1988. Originally established as an umbrella organization that included cultural and political groups such as Suverenitet (Sovereignty), Azatlyk, Ittifak, Iman (Faith), Marjani Society, and the Republican Party of Tatarstan,[36] TOTs put forward a moderate program supporting the establishment of a sovereign, multiethnic republic. The primary goal of the nationalist movement was to win republican sovereignty, but the meaning of this concept evolved over time. Before the Soviet Union collapsed, TOTs defined sovereignty as raising the status of the republic from autonomous to union, since a higher position in the country's ethnoterritorial administrative ranking would provide Tatarstan with greater rights, resources, and status. After 1991, taking advantage of the dramatically changed political context, the nationalists

---

36. For the history and program of each group, see Damir Iskhakov, "Neformal'nye ob"edineniia v sovremennon tatarskom obshchestve" [Informal Associations in Currrent Tatar Society], in *Sovremennye natsional'nye protsessy v Respublike Tatarstan,* Vol. I, ed. D. M. Iskhakov and R. N. Musina, 1992, 5–52.

interpreted sovereignty to mean independent statehood.[37] As the main national-ist organization in the republic, TOTs articulated several issues, all of which were linked to the overarching goal of state sovereignty. These included Tatar cultural revival (primarily language revival), economic autonomy from Moscow, greater political representation for Tatars at the federal level, assistance and representa-tion for the ethnic Tatar "diaspora" outside Tatarstan, and increased representa-tion for Tatars in the republic's economy.

For the nationalists, reviving the Tatar culture meant above all spreading the use of the Tatar language. The TOTs program of 1989 advocated increasing Tatar-language education in primary and secondary schools as well as at the university level. Somewhat more controversially, the nationalist program also promoted making Tatar an official state language of the republic.[38] The nation-alists also sought to renew national culture by creating more opportunities for publishing and radio broadcasts in the Tatar language and by establishing a new Tatar theater and restoring Tatar architecture. TOTs also emphasized Islam but conceived of the religion as an attribute of Tatar culture. The TOTs program advocated restoring old mosques, sending Muslim youth abroad for religious training, and establishing a Muslim council of elders, *madrassas* (secondary Is-lamic schools), and an Islamic university.[39] Yet Islam never became a central part of the nationalists' program. TOTs devoted little attention to the Soviet state's campaign against Islam despite an available history of harsh repression by Mos-cow[40] and despite the fact that in the early twentieth century Tatarstan was home to the Islamic reformist movement known as jadidism.[41] An Islamic revival was

---

37. This position was laid out in resolution no. 2, "On the Status of the Tatar Republic," of the TOTs founding congress in *Suverennyi Tatarstan* [Sovereign Tatarstan] vol. 2, ed. D. M. Iskhakov and M.N. Guboglo (Moscow: Russian Academy of Sciences, 1998), 186, and in the TOTs second program in 1991. See Iskhakov, "Neformal'nye ob"edineniia," 10, 11.

38. The republic's supreme soviet passed a law on languages in 1992 only after prolonged debate. The law made both Tatar and Russian official state languages and established a rather long implemen-tation period of ten years. See Zakon Respubliki Tatarstan o iazikakh narodov Respubliki Tatarstan [Law on Languages of the Republic of Tatarstan], 8 June 1992. For TOTs's position on the language law, see R. Tufitulovoi, "Iazyk—sredstvo vzaimoponimaniia a ne otchuzhdeniia" [Language—Means of Mutual Understanding, Not Alienation], *Vecherniaia Kazan'*, April 16, 1990.

39. "Rezoliutsii i obrashcheniia II s"ezda Tatarskogo Obshchestvennogo tsentra [Resolutions and Appeals of the second Congress of the Tatar Public Center], in *Suverennyi Tatarstan*, 2: 200–202.

40. The Bolsheviks closed Muslim schools in the countryside; changed the Tatar script from Arabic to Cyrillic; forbade religious contacts with Turkey; and perhaps most important, put an end to the Islamic jadidist movement—which they viewed as having pan-Arab aspirations—in part by killing its leader, Mir Said Sultangaliev. See Shnirelman, *Who Gets the Past?* 1996.

41. However, by the late 1990s, Tatarstan's government and former nationalist leader, Rafael Kha-kimov, had spent considerable effort and resources articulating the concept of "Euro-Islam" based on some jadidist ideas. See Katherine Graney, "'Russian Islam' and the Politics of Religious Multicultur-alism in Russia," in *Rebounding Identities: The Politics of Identity in Russia and Ukraine,* ed. Domin-ique Arel and Blair A. Ruble (Washington, D.C.: Woodrow Wilson Center Press, 2006), 89–115.

under way in the republic at the time as some of the younger generation were becoming practicing Muslims.[42] But among urban educated Tatars, and within the nationalist movement itself, Islamic belief was quite weak.[43] Eventually, the Muslim organizations that had joined the nationalist movement went their separate ways. As Valyulya Yakup, leader of the group Iman, stated in the mid-1990s, "We are...worried about the national problem—but we decided that you can resolve the national question through Islam."[44]

In terms of economic autonomy from Moscow, Tatar nationalists sought increased control over local economic resources and the republican budget.[45] They maintained that the republic's government should take over the administration of enterprises located on republican territory and called for control over tax policy and an end to the dual-channel structure in which the center collected all taxes and then returned a portion to the regions. TOTs argued that the republic—not Moscow—should control the natural resources located on Tatarstan's territory and focused particular attention on controlling one of its most lucrative resources, oil.[46] For example, TOTs, together with two other nationalist organizations, sponsored demonstrations at the oil extraction complex Druzhba (Friendship) in the city of Al'met'evsk in April 1991. The demonstrations encouraged workers to strike in protest of Moscow's "appropriation" of the complex's oil. Nationalists carried placards saying, "Hands off our Sovereignty" and even clashed violently with police at one point as demonstrators tried to climb over gates onto factory grounds.[47] TOTs positioned economic autonomy as a good that would benefit all citizens, regardless of ethnicity, while the radical wing of the nationalist movement led by Ittifak sought to establish an ethnic state in which resources would be directed primarily toward ethnic Tatars. As one such leader

---

42. Tatars who considered themselves Muslim grew from only 15.7 percemt in 1980 to approximately 69.6 percent in 1997. Author's survey of the general population (N=300), Kazan, Naberezhnye Chelny, 1997. Also see Walker, "The Dog That Didn't Bark."

43. Islamic belief and practice were stronger among Tatars in the rural regions. Several secular Tatar informants stated that they had recently learned that their grandfathers or other ancestors had been mullahs but that their families decided to hide this fact and abandon Islam rather than risk discrimination, persecution, or even death.

44. Interview with Valyulya Yakup, a mullah and head of Iman, Kazan, February 7, 1997.

45. The nationalists also backed the vaguely sketched-out goals of creating a market economy and establishing a national state bank.

46. For a review of Tatar nationalist attitudes toward republican oil, see "Kazhdyi narod dolzhen zhit' v svoei Litve" [Each Nation Should Live in Its Own Lithuania], Vecherniaia Kazan', April 16, 1991. Throughout the 1990s, TOTs continued to stress the lack of oil rights. In the words of one of the current leaders of TOTs, "If we [Tatarstan] could keep all of the proceeds from the sale of our oil, we'd be so rich we would all have toilets made of gold." Interview with Zaki Zainuillin, Kazan, January 22, 1997.

47. "Miting v Al'met'evske: "Nam ne nuzhna takaia 'Druzhba'" [We Don't Need That Kind of "Friendship"], Vecherniaia Kazan', April 23, 1991.

stated, "Tatarstan has oil, forests, many natural resources; we want to use these in the interests of Tatars. Russians can leave if they want to at any time and go back to Tver, Ryzan, and so on, but Tatars can't. This is their historical homeland. So we promote laws that defend the indigenous nationality."[48]

Tatar nationalists also raised the issue of greater political representation for ethnic Tatars in the country's federal institutions. They claimed that there were too few Tatar politicians in Moscow legislatures representing both the Tatar population in Tatarstan and the 6.6 million Tatars in total who lived throughout the Soviet Union. As one nationalist arguing for better representation in Moscow stated, "Of the six people's deputies of the USSR from Kazan, there is not a single Tatar, although Tatars are almost half the population of the city of Kazan."[49]

The issue of political representation was connected to another main nationalist concern: how to improve the status and cultural level of the so-called Tatar diaspora. The nationalists repeatedly pointed out that three-quarters of the Tatar nation lived outside the borders of Tatarstan, including the more than one million Tatars in the neighboring Bashkir republic. According to the TOTs program, these people should be able to receive educations and consume mass media in the Tatar language and should have a voice through formal representation in federal political institutions. The Republic of Tatarstan, as the national homeland, "should be responsible for the cultural and linguistic joining of all groups of Tatars."[50]

TATAR ECONOMIC INEQUALITY

In addition to the issues outlined above, the nationalist movement demanded that the rights of Tatars and Russians in the republic's economy be equalized. Specifically, both TOTs and Ittifak framed the issue of ethnic group representation in the economy as an ethnic division of labor in order to construct a grievance about Tatars' subordinate socioeconomic status.

Tatar nationalists expressed several themes in constructing this grievance. First, they claimed that Tatars lagged behind Russians in occupational achievement and were thus blocked from fulfilling their potential inside their own republic. Second, they either ignored or criticized ethnic quotas and the role of the Soviet state in facilitating Tatar mobility. This position served to delegitimize the achievements that Tatars had made during the Soviet period and also

---

48. Interview with Khakim Abdulovich Gainuillin, chairman, Republican Party of Tatarstan, Kazan, January 31, 1997.

49. The author went on to advocate the passage of a law stipulating proportional representation according to population percentage. Kh. Saifullin, "Kto zhe provotsiruet natsionalizm?" [Who Is Provoking Nationalism?] *Vecherniaia Kazan'*, August 7, 1990, 2.

50. Iskhakov "Neformal'nye ob"edineniia," 10, 12, 13.

placed blame for problems facing Tatars on the central state and to a lesser degree on republican authorities. Next the nationalists outlined specific policies to improve the socioeconomic status of Tatars. Finally, they linked all these points to the overarching need to topple the unjust status quo and establish republican sovereignty.

In its founding charter, TOTs defined social conditions facing Tatars as unjust and described Tatars as socially disadvantaged vis-à-vis Russians. It claimed that this fact endangered the future of the Tatar nation. Since the beginning of the Soviet era and lasting to the present day, the TOTs charter stated, Tatars outnumbered Russians in rural areas and experienced a slower rate of urbanization, "lower qualifications," and a subordinate social status. Next, the charter identified specific solutions: rural Tatars must secure employment in the urban economies of Tatarstan's cities to ensure the "full-fledged development of the Tatar nation." It focused on occupational equality ("The optimization of social-professional status of the population in the republic cannot be achieved without the creation of job placement in all economic spheres") and advocated providing Tatars with preferences and set-aside positions in the republican economy and free job placement in "any economic sphere." The document also recommended regulating the "national composition of higher educational institutes."[51] Thus, in addition to the general goal of sovereignty, TOTs offered a specific picture of how the position and status of Tatars would be improved in a sovereign state.

The Tatar Public Center articulated these issues at demonstrations and rallies. For example, the group exhorted state organs to provide jobs for Kazan's unemployed and for Tatar migrants from outside the republic at the new automobile plant under construction in the city of Elabuga. TOTs passed a resolution asking Tatarstan's government and supreme soviet to disallow "discrimination along national lines" in laying off employees.[52] In a newspaper article, a TOTs leader stated that the group was receiving letters from many Tatars living outside the republic expressing a desire to migrate to Tatarstan. At the same time, TOTs claimed that the Elabuga plant, other enterprises, and state farms were all hiring workers (*orgnabor rabochii*) from Central Asia and the Caucausus to work for them. "It seems to us," stated TOTs leader Farit Sultanov in an interview, "that it would be more sensible to steer work toward Tatars from outside the republic, especially in

---

51. Ibid., 14.

52. "Rezoliutsiia mitinga TOTs" [Resolutions of TOTs demonstration], *Vecherniaia Kazan'*, March 19, 1991, 1, and "Programma (Platforma) Vsesoiuznogo Tatarskogo obshchestvennogo tsentra—" [Platform of the Tatar Public Center in *Suverennyi Tatarstan* [Sovereign Tatarstan], Vol. 2, ed. D. M. Iskhakov and M. N. Guboglo (Moscow: Russian Academy of Sciences, 1998), 133.

Central Asia."[53] In this way, TOTs tied the issue of professional achievement to the future flourishing of the Tatar nation.

The Tatar Public Center did not consistently demand special privileges for Tatars, often stating that it merely wanted protection for the Tatar nation or an equalization of the status of Tatars and Russians. For example, the second TOTs program favored "providing equal access to education...under market conditions..."[54] The Naberezhnye Chelny TOTs program also announced that it opposed all forms of "national privilege...and great power chauvinism [i.e., Russian nationalism] as well as local nationalism and national nihilism [i.e., Tatar nationalism and self-hating Tatars]."[55] The republic's more radical nationalist groups, on the other hand, did not equivocate on this issue. Ittifak, which broke off from TOTs in 1991, maintained that Tatar should replace Russian as the sole official state language and advocated state independence for Tatarstan. Ittifak's leader, Fauzia Bairamova, whose public persona vacillated between that of a demure Muslim woman in a head scarf and a firebrand activist, articulated an exclusivist "Tatarstan for Tatars" position, criticizing Russians regularly in the press. She eventually went as far as condemning Russian-Tatar marriage and called Tatars involved in such marriages *mankurty* (betrayers) of the nation.[56] Ittifak also framed the issue of ethnic group professional achievement as an injustice that damaged the future of the Tatar nation. Bairamova offered her view on the subject in an early editorial in Tatarstan's main newspaper:

> There is an overt disproportion in the number of specialists with higher educations in the economy. Russians comprise 55 percent of them and Tatars 37 percent, although the population of the republic is 47 percent Tatar and 44 percent Russian. It is necessary to provide assistance to Tatars....Currently, the number of Tatars studying in higher educational institutes is decreasing every year...except [for those in] agricultural institutes: there indigenous residents comprise 75 percent. Thus the [Tatar] nation is developing in a one-sided, agrarian direction.[57]

---

53. A large number of Tatars who had been living in Central Asia were migrating to Tatarstan during this period. Talgat Bareev, "Teper'—V polnyi rost" [Now—At Full Growth], *Vecherniaia Kazan,* July 27, 1989, 3.

54. Iskhakov, "Neformal'nye ob"edineniia,"14.

55. "Programma Naberezhno-Chelninskogo otdeleniia TOTsa" [Program of Naberezhnye Chelny Branch of TOTs], 4.

56. The Kyrgyz writer Chingiz Aitmaitov used the term *mankurt* to refer to Kyrgyz who had renounced their Kyrgyz identity in favor of a Russian one.

57. Fauzia Bairamova, "'I tot li narod svoikh prav ne dostoin?'" [Don't the People Deserve Their Rights?] *Vecherniaia Kazan,* September 27, 1988.

Bairamova's comments are descriptively accurate, but the fact that she presented data on Tatars' educational achievements from a single point in time rather than over a longer period served to undercut all the achievements won during the Soviet era and legitimized an appeal for radical change. Other Tatar organizations added their voices. The Writers' Union and the Mardjani Society drafted an open letter complaining of the insufficient number of Tatar school principals in Kazan: "Out of 139 schools, only 19 are run by Tatars. These numbers do not accord in any way with the policy of internationalism in our state."[58] Picking up on the themes articulated by the nationalists, the main democratic newspaper in the republic, *Vechernaia Kazan* (Evening Kazan), published articles addressing issues of resource allocation among ethnic groups and ethnic representation with titles like "Who Is Studying in Institutes of Higher Education?"[59]

Nationalist groups were not constructing the issue of professional representation in a vacuum. Rather, they were in dialogue with Moscow, which had been trying to set the terms of the debate as soon as ethnic complaints began to emanate from the republics. Gosplan, the state planning agency in Moscow, published the results of a 1989 research study stating that titular nationalities were well represented in the management structures of major enterprises located in the ARs. In response, TOTs offered its own interpretation, reporting that Tatars occupied a lower percentage of the management positions at KamAZ.[60] In the city of Naberezhnye Chelny, as the next chapter describes, the local TOTs and Ittifak affiliates paid particular attention to the relative occupational achievement of Tatars and Russians at KamAZ.

How could Tatar nationalists make such strong claims about occupational discrimination against ethnic Tatars when Tatars dominated political institutions in the republic, including the Communist Party? Many Tatars did not consider political representation an issue of occupational opportunity but the natural state of affairs in an ethnic republic. In fact, as mentioned above, some Tatar nationalists—accepting the Soviet norm of proportional representation—made the argument that Tatars were underrepresented in republican politics because the size of the Tatar population in the country as a whole, not just in Tatarstan, should determine the proper number of political representatives. As a former nationalist supporter explained to me, "If our electoral system were based on proportional representation, then there should be more Tatars in the federal Duma

58. "Ravnopraviia poka net" [There Is No Equality Yet], *Vecherniaia Kazan'*, July 18, 1990.

59. "Kto uchitsia v vuzakh?" [Who Studies in VUZy?], *Vecherniaia Kazan'*, November 16, 1989.

60. TOTs's analysis was based on data collected by the research division of KamAZ. At this time TOTs was restricted from publishing within Tatarstan and published the results in a Lithuanian periodical. Paul Goble reported on the general phenomenon of Russian over-representation in republican enterprises in "Ethnicity and Economic Reform," *RFE/RL Research Report,* February 16, 1990, 24.

and other state structures...just like you have in America—quotas for blacks, Mexicans, etc. in every part of government." When I asked whether the majority of Tatarstan government officials weren't ethnic Tatars, he replied, "Yes, but our population here is only one and a half million Tatars—a very small part of the total number. There are more than six million Tatars in Russia."[61] Tatar nationalists could unself-consciously rail against discriminatory ethnic representation in the economy while ignoring the fact of Tatar dominance of local government.

Nationalist entrepreneurs articulated issues of blocked Tatar mobility not because they thought this issue would be successful in attracting popular support but because their worldview shaped how they perceived the situation of Tatars in the republic. For them, occupational underrepresentation was not the only way in which Tatars were subordinate in the republic, but it was a central problem, given their own concern with professional success and social status as educated professionals. The fact that Tatar nationalists chose to focus on issues of equality of ethnic representation in the economy suggests that they, like other Soviet citizens, had internalized their society's values of urbanization, higher education, and prestigious employment.

It is clear from interviews I conducted with the nationalists that their perceptions represented a genuine set of beliefs, not a strategic calculus about which issues would attract the most mass support. Even after the period of nationalist mobilization had ended, many were still committed to the belief that Tatars faced limited opportunities, continuing to lament ethnic economic inequality in interviews that took place in 1996 and 1997. For example, a leader in the Naberezhnye Chelny branch of the nationalist youth group Azatlyk denied the existence of quotas for Tatars during the Soviet era. In response to my question about Soviet support for national cadres, Talgat Amadishin responded vehemently, "No, there wasn't anything like that." He added, "There isn't anything like that now either."[62] For Amadishin, Tatars' achievements were due to their own skills and abilities. Another nationalist leader, Rimzel Valeev, who headed the Tatar cultural organization Vatan, continued to be concerned with the supposed underrepresentation of Tatars in the republic's economy, stating,

> We have formal equality, but how can it be real equality when Tatars in the rural regions don't have computers in their schools, don't have money and so can't send their kids to law school or university? How can it be equal? In America you have a situation where blacks get privileges,

---

61. Interview with Khaidar Tuktarov, construction firm owner, Naberezhnye Chelny, May 27, 1997. The respondent's name has been changed.
62. Interview with Talgat Amadishin, Azatlyk, Naberezhnye Chelny, May 24, 1997.

right?...a system where if two people apply for the same job and are equal in ability, the black one will get the job. That system of quotas and privileges should exist here for Tatars....We wish that policies privileging Tatars were here. For example, they sell automobile gas to anyone, but it should go to Tatars first.[63]

Popular Support for Tatar Nationalism

The nationalist articulation of a grievance about economic inequality and Tatar socioeconomic subordination resonated with many Tatars. Popular support for nationalism rose steadily, as evidenced by growing participation in nationalist rallies and demonstrations, the rising popularity of nationalist politicians, and popular attitudes backing nationalism expressed in opinion polls. Nationalism in Tatarstan peaked in 1991 and early 1992 and then began to decline during 1992 and 1993.

What did Tatars think about the issue of ethnic representation in the economy? First, with regard to Soviet korenizatsiia policies and ethnic quotas, there was a diversity of attitudes among Tatars. Many were simply unaware of the particular role played by the state in assigning occupations. People who were aware of quotas for Tatars expressed ambivalence; some accepted them as normal and fair in the Tatar homeland. Others discounted their importance believing that all policies enacted by the Soviet central state failed to benefit, or actively hurt, national minorities.

Public opinion data on occupational representation during the peak period of nationalist mobilization unfortunately do not exist. However, a survey of the general population I conducted in Kazan and Naberezhnye Chelny in 1997 (N=300) addressed these issues.[64] Although the survey was conducted several years after nationalist mobilization in Tatarstan had ended, it may shed light on popular attitudes from that period. According to my survey, many Tatars had difficulty recognizing the fact that they had benefited from Soviet state policies.

---

63. Interview with Rimzel Valeev, leader of Vatan, Kazan, February 3, 1997.

64. Conducted in April–May 1997 with the assistance of the Department of Ethnology of Kazan State University led by Guzel Stoliarova, three hundred randomly selected respondents in Kazan and Naberezhnye Chelny were interviewed in their homes. To capture diversity among the population, I selected five streets representative of various socioeconomic environments in each of three regions of Kazan: the city center, an industrial region, and a "bedroom" (spalnyi) region. In Naberezhnye Chelny, which is organized into large residential complexes (kompleksy) with their own schools, respondents living in separate buildings in each of fifteen residential complexes were interviewed in both the "old city" and the "new city."

Respondents were asked whether they agreed with the statement "Soviet state policies helped Tatars receive certain jobs." In general, more Tatars than Russians responded negatively. Thirty-seven percent of Tatars compared with 23 percent of Russians disagreed with this statement, whereas more Russians (27 percent) than Tatars (15 percent) agreed with it (significant at $p<0.05$). Overall, however, respondents' awareness of the issue of Soviet state assistance was quite low; approximately half answered the question with "difficult to say." Thus large numbers of Tatars reported either that they had no knowledge of Soviet state quotas or that they had not received assistance from the Soviet state in obtaining certain jobs—a position that largely corresponds with how nationalists had framed the issue of Soviet korenizatsiia policies during the early 1990s.

Many Russians, on the other hand, openly expressed opposition to privileges for Tatars, beginning with the policy of korenizatsiia and passport identity under Soviet rule. In an editorial in *Vechernaia Kazan,* a Russian made a direct plea for the state and enterprise employers to consider individual merit rather than ethnic group affiliation in allocating jobs:

> Recently, the issue of the notorious fifth line of the passport [describing nationality] has been raised several times. [The fifth line is] raw data [*iskhodnom material*] for training bureaucrats in their "struggle in the purging of cadres." I think that cadres should be selected according to merit; information about nationality should remain only on census forms and voting lists....All of this would emphasize the equality of citizens of our country and not in any way harm national consciousness.[65]

In another example, a Russian musician writing a letter to the editor verbalized his fear that preferences for Tatars would increase in an independent Tatarstan: "I wouldn't want the work collective to take into account my national character and psychology. The memory of these thorough record-takings is still vivid in the memories of citizens of my country. It's criminal that our country has a passport system with an entry noting 'nationality.'"[66]

Extremist Russian nationalist groups such as Pamiat' attempted to exploit these fears and incite Russians against Tatars. At a rally held in 1990, a Pamiat' leader (a local professor) reported that he had counted the number of Jewish, Tatar, and Russian department chairmen at his institute and found that Russians were outnumbered by the others. He lamented, "And it's the same picture with

---

65. D. Shapiro, "Na usloviiakh vseobshchego ravenstva" [Under Conditions of General Equality], *Vecherniaia Kazan',* November 17, 1989.

66. Iu. Orlov, "Kritika sotsiologii bolevikh oshchushchenii" [A Critical Sociology of Pain], *Vecherniaia Kazan',* January 12, 1990.

other bosses and managers. And also with the leaders of the republic. They are stifling the Russian foreigners [*russkiie inorodtsi*]!"[67] Thus a divergence of opinion developed around the issue of occupational representation and contributed to the polarization of republican politics. This in turn prompted greater numbers of Tatars to support the nationalists' call for equalization of opportunity.

My 1997 survey asked respondents which nationalities "obtain the most prestigious professions and occupy the most prestigious positions in Tatarstan?" (table 4.6). Again, though we cannot accept answers from the survey as definitive evidence of attitudes in the early 1990s, the responses may approximate earlier opinions about socioeconomic status. The position of Tatars had changed slightly by 1997. In two somewhat divergent trends, the post-Soviet state ended quotas for Tatars, but Shaimiev's government facilitated the placement of more Tatars than Russians into government positions. Because a certain degree of Tatarization of the state was taking place in post-Soviet "sovereign" Tatarstan, we might expect Tatar respondents to have recognized that Tatars held the high-status jobs in the republic. However, only 14.4 percent of Tatars expressed this opinion. On the other hand, a majority of Russians (64 percent) did.[68] Both Russians and Tatars agreed that Russians did not occupy the most prestigious professions: only 0.7 percent of Russians and 4 percent of Tatars thought they did (significant at p<0.001). Tatars found it more difficult than Russians to recognize the fact of Tatar professional achievement. If they held the same opinions during the period of national revival (when their domination of the government was less conspicuous), this would suggest that they were convinced by nationalists' claims about the absence of Tatar achievement and privilege.

Ethnic Tatars I talked with often claimed that individual merit and ability counted more than ethnic identity, especially in their own profession. One Tatar professor described the situation at her own university: "You can't say that Tatars just received privileges everywhere....Kazan State Technical University is a Russian institute and there are no privileges; it's about merit. Wherever there is a need for specialists in Kazan, even in government, then it's about ability, not nationality."[69]

Overall, attitudes about Tatar underrepresentation in the republican economy translated into support for other key nationalist policies, such as having an ethnic Tatar president and, above all, republican sovereignty. Data from a major

---

67. "Pozdravim sebia?" [Should We Be Congratulated?] *Vecherniaia Kazan'*, August 27, 1990, 1.

68. Of other nationalities in Tatarstan, 39 percent also believed that Tatars obtained the most prestigious positions.

69. Interview with Taslima Gaissevna Islamchiva, professor, Department of Sociology and Political Science at Kazan State Technical University (KGTU), Kazan, March 11, 1997.

Table 4.6 The effect of ethnicity on which group obtains the most prestigious professions in Tatarstan

	RUSSIANS	TATARS	OTHER	DIFFICULT TO SAY
Russians	7%	64%	0	35%
	1	92		50
Tatars	3.60%	14.40%	0.90%	81.10%
	4	4	1	90
Others	0	38.50%	0	61.50%
		10		16

Note: N=300, Pearson χ2= 66.06, d.f.=6, p=0.000. The left column represents respondents' answers to the question "Which nationalities obtain the most prestigious professions and occupy the most prestigious positions in Tatarstan?" Author's survey of the general population, Tatarstan, 1997. The table contains missing values due to respondents who did not answer this question.

1993 survey indicate that significantly more Tatars than Russians (65 percent vs. 25 percent) "agreed" or "more or less agreed" that the president should be an ethnic Tatar (significant at p<0.001).[70] This attitude remained even after the decline of the nationalist movement. Thus in my survey of the general population in 1997, 73 percent of Tatars reported that they thought the president of the republic should be an ethnic Tatar.[71] The next section provides context for these microlevel attitudes by describing the chronology of nationalist mobilization in Tatarstan.

Achieving National Sovereignty in Tatarstan

The Tatar nationalist movement consistently focused its efforts on republican sovereignty, the meaning of which, as mentioned above, shifted over time from acquiring union republican status to achieving independent statehood. Soon after its founding, TOTs promoted its program by sponsoring mass political acts. It held meetings and small demonstrations and in early 1990 circulated a petition that collected one hundred thousand signatures in support of UR status. As nationalist issues became subjects of debate in newspapers, in the workplace, and on public transportation, the size and frequency of nationalist demonstrations grew.

---

70. Survey results are from the Laitin/Hough NSF survey, "Language and Nationality in the former Soviet Union," conducted in 1993 (N=3000). The survey did not include explicit questions about support for Tatar nationalism or nationalist organizations. However, it did include questions addressing issues that were part of the nationalist agenda.

71. Interestingly, the preferences of ethnic Russians on the issue had changed: a greater percentage of Russians (56 percent) now also believed that the president should be Tatar (significant at p<0.005). This shift might have been due to Russians' decreasing fear of a nationalizing Tatar regime in post-Soviet Tatarstan. Author's survey of the general population in Tatarstan, 1997.

The rising popularity of the Tatar nationalist program is shown by the influence of nationalist ideas and deputies sympathetic to those ideas in Tatarstan's supreme soviet. Following the first semifree elections held in March 1990, the republic's soviet transformed from a rubber-stamp legislature into a parliament with several nationalist, prodemocracy, and independent deputies. In the election itself, TOTs fielded very few candidates since political parties were illegal at this time and few individuals were willing to risk running for office as openly nationalist candidates. However, a majority of those who did run as nationalists won the right to represent their districts.[72] Nationalist candidates won only 14 out of 250 districts, but their presence in parliament introduced new issues into the debate and influenced the opinion of other deputies. Eventually a large parliamentary bloc formed that was known as the Tatarstan faction. According to Rafael Khakimov, a founder of TOTs and later adviser to the president of the republic, the Tatarstan faction backed the TOTs program and included approximately 120 out of 250 votes in the supreme soviet. Another voting bloc—Soglasie (Agreement)—formed to oppose the Tatarstan faction. Composed mainly of ethnic Russians, it controlled seventy to eighty votes in the soviet.[73]

Throughout 1990, Tatar nationalists, both within and outside the newly reconstituted supreme soviet, advocated a republican declaration of sovereignty. Their demands became more insistent following the RSFSR's declaration of sovereignty that summer. Nationalist activists held daily mass demonstrations in order pressure the republican administration and supreme soviet. According to Damir Iskhakov, a cofounder of TOTs and later a leading specialist on Tatar ethnic politics, as many as thirty thousand people attended these prosovereignty demonstrations.[74] Then, in August 1990, Boris Yeltsin made a campaign swing through the Volga republics in an attempt to turn the ARs into allies in his power struggle with Gorbachev. Seeking popular support on the streets of Kazan, Yeltsin made the now well-known statement that would be taken with utmost seriousness by the nationalists: "Take all the sovereignty you can handle."[75] He declared, "We will welcome whatever independence the Tatar ASSR chooses

72. See Gorenburg's discussion on elections in Tatarstan in *Minority Ethnic Mobilization*, 133–38.

73. Rafael Khakimov, "Politicheskaia zhizn" [Political Life], in *Tatary i Tatarstan* [Tatars and Tatarstan] (Kazan: Tatarskoe knizhnoe izdatel'stvo 1993), 96.

74. Damir Iskhakov, "Sovremennoe Tatarskoe Natsional'noe dvizhenie: Pod'em i krizis" [The Current Tatar National Movement: Ascent and Crisis], *Tatarstan* 8 (1993): 27, cited in Beissinger, *Nationalist Mobilization*, 265.

75. *Vecherniaia Kazan'*, August 23, 1990. Yeltsin repeated this statement during his campaign stop in Ufa, Bashkortostan, saying, "Take all the sovereignty you can swallow."

for itself....I will say: if you want to govern yourselves completely, go ahead."[76] Soon thereafter, with 241 out of 242 deputies voting in favor, Tatarstan's supreme soviet passed a declaration of republican sovereignty.[77] The declaration deleted the word "autonomous" from the republic's name and announced that the republican laws and constitution took primacy over those of the Soviet Union.[78] Mintimir Shaimiev, a longtime apparatchik who had only recently been appointed first secretary of the Tatar Communist Party, proclaimed that Tatarstan was no longer part of the RSFSR and then resigned his position, sensing the party's increasing political irrelevance. However, he held on to his position as chair of the supreme soviet and thus remained de facto leader of the republic.

Support for the nationalist movement was growing. In a state under single-party control for seventy-four years, the nationalist opposition had quickly attracted relatively significant levels of support. Polls showed that 21 percent of the republic's population supported TOTs in late 1990 and early 1991 and that popular trust was higher for the nationalist organizations (12 percent) than for the Communist Party (9.4 percent).[79] Support for the nationalist goal of republican sovereignty was even higher. According to surveys conducted by the Russian polling organization VTsIOM (All Russian Public Opinion Research Center), more than 70 percent of ethnic Tatars and approximately 50 percent of ethnic Russians favored the upgrade to UR status. Mass support for republican sovereignty among ethnic Tatars rose even further during the several-month period following the August 1991 coup attempt in Moscow and prior to the collapse of the Soviet Union. Another VTsIOM survey indicates that the portion of Tatars backing UR status rose to 80 percent, while Russian support dropped to 23 percent. Most strikingly, whereas the possibility of independence for Tatarstan had been unthinkable just months earlier, VTsIOM surveys conducted from December 1990 to November 1991 show that significant support had developed among Tatars for independent statehood over the course of just one year. A majority of

---

76. E. Chernobrovkina, "Reshat' vam samim" [Decide for Yourselves], *Vecherniaia Kazan'*, August 10, 1990.

77. M. Medvedeva and E. Chernobrovkina, "Garantiruia ravnie prava" [Guaranteeing Equal Rights], *Vecherniaia Kazan'*, August 31, 1990.

78. The TASSR renamed itself the Tatar Soviet Socialist Republic—The Republic of Tatarstan.

79. Iskhakov, "Sovremennoe Tatarskoe natsional'noe dvizhenie," 29, 31. However, a research team from Shaimiev's administration later published a study claiming that popular support for nationalist organizations in 1991 was lower: 8 percent of the population supported TOTs and Ittifak, while between 4 and 12 percent supported the Russian federalist DPR. Slightly more than half of Tatarstan's population, they reported, remained apolitical in 1991. See *Tatarstan: na perekrestke mnenii* [Tatarstan: At the Crossroads of Opinion]. Kazan: Tatarstan Supreme Soviet, 1993), 33–51.

Russians, on the other hand, opposed full independence, though many continued to support increased republican autonomy.[80]

In 1991 the nationalist movement became more radical, declaring that sovereignty now required independent statehood. Throughout the year, the movement focused its opposition on the RSFSR and its new leader, Boris Yeltsin. The republic's nomenklatura-dominated administration, however, continued to support the former conception of sovereignty in which Tatarstan would enjoy UR status in a reconstituted Soviet Union after Gorbachev's passage of the union treaty. In the spring, when Shaimiev announced that elections to the newly created RSFSR presidency would be held on the territory of Tatarstan, the nationalists sponsored a series of rallies challenging this position and urging a boycott. Nationalist activists staged a successful two-week hunger strike led by Baraimova on Freedom Square in Kazan. The strike, in its novelty and militance, attracted enormous attention and won increased support for the movement. It ended with a large demonstration attended by fifty thousand people at which nationalists proclaimed support for the presidential candidacy of former party first secretary Shaimiev and denounced the upcoming elections for the presidency of the RSFSR as illegal.[81] Pushed by the nationalists, the republic's administration established the post of republican president and held elections with Shaimiev as the only candidate in early June. Although elections for the presidents of both the RSFSR and Tatarstan took place concurrently, the influence of the nationalists was evident in the fact that more republican residents chose to vote in the local election for Shaimiev (66 percent) than in the RSFSR election for Yeltsin (37 percent).[82] With the full support of TOTs, Mintimir Shaimiev was elected Tatarstan's first president.

Nationalist groups began to sponsor increasingly radical activities. They mounted frequent, large-scale protests in front of the Tatar supreme soviet building on Freedom Square, and organized strikes at the KamAZ truck factory in Naberezhnye Chelny and at the tire production plant in Nizhnekamsk. The Russian federalist opposition, headed by the Tatarstan branch of the Democratic Party of Russia (DPR), though less activist than the nationalists, sponsored counterrallies advocating the unity of Russia. During 1991 and 1992, thousands of people regularly gathered on Freedom Square, increasing the influence that opposition

80. Unpublished data from VTsIOM survey of December 1990; Leonid Tolchinskii, "Tatarstan: Uzly problem i perspektivy dvizheniia" [The Crux of the Issues and the Future of the Movement] *Vechernaia Kazan,* February 27, 1991.

81. Damir Iskhakov, "Khronika natsional'nykh dvizhenii (1980-e gody-avgust 1992 g.) [Chronicle of the Nationalist Movement], in *Suverennyi Tatarstan,* Vol. 1:241.

82. Walker, "The Dog That Didn't Bark," 13.

groups could bring to bear on republican politics.[83] Azatlyk formed in solidarity with the goals of Ittifak and began advocating the use of force.[84] It claimed that it had organized a people's militia in order to "stop provocations on the part of the supporters of imperial ambitions" (by which it meant Russians and federalist organizations).[85]

The leaders of the radical wing of the nationalist movement perceived that their groups enjoyed relatively significant popular support. Bairamova of Ittifak reported that more than 33 percent of the population supported her organization from 1991 to 1993.[86] Ramai Yuldashev, the leader of Azatlyk, claimed that as a result of the group's sponsoring rallies, speaking on television and radio (in both Russian and Tatar languages), and propagandizing in schools and institutes of higher education, 22–25 percent of Tatar youth supported his group.[87]

The attempted coup d'etat against Gorbachev by hard-line party conservatives in Moscow in August 1991 suddenly changed the political situation in the republic, creating an opening for the nationalist opposition to win power. President Shaimiev miscalculated the situation and sided with the leaders of the coup, the State Committee for the State of Emergency (Gosudarstvennyi Komitet po Chrezvichainomu Polozheniyu, or GKChP). Resorting to Soviet-era repression techniques, he arrested many of the democrats and nationalists who demonstrated on Freedom Square in support of Gorbachev and democracy and suppressed information about what was happening. When it became clear that the coup had failed, palpable anti-Shaimiev sentiment erupted in the republic. The democratic opposition movement began a grassroots campaign gathering signatures to impeach the president, while many nationalist organizations, democratic groups, and other organizations lined up to demand the resignations of both Shaimiev and the supreme soviet.[88] Political leadership in Tatarstan was up for grabs.

---

83. Interview with Vladimir Alexandrovich Belaev, chairman of Department of Sociology and Political Science at KGTU and leader of Soglasie, Kazan, June 20, 1997.

84. For more on the programs of Ittifak and Azatlyk, see Iskhakov, "Neformal'nye ob"edineniia,"

85. Guzel Faisullina, "Tatar Patriots Recall Ivan the Terrible," *Kommersant*, no. 22 (1991): 12, in *CDSP* 53, no. 21 (1991): 24; N. Morozov, "Tatarstan—A People's Militia is Being Created," *Pravda*, October 16, 1991, 1, in *CDSP* 53, no. 42 (1991): 28; "Tatarstan—Freedom Square Seethes," *Pravda*, October 17, 1991, 1, in *CDSP* 53, no. 42 (1991): 29.

86. Interview with Fauzia Bairamova, leader of Ittifak, Kazan, January 21, 1997.

87. Azatlyk established branches in cities throughout Tatarstan, including Almetevsk, Naberezhnye Chelny, Aznakaev, and Baltashai, as well as in cities outside the republic such as Ufa, Yaroslavl, Moscow, St. Petersburg, Samara, Uzhevskii, Chelyabinsk, and Omsk. Interview with Ramai Zagidyulovich Yuldashev, head of Azatlyk, Kazan, January 22, 1997.

88. Iskhakov, "Khronika natsional'nykh dvizhenii," 247–48.

In the wake of the coup, as the union republics were asserting their independence from the USSR, the Tatar nationalist movement began issuing strong appeals for independent statehood. Nationalist demonstrations took place throughout the fall culminating in October as the supreme soviet met to consider declaring republican independence. Nationalist demonstrators had been gathering for days in Freedom Square, timing their rallies to commemorate the anniversary of Ivan the Terrible's sacking of Kazan. They agitated for the supreme soviet to declare independence and called for its dissolution and the resignation of President Shaimiev if the soviet refused.[89] When demonstrators, some of whom were armed, heard that the legislators had voted against independence, they rushed the parliament building. Several demonstrators and policemen were seriously injured. One soviet deputy remembers this critical time as follows:

> I was a an eyewitness to very serious events in...Tatarstan....I will never forget how the crowds, the multithousand-person crowds surrounded our parliament building on Freedom Square from morning till night and how they idolized Fauzia Bairamova, who was advocating secession from Russia. It was quite frightening. I was afraid that such events might scandalously develop into a civil war. I remember...that when...we [the deputies] exited the parliament, the militia was holding back the crowds with much difficulty...and they were throwing pieces of broken glass and nails at us.[90]

The "storming" of parliament further polarized politics along ethnic lines. Comments made by the leader of one of Tatarstan's democratic opposition organizations indicated the degree of ethnopolitical polarization in the republic and suggested that Shaimiev's administration was losing legitimacy:

> We Tatars are suffering from the tragedy (the recent developments in Tataria) even more than Russians....Not long ago, M. Muliukov [a TOTs leader] held talks with us on the possibility of unification. But now we can hardly sit at the same table with them....But we also do not accept the arrogance and definite extremism of some democratic parties. Why, for example, did members of the Democratic Party of Russia go out onto Freedom Square at the very height of the nationalistic orgy, and with a Russian flag, no less? In effect, they provoked the extremists to an act of vandalism against the flag....If the nationalists aggravate the situation

---

89. Ibid., 249.
90. Interview with Boris Leonidovich Zheleznov, professor of law, Kazan State University, June 6, 1997. Conducted by Jeffrey Khan.

and the authorities do nothing, we will call on the working people...to express our lack of confidence in the republic's leadership.[91]

The nationalist movement experienced its strongest degree of popular support at this time. According to public opinion polls, 86 percent of the Tatar population backed independence, whereas 24 percent of Russians did.[92] President Shaimiev, responding to popular opinion, announced that a referendum on state sovereignty would be held in March 1992. In the lead-up to the vote, Shaimiev spoke about sovereignty as a public good that would benefit all citizens of the republic rather than as an ethnic good benefiting only Tatars. The vague wording of the referendum made it difficult for observers in both Tatarstan and Moscow to know whether the referendum was intended as a vote for independence and a prelude to secession. It asked citizens, "Do you agree that the republic of Tatarstan is a sovereign state, a subject of international law, building its relations with the Russian Federation and other republics and states on the basis of treaties between equal partners?" The sovereignty referendum passed with a majority of the republic's population (61 percent) voting yes. The results show that popular support existed for what had been the focus of the nationalist movement's efforts: achieving republican sovereignty.[93]

In early 1992 the radical wing of the nationalist movement challenged the authority of Tatarstan's supreme soviet by organizing an all-Tatar *kuraltai* (congress) that brought ethnic Tatars from throughout the former Soviet Union to Kazan. The *kuraltai* issued a declaration of independence and announced the formation of the *Milli Mejlis,* or Tatar National Assembly.[94] Over the next several months the Milli Mejlis attempted to wrest political power away from the supreme soviet. In the opinion of a former chairman of the assembly, "At that time, the Milli Mejlis had a lot of power, public opinion was on our side. The Milli Mejlis could have criticized any leader in the republic for going to Moscow and sitting in some ministry all day waiting for permission to do something instead of being in Tatarstan."[95] This bid to place Tatarstan's legislative and political power in the hands of radical Tatar nationalists, although an important event

---

91. A. Fazliyeva, chairwoman of the executive committee of Tatarstan's Democratic Reform Movement, quoted in Yevgenii Skukin, "Ordinary Ittifak Fascism?" *Rossiiskaia gazeta,* November 28, 1991 in *Current Digest of the Soviet Press,* 53, no. 47 (1991): 5.

92. Beissinger, *Nationalist Mobilization,* 267.

93. See Giuliano, "Who Determines the Self in the Politics of Self-Determination? Identity and Preference Formation in Tatarstan's Nationalist Mobilization," *Comparative Politics* 32, no. 3 (April 2000): 295–316.

94. The Milli Mejlis was named after the original Tatar National Assembly established by Tatar intellectuals who attempted to found the Idel-Ural republic following the 1917 Revolution.

95. Interview with Talgat Midkhatovich Abdullin, president of Ak-bars Bank and former chairman of Milli Mejlis, Kazan, June 30, 1997.

in symbolic terms, was ultimately unsuccessful. In June of that year President Shaimiev began to adopt parts of the nationalist program. He organized another conference, called the World Congress of Tatars, which also brought together diaspora Tatars and served to undermine the kuraltai's legitimacy while trading on its popular goal of supporting ethnic Tatars living outside the republic.

In general, after nearly being deposed from power, Shaimiev became significantly more responsive to the Tatar nationalist movement. He responded to its initiatives, adopted some of its policies, and began to co-opt its most influential leaders. The relationship between the nationalists and Shaimiev's administration was a complex and evolving one. The nationalist movement for the most part backed Shaimiev, believing that as an ethnic Tatar he supported the interests of the Tatar nation. Shaimiev's government, however, was made up of communist-era nomenklatura elites resistant to any kind of change. Some observers maintain that Shaimiev supported nationalism in order to use the threat of large-scale unrest as leverage during negotiations with Moscow. For example, according to several nationalist leaders, his administration provided financial support—including office space in the center of Kazan—to several nationalist groups from the end of 1991 to March 1992.[96] Other leaders vehemently denied this.[97] While Shaimiev found it useful to let Moscow know that he was constrained by popular nationalism, he controlled neither the activity of the nationalist movement nor the large public support that it commanded. As his behavior during the coup attempt shows, Shaimiev initially chose to side with Soviet conservatives opposed to reform. Ultimately his administration adopted some nationalist policies and made secessionist demands on Moscow, but only after it was pressured to do so by the strong support for Tatar nationalism among the population.

Throughout 1992 the relationship between Tatarstan and Moscow soured despite the fact that Yeltsin entered into negotiations with Kazan concerning each side's rights and jurisdiction. That spring the Tatar supreme soviet passed legislation declaring fiscal sovereignty and establishing a single-channel tax structure. Moscow angrily cut central disbursements to the republic; Tatarstan retaliated by failing to remit taxes to the center.[98] Tatarstan defied Moscow again when it refused to sign Yeltsin's federation treaty. (The only other republic unwilling

---

96. Interview with Damir Iskhakov, Tatar historian and cofounder of TOTs, Kazan, December 19, 1996; interview with Amir Gubaevich Makhmutov, head of Suverenitet (Sovereignty), Kazan, January 23, 1997.

97. These leaders included Fauzia Bairamova of Ittifak, January 21, 1997; Zaki Zainuillin of TOTs, January 22, 1997; and Khakim Abdulovich Gainuillin of the Republican Party of Tatarstan, January 31, 1997, all interviewed in Kazan. In general, nationalist organizations were funded by private individuals and associations.

98. Lapidus and Walker, "Nationalism, Regionalism, and Federalism."

to sign was Chechnya.) Several months later, in November, Tatarstan adopted a constitution, declaring itself a subject of international law and proclaiming dual citizenship with Russia for republican residents.

During 1993 Yeltsin was engaged in a protracted power struggle with the conservative state Duma in Moscow. He organized a nationwide referendum on his leadership and reform policies to resolve the conflict, but Tatarstan called on its citizens to boycott the vote. They heeded Shaimiev's appeal, and voter turnout—at less than 15 percent of the population—was too low to count. Chechnya was the only other republic to exhibit equally low levels of participation.[99] At the end of the year, Tatarstan again asked its population to boycott Russian federal elections, this time for the state Duma. The majority of the republic's population complied, with only 14 percent of Tatarstan's voters participating.

When Yeltsin finally resolved the conflict with the Duma by shelling the parliament building in September 1993, Tatarstan remained disengaged, as if events in distant Moscow were of no concern in the republic. As the rest of the country was up in arms issuing statements of support for or against Yeltsin, Tatarstan's prime minister announced, "We're very sorry, but honestly, we aren't in the mood for this. Tatarstan has to finish harvesting its grain crops, potatoes and beets." President Shaimiev and the chairman of Tatarstan's supreme soviet purposely continued their vacation in the Tatar countryside.[100] At the end of the year Yeltsin put forward a new Russian constitution, but republican leaders protested that it did not grant sufficient power to the republics. Russia held another referendum throughout the country for the adoption of the constitution, and Tatarstan again urged its residents not to vote; only 13.8 percent of the population participated.

Suddenly, in February 1994, Shaimiev's government announced that it had achieved a breakthrough in the ongoing negotiations with Moscow for a bilateral treaty. The treaty—actually a series of agreements—granted Tatarstan the right to set its own budget and taxes, establish republican administrative bodies, and conclude economic and political relations with foreign states and with other subjects of the Russian Federation.[101] With the signing of the treaty, Shaimiev consolidated his political power in Tatarstan. His administration took credit for achieving sovereignty as well as other goals that the nationalists had introduced into the political agenda. Over time, Shaimiev attributed the republic's ability to avoid interethnic conflict to his own policies and to the existence of sovereignty. As his control increased, the nationalists, as well as the democratic opposition,

---

99. Elizabeth Teague, "Russia and Tatarstan Sign Power-Sharing Treaty," *RFE/RL Research Report,* April 8, 1994, 25.

100. "Who Thinks What about the President's Decree?" *Nezavisimaia gazeta,* September 23, 1993, 3 in *Current Digest of the Post-Soviet Press,* 55, no. 38 (1993): 11.

101. Walker, "The Dog That Didn't Bark," 25.

were shunted aside. Negative press campaigns and the gerrymandering of electoral districts prevented opposition candidates from winning seats in parliament. Although nationalist groups continued to exist after 1994, their influence
among the general population, which had been declining since the movement's
peak in 1992, further receded. Some groups that had been part of the nationalist
movement turned their attention from politics to religious or cultural pursuits.
Other groups, including the main nationalist organizations, split into smaller
and smaller factions. The Tatar Public Center in 1996 was a pale reflection of
its former self. First-generation TOTs leaders had been replaced by uncompro-
mising, radical nationalists. The group's extremism provoked such antipathy
from the Shaimiev administration that at the time of my research in 1997, the
group was threatened with eviction from its unheated office space in the center
of Kazan. Ittifak, meanwhile, had put aside its goal of national independence to
join forces with the opposition communist party to battle the "mafia-nomenkla-
tura structures" of Yeltsin and Shaimiev.[102] The Tatar nationalist movement had
disintegrated.

The case of Tatarstan shows that even when the professional mobility and
socioeconomic status of a minority group improve over the course of several
decades, and even when central state policies are largely responsible for that im-
provement, group grievances can be constructed in which people nevertheless
blame the central state for blocked mobility. When Tatar nationalists articulated
issues of ethnic economic inequality, people responded, since they were becoming increasingly worried about their professional futures as the state-controlled
economy entered a major economic crisis. In the story of national revival in
Tatarstan, worsening macroeconomic conditions mattered, but not in the way
most observers would have expected. People with ethnic affiliations responded
to nationalist leaders not because those leaders were describing an economic crisis and representing ethnic interests but because particular issues found a receptive audience among people psychologically affected by the crisis. In response to
the nationalist message of blocked Tatar mobility and socioeconomic subordination to ethnic Russians, many people with Tatar identities became convinced
that their ethnicity negatively affected their personal life chances and that the
only way to put an end to this problem was for the Tatar nation to obtain sovereignty. The nationalists constructed a grievance that allowed a sense of Tatar
nationhood to crystallize for a brief period in the early 1990s. Aggrieved and
eager for change, people took to the streets to demand sovereignty for the Tatar
nation and Republic of Tatarstan.

---

102. Bairamova interview, Kazan, January 21, 1997.

5

NATIONALISM IN A SOCIALIST COMPANY TOWN

Tatars, Russians, and the Kamskii Automobile
Works in Naberezhnye Chelny

> **The Kama River Truck Plant [KamAZ] is the Soviet crash project
> par excellence, the showpiece of the 1971–1975 Five-Year Plan.
> I've seen other Soviet installations,...[b]ut none...matches the
> Kama River Truck Plant as an archetype of the gigantomania of
> Soviet planners, as a symbol of Soviet faith that bigger means better
> and the Soviet determination to have the biggest at any cost.... It
> embodies industrial might created from a vacuum and materialized in
> a furious five-year flurry of storming. It emanates brute strength.**

—Hedrick Smith, *The Russians*

In 1969, Naberezhnye Chelny, named Brezhnev at that time, was a small rural town located in northeast Tatarstan with a population of thirty-eight thousand and no infrastructural links to the rest of the country. Soviet central planners, in a less than rational moment, decided this was the ideal spot to construct the USSR's newest and largest truck and automobile production complex. So construction began on the all-union enterprise, Kamskii Automobile Works, or KamAZ. Technical training schools appeared, and enormous housing complexes were thrown up, each with its own stores, schools, and child-care centers. Young workers poured into the city, persuaded by the rhetoric of building the socialist future and attracted by the promise of large new apartments. In less than a decade, a small town had been transformed into the second-largest city in Tatarstan, as well as one of the Soviet Union's major industrial sites. By 1990, the population had reached more than half a million people.[1]

The enthusiasm of the era is recorded in the City History Museum, where an exhibit dedicated to the construction of KamAZ shows smiling brigade workers busily constructing factory buildings and living in dormitories. The atmosphere portrayed at the museum of one very long and festive barnraising was

---

1. The city's population was 506,000 in 1990 and grew to 525,000 by 1996. *Statisticheskii ezhegodnik Respublika Tatarstan 1995* [Statistical Handbook of the Republic of Tatarstan, 1995] (Kazan: Goskomstat Respubliki Tatarstan, 1996).

not simply propaganda. Passing comments made by sixty-year-olds reminiscing about the faith they had had in the future while working at KamAZ in the early 1970s suggest how well the Soviet central planners' campaigns succeeded in channeling willing labor to new production sites in somewhat obscure parts of the country.[2]

During the Soviet era, Naberezhnye Chelny was the quintessential company town. KamAZ owned and managed not merely the factory, but city schools, residential buildings, services, public transport, clinics, and entertainment complexes. The enterprise employed approximately 80 percent of the city's population. When macroeconomic contraction set in and demand for KamAZ cars and trucks began to shrink, KamAZ cut production, and people began to fear for the continued supply of positions and promotions. Because KamAZ was a monopoly employer in the city, residents faced a lack of viable alternative employers and job opportunities. Although moving out of the city was possible, the challenge citizens faced in obtaining residence permits and securing apartments and services in other cities made moving an undesirable option. Residents of Chelny therefore experienced increasing apprehension about jobs, promotions, education, and training, and anxiety about the prospects for their children. As economists Vladimir Gimpelson and Douglas Lippoldt state, the many Soviet citizens living in company towns or "enterprise-linked residential areas" were accustomed to a life in which loyalty to the enterprise was rewarded, and benefits and social activities depended on the workplace. Such households "found it extremely difficult to accept any disruption to these ties."[3] Given the precarious position of residents of Chelny, we might expect them to have conservatively clung to the status quo and to have supported the system of central planning in which their jobs, apartments, and services would remain secure. Instead, during the period of national revival, Naberezhnye Chelny had the highest levels of mass nationalism in Tatarstan. It was labeled the headquarters of the nationalist movement by locals, and a sizable portion of the Tatars living there supported the nationalist movement. Why?

The case of Naberezhnye Chelny clearly illustrates the argument of this book concerning the disconnect between economic conditions and people's perceptions of those conditions. In the labor market in Naberezhnye Chelny—where the main employer was KamAZ—many Tatars were disadvantaged by comparison with Russians. They held a majority of blue-collar assembly-line jobs, while Russians dominated white-collar management. However, at the same time, Tatars in Naberezhnye Chelny experienced significant social mobility as a result

---

2. Field notes, Naberezhnye Chelny, 1997.
3. Gimpelson and Lippoldt, *The Russian Labour Market*, 7.

of Soviet development and ethnic affirmative action policies. The Soviet state encouraged Tatars to move to the city to work at KamAZ and established preference policies for Tatars at the factory as well as in the city's feeder educational institutes. Therefore, many Tatars who migrated to the city for work rapidly moved up the professional ladder. In this sense, Tatars were more privileged in the city's labor market than Russians. Thus, there were two economic realities for Tatars. The nationalists, however, chose to focus on only one: Tatar underrepresentation and blocked opportunity. The nationalist movement communicated the message of ethnic economic inequality, and a substantial portion of the Tatar population in the city responded. Despite friendly relations with ethnic Russians in the workplace for the most part, many Tatars started to support the program of the Tatar Public Center and its call for republican state sovereignty. Apprehension about future job security and employment prospects was arguably more severe in Naberezhnye Chelny than in Kazan. At the same time, nationalist leaders in Chelny strongly emphasized the point about ethnic economic inequality at KamAZ. These two variables interacted to produce a rise in mass support for Tatar nationalism.

There was, however, an alternative explanation for the high level of nationalist mobilization in the city. Many Tatars living in Naberezhnye Chelny migrated to the city from the republic's rural countryside during the 1970s and 1980s to work at KamAZ. Two-thirds of the city's Tatars were relatively recent arrivals, or in local parlance, "first-generation" residents, who spoke Tatar as their native language.[4] In comparison with Kazan, a city in which most Tatars had lived for several generations and spoke Russian fluently, Naberezhnye Chelny was far less Russified.

Thus, several informants in Tatarstan offered another explanation for the city's support of nationalism: the strong ethnic consciousness of the Tatars living there and their proximity to traditional ethnic culture. For example, Ramai Zagidyulovich Yuldashev, a young leader of Azatlyk, explained that Chelny's Tatars supported nationalism because they were former agricultural workers (i.e., workers on collective farms) who hadn't forgotten their culture.[5] Another nationalist leader, Talgat Amadishin of the Naberezhnye Chelny branch of Azatlyk, echoed

---

4. Roza Musina, "Etnokulturnie orientatsii i mezhnatsional'nye otnosheniia," in *Sovremennye natsional'nye protsessy v Respublike Tatarstan,* Vol. II (Kazan: Tatarstan Academy of Sciences, 1994). The Russian population in the city was also composed of relative newcomers, but they migrated primarily from outside the republic of Tatarstan. Only 35 percent of Chelny's Russians were natives of Tatarstan. Also see Yagfar Garipov, "Sotsial'no-etnicheskaia struktura rabotnikov i mezhnatsional'nye otnosheniia na KamAZe," in *Sovremennye natsional'nye protsessy v Respublike Tatarstan, Vol. I* (Kazan: Russian Academy of Sciences, Kazan Scientific Center, 1992), 68.

5. Interview with Ramai Yuldashev, Azatlyk, Kazan, January 22, 1997.

this view: "People from the countryside supported us because people there kept their national traditions."[6] A government official and former academic in the Department of Interethnic Relations thought along the same lines. According to Raman Yurevich Belyakov, Tatars in Chelny supported the nationalists because of their common cultural identity. They were essentially rural dwellers and as such possessed "a different mentality" and culture than the urban Tatars. He told me, "The rural population knows their own language and supported the nationalists, of course, because if it weren't for them, the Tatar national culture would have died out long ago."[7] Yuldashev, Amadishin, and Belyakov all believed that people's ethnic identities and culture directly determined their political choices. Rural inhabitants and, by extension, rural migrants to the city, they argued, naturally supported a nationalist program because they embodied and reproduced authentic Tatar culture. This is standard party line for nationalists everywhere, and it is also a common assumption of Western analysts. Results from a research survey conducted by Leokadia Drobizheva, however, show that there was little support for nationalism among rural Tatars. Another scholar at the Tatarstan Academy of Sciences reported the same thing: "In the countryside, nobody cares about politics, and nobody participates. When our survey asked people which nationalist groups they supported, they had only heard a little bit about them."[8] But because it is a standard nationalist belief to see a rural ethnic community as the embodiment of indigenous culture and the site of its current reproduction, it was difficult for some nationalists to square their expectations of rural Tatar support for nationalism with their observation of low nationalism in the countryside. As one nationalist explained, "There is a Tatar-speaking Tatar population here and a Russian-speaking Tatar population, and the real bearers of nationalism are the Tatar-speaking Tatars. But I think that the Tatar-speaking Tatars did less than Russian-speaking Tatars for the nationalist movement. I chided many of them for this."[9]

A significant number of ethnic Tatars who were born in the countryside demonstrate the point that social origins do not directly determine interests. Local administrative and Communist Party leaders benefited from knowing the Tatar language, growing up in the countryside, and then learning Russian. Tatar-speaking Tatars in the countryside held many high-status positions as party administrators and chairmen of collective farms. Political leadership in

---

6. Interview with Talgat Amadishin, Azatlyk, Naberezhnye Chelny, May 24, 1997.

7. Interview with Raman Belyakov, Department of Interethnic Relations, Presidential Apparat, Kazan Kremlin, February 15, 1997.

8. Interview with Lilia Sagitova, Tatarstan Academy of Sciences, Kazan, December 19, 1996. For more evidence of low nationalist support among rural Tatars, see Leokadia Drobizheva et al., *Natsional'noe samosoznanie i natsionalizm v Rossiiskoi Federatsii nachala 1990-kh godov*.

9. Interview with Rustem Sultanovich Korzhakov, economist, Kazan, April 1, 1997.

rural Tatarstan became "indigenized" as a result not only of korenizatsiia but also, as mentioned in the previous chapter, of the process of zemlyachestvo. In the 1960s under Oblast Party Committee (Obkom) first secretary Talbaev, rural Tatars began to enter posts in local and city administration through a system of clientelist networks based on region of origin. This meant that the majority of political cadres in the republic, in both country and city, were so-called first generation city residents born in the Tatar countryside. They spoke Tatar as their native tongue, usually received their early education in the countryside, learned to speak Russian, and then began a career in government administration. A Tatar sociologist writes, "For several decades, the political elite recruited new members from agrarian regions of the republic....It still relies on a continuity of succession in which higher-ups find their cadres in the 'provinces.'"[10]

Zemlyak networks tied Tatar-speaking Tatar administrative leaders in Kazan—led by former Obkom first secretary (and later president) Mintimir Shaimiev—to those in republican cities and rural regions. The administrators were district or city party secretaries (i.e. leaders of a raion party committee [*raikom*] or a city party committee [*gorkom*]) who became "heads of administration" (*glav administratsiia*) in 1993. Local party secretaries in turn mediated between Tatar-speaking Tatar kholkhoz chairmen, who then governed their local collective farms—communities made up of Tatar-speaking Tatars. The Soviet policy of indigenization of political cadres fused with local zemlyachestvo networks to produce a Tatar-speaking Tatar elite running the republic.

The nationalist movement, however, was composed of an elite from a very different social and geographic stratum: the republic's urban intelligentsia. If the nationalist cohort of Russified Tatars were to take power in the republic, the positions and zemlyak network of elite rural Tatars would come under threat. Members of the rural, Tatar-speaking Tatar community who had done extremely well for themselves under the current zemlyak system but did not know what to expect with a new nationalist state preferred to maintain the status quo. Political scientist Mary McAuley argues that party leaders and nomenklatura administrators in Tatarstan more generally were "desperate to hold onto their positions" because they were unable to move into lateral positions outside their republic: "Careers had to be made at home and the costs of failure were high."[11]

For a part of the rural Tatar nomenklatura, embracing the nationalists' call for a full-scale Tatar language revival might place the zemlyak system in jeopardy. The republic would be confronted with a sudden influx of new Tatar speakers

10. Akhmetov, "Elita tatar," 123.
11. Mary McAuley, *Russia's Politics of Uncertainty* (Cambridge: Cambridge University Press, 1997), 88.

into republican politics at all levels, rural and urban. This would destroy the rural Tatar elite's monopoly on speaking Tatar—a skill it used in mediating between urban and rural elites. Within the space of a few years, highly educated, bilingual newcomers could build new lines of direct communication to the countryside that would render the zemlyak networks impotent. The newcomers, furthermore, might introduce the attributes of merit and ability, rather than connections and custom, as preconditions for administrative appointments. Therefore, contrary to the expectations of nationalists, an important segment of the Tatar rural population—administrative elites—was predisposed to oppose full-scale Tatar language revival. The point here is that cultural attributes should not be assumed to directly guide people's political preferences toward support of nationalism. Even the seemingly fundamental and straightforward attribute of native language can establish varied preferences among people who speak that language.

Tatar language revival struck more of a receptive chord among urban, Russified Tatars than among rural, Tatar-speaking Tatars. According to the Tatar scholar Rustam Gibadullin, who conducted a survey of 694 Tatars in Naberezhnye Chelny from 1991 to 1992—the period in which popular support for nationalism peaked—the total percentage of respondents who favored linguistic Tatarization was rather low. Only 30 percent of even those respondents who had attended Tatar-language grade schools supported making Tatar the sole state language of the republic (as opposed to having both Tatar and Russian share official state status). More Tatars from the countryside who had migrated to Naberezhnye Chelny (28 percent) than Tatars from urban areas (13 percent) reported that they backed Tatar as the sole state language. Still, these data show that overall, a majority of Tatar respondents favored having both Russian and Tatar as Tatarstan's official state languages.[12]

Finally, despite the fact that Tatar nationalists viewed rural Tatars as "true representatives of the Tatar nation," distinct differences existed between urban and rural Tatars that challenge the nationalist idea that Tatars formed a cohesive ethnic group. Many urban Tatars in fact recognized that there were differences in attributes, mentality, social milieu, and interests between the rural and urban populations, and they variously described such differences as a psychological divide, a rural inferiority complex, a different way of thinking, a different mentality, and even a different culture. When I asked urban Tatars during interviews whether they had been born in the countryside, they consistently reacted in an offended and surprised tone. The lower social status of rural Tatars was

---

12. R. M. Gibadullin, *Tatarskoe naselenie naberezhnykh chelnov v tsifrakh etnosotsiologii, 1992 g.* [The Tatar Population of Naberezhnye Chelny: An Ethnosociology in Numbers, 1992] (Naberezhnye Chelny: Magrifat, 1993), 43.

reinforced by their inability to speak Russian. Even urban Tatars who advocated Tatar language revival took pride in the fact that they spoke Russian, as revealed in comments made by Akhat Mushinskii, the leader of the Tatar branch of the International PEN club—an organization whose goal was to elevate Tatar literature to its rightful place in world literature.[13] Mushinskii proudly and without a hint of irony told me, "I'll let you in on a secret. Only people born in the countryside write in Tatar. Nobody born in Kazan does. I write in Russian, like Chingiz Aitmaitov."[14] Tatar nationalists failed to recognize that rural-urban, intraethnic cleavages could mean that rural Tatars did not share the interests and preferences of urban Tatars and might not perceive any connection between the social practices and beliefs of their daily lives and the nationalist program of urban intellectuals.

Tatar nationalist organizations, in fact, made very limited attempts to reach rural Tatars. They concentrated the bulk of their activity in the republic's urban regions. As a result, Tatar-speaking Tatars responded weakly to the nationalist appeals. According to a local sociologist, Guzel Stoliarova, urban Tatars' concerns simply did not resonate with the rural Tatars. This is not to claim that rural Tatars did not support any of the nationalist goals. On the contrary, the rural Tatar regions solidly voted for republican sovereignty in the 1992 Referendum on Tatarstan's State Sovereignty. For example, the rural, majority-Tatar Aktanishskii, Arskii, Leninogorskii, and Sabinskii districts voted yes to sovereignty almost unanimously.[15] However, as McAuley points out, soon after this vote, rural Tatars also voted for President Shaimiev and other nonnationalist candidates in elections to the Russian Federation Duma and Federation Council elections. McAuley hypothesizes that rural residents engaged in "ritual voting," unlike urban residents, who practiced "preference voting behavior." Voting in the countryside, she argues, represented "ritual participation in a collective

---

13. The International PEN club is a "worldwide association of writers...promot[ing] friendship and intellectual cooperation among writers.... [It] exists to fight for freedom of expression and represent the conscience of world literature." http://www.internationalpen.org.uk/index.php?pid=2.

14. Aitmaitov is a famous writer and Russified Kyryz who led Kyrgyzstan's national revival and then left the nationalist movement. Interview with Akhat Mushinskii, Tatar PEN Club, Kazan, March 4, 1997.

15. Data on the ethnic breakdown of the sovereignty vote either are not published or simply do not exist. I compiled this data by comparing the percentage of voters supporting sovereignty in each raion (from the official voting results) with data on the percentages of ethnic groups and rural population in each raion (from a statistical handbook). See Dokumenty (Protokoly, informatsiia, itogovye resul'taty) po resul'tatam golosovaniia na referendume Respublike Tatarstana 21 Marta 1992 goda [Documents on the results of a referendum on the Republic of Tatarstan], fond no. P2297, op. no. 2, delo no. 2, and M. R. Mustafin and R. G. Khuzeev, *Vse o Tatarstane: Ekonomiko-geograficheskii spravochnik* [All about Tatarstan: Handbook of Economy and Geography] (Kazan: Tatarskoe knizhnoe izdatel'stvo, 1994).

activity"—something expected of rural residents by their kholkhoz chairmen and local political leaders.[16]

I make the arguments here about rural regions to emphasize first, that rural nationalism was not an automatic outcome and second, that if rural Tatars did not automatically support nationalism simply because of their identity and culture, we cannot assume that rural Tatar migrants to the cities supported nationalism for these reasons either.

Ethnicity and the KamAZ Labor Force

By the early 1990s, the population in Naberezhnye Chelny was almost evenly split between the two largest ethnic groups there: Russians, who comprised 48.7 percent of the population, and Tatars, who made up 40.6 percent.[17] Was the city's ethnodemographic structure reflected in the factory? First, ethnic Russians clearly dominated the highest levels of management at KamAZ. The thirteen directors of KamAZ's factories received their education and early training in various technical centers of the Soviet Union before moving into top positions at KamAZ.[18] Nikolai Bekh, the president and general director, and the two deputy general directors, Vadim Paslov and Vladimir Sigal, were also ethnic Russians. The professional positions of these men only hint at their power, however, since KamAZ directors acted as de facto political leaders of Naberezhnye Chelny.[19] Whereas Russians dominated top factory management, ethnic Tatars ran the city's party structures and local administration. This arrangement was typical of many cities in republics throughout the USSR and was considered entirely appropriate, since these enterprises were all-union projects from their inception and were administered by central planners in Moscow.

The ethnic makeup of the middle and lower tiers of the KamAZ workforce differed from that in upper management. First, there was a lopsided situation in midlevel management as of the early 1990s: more than twice as many Russians as Tatars were "specialists," a category that included section (*tsekhi*) managers,

---

16. Eighty percent of rural voters voted for Shaimiev for the Federation Council. McAuley, *Russia's Politics*, 104–8.

17. The next three largest nationalities are Chuvash (2.5 percent); Ukrainians (2.3 percent), and Bashkir (1.9 percent). Mustafin and Khuzeev, R.G. *Vse o Tatarstane*, 90.

18. In addition to KamAZ's thirteen factories in Tatarstan, it has five more located in Bashkortostan, Ukraine, Kazakhstan, and Russia.

19. The KamAZ anniversary book recognizes Bekh's power. The caption to a photograph of Bill Clinton, Boris Yeltsin, and Nikolai Bekh standing together reads, "A Meeting of Three Presidents." *Kamaz 25*, 137. McAuley describes the close tie between the Communist Party and KamAZ. *Russia's Politics*, 93.

foremen (*masteri*), engineers, technical workers, and supervisors (*rukovoditeli*), and white-collar workers/clerks (*sluzhaschii*). Of 22,437 specialists, approximately 60 percent (13,552) were Russian, and 28 percent (6,354) were Tatars.[20] Moreover, within the category of specialist, Russians occupied the higher positions (head of section and assistant head of section), whereas Tatars occupied the middle and lower levels.[21] Some of this ethnic imbalance could have been due to the fact that there were more Russian than Tatar employees at KamAZ overall: the workforce was 48 percent Russian and 39 percent Tatar.[22] However, the ethnic composition of the blue-collar workforce nullifies this explanation because these workers were almost evenly split between Russians (44 percent) and Tatars (42 percent) (table 5.1).[23]

These statistics show that there were fewer Tatars than Russians in midlevel management at KamAZ. However, they fail to capture the fact that Tatars had been moving into the KamAZ workforce from the moment the factory opened in the early 1970s. Tatar social mobility was a direct result of policies enacted by the Soviet state in conjunction with KamAZ. Training institutes were established in the city as feeders for the factory. The most important of these was KAMPi (KamAZ Polytechnical Institute), where the language of instruction was Russian. Tatars from the countryside were given preferences in admission to the training institutes, such as extra points on their entrance exams and allowances for poor Russian-language ability. The majority of students at KAMPi came from the Tatar countryside.[24] KamAZ itself developed a system of ranks for all employees to follow in order to advance professionally and obtain better salaries and nonmonetary side payments critical to the Soviet system. Farida Orlova, an ethnic Tatar and the head of the Department of Social Regulation at KamAZ explained, "A worker straight from school without higher education has to start

20. Yu. V. Platonov and G. A. Kulakova, "Otchet po resul'tatam oprosa obshchestvennogo mneniia rabotnikov tatarskoi natsional'nosti po nekotorym problemam natsional'nogo razvitiia" [Report on the Results of a Public Opinion Survey of Tatar Workers on Issues of National Development], KamAZ Center for Sociological Research, Naberezhnye Chelny, 1992.

21. Interview with Glusyia Akhatovna Kulakova, assistant director, KamAZ Center for Sociological Research, Naberezhnye Chelny, May 27, 1997.

22. A. Platonov, "Spravka: Nekotorye aspekty mezhnatsional'nykh otnoshenii v kollektive AO KamAZa" [Several Aspects of Interethnic Relations in the KamAZ Workforce], KamAZ Center for Sociological Research, Naberezhnye Chelny, 1991. Platonov is the director of the center.

23. Other nationalities, especially Ukrainians and Chuvash, form the remainder of the workforce. Data are from a 1996 KamAZ Center for Sociological Research survey, "Otchet o komplektovanii i rasstanovke kadrov aktsionernogo obshchestva KamAZa na 01.01.96 goda" [Report on the Organization and Composition of the Personnel of the Joint Stock Company KamAZ, January 1, 1996]. The same figures were found in a 1990 survey conducted by the KamAZ Center. The 1990 survey results are analyzed in Garipov, "Sotsial'no-etnicheskaia struktura."

24. Interview with Nailia Ildanovna Iskhakovna, vice chairman of public relations, TOTs, Naberezhnye Chelny, May 20, 1997.

Table 5.1 Ethnic composition of KamAZ workforce, 1989

	RUSSIANS	TATARS	OTHER	TOTAL
Total KamAZ workforce	48%	39%	13%	100%
White-collar workers	60%	28%	12%	100%
Blue-collar workers	44%	42%	14%	100%

Source: Yu. V. Platonov and G. A. Kulakova, "Otchet po resul'tatam oprosa obshchestvennogo mneniia rabotnikov tatarskoi natsional'nosti po nekotorim problemam natsional'nogo rasvitiia" [Report on the Results of a Public Opinion Survey of Tatar Workers on Issues of National Development], KamAZ Center for Sociological Research, Naberezhnye Chelny, 1992.

at the bottom of the ranks. The hierarchy is: assembly line worker, skilled worker, foreman, shop head, head of department, manager. It takes twenty years to climb through the ranks." The responsibilities and requirements necessary for individuals to advance professionally through each rank were clearly delimited. But KamAZ offered night school classes to Tatars that allowed them to skip several ranks. According to Orlova, "In this way, Tatars went from being a worker directly to head of department."[25] These policies and institutions helped Tatars catch up to the Russians' level of professional achievement.

The efforts of KamAZ to educate, employ, and assimilate Tatars into urban factory life took place because it was a socialist enterprise operating in a centrally planned, rather than a capitalist, economy. Soviet enterprises operated under a soft budget constraint, meaning that directors were under no obligation to minimize costs and maximize profit. They had little interest in locating and maintaining a constant supply of cheap, blue-collar labor. Therefore, instead of drawing on the Tatar population as a relatively uneducated and thus inexpensive source of labor, the factory assumed the cost of educating and training Tatars so that they would become white-collar managers as well as factory workers. Ironically, because the socialist workers' state was deeply concerned with establishing ethnic egalitarianism, the system institutionalized career advancement for Tatars, providing incentives to alter the life course of rural Tatars. From farmer to skilled worker and even brigade leader within one lifetime, the system tied Tatars to the factory's assimilationist ideal. By the late 1980s, large numbers of Tatars were working side by side with Russians in almost all tiers and departments of the factory, though they were still outnumbered in white-collar management posts.

The static percentages of Tatar and Russian representation in the KamAZ workforce fail to capture how Tatars took advantage of the privileges granted them by the Soviet state to move into white- and blue-collar sectors of Naberezhnye

25. Interview with Farida Orlova, head of Department of Social Regulation, KamAZ, Naberezhnye Chelny, May 23, 1997. Respondent's name has been changed.

Chelny's economy. Yet it was these frozen-in-time statistics that nationalists used to mobilize Tatars against an allegedly unjust status quo.

The Nationalist Movement

In the founding charter of the Naberezhnye Chelny branch of the Tatar Public Center, the group directly advocated placing Tatars in professional jobs. TOTs announced its goals—"train and promote national cadres [i.e. Tatars] for management positions [*rukovodiashchie dolzhnosti*], [and] to provide proportional representation of Tatars."[26] TOTs drew attention to this issue via grassroots tactics, such as holding demonstrations and sponsoring strikes at the factory and picketing KamAZ to get the management removed. According to the KamAZ sociologist Glusyia Kulokova, "The group claimed that [General Director] Bekh and all the others were Jews and that national cadres should run KamAZ. They wanted to remove all the directors." She added, "They weren't totally mistaken about this." According to Kulakova, though the claim made by TOTs was rather extreme, the group was correct in asserting that most of the managing directors of the factory were not Tatars.

A study by TOTs of the ethnic composition of the KamAZ workforce found that a majority of the management positions at the factory were held by Russians.[27] Publications by sympathetic Tatar intellectuals helped to bolster the nationalist claims about limitations facing Tatars. According to a study by Yagfar Garipov, Tatars were at a general disadvantage vis-à-vis Russians because they had not been working at KamAZ as long as Russians had. Three times as many Russians as Tatars had an employment term (*stazh*) of fifteen years or more, whereas one-third of Tatars had an employment term of five years or less. Garipov argues that this fact limited Tatars because longer employment terms facilitated employees' advancement through the professional ranks and helped them in resolving residential problems or other daily bureaucratic needs.[28] TOTs began to lobby for the promotion of more Tatars into management positions, and according to one nationalist leader, General Director Bekh occasionally responded positively.[29] The TOTs leadership became more radical than the leaders in Kazan and organized many rallies and demonstrations in Naberezhnye Chelny, as well

---

26. "Programma Naberezhno-Chelnynskogo otdeleniia Tatarskogo obshchestvennogo tsentra" [Program of the Naberezhnye Chelny Branch of the Tatar Public Center], 4.

27. The TOTs study began as a response to a report issued by Gosplan in Moscow stating that titular nationalities were well represented in management structures of major enterprises in the autonomous republics. See Goble, "Ethnicity and Economic Reform," 24.

28. Garipov, "Sotsial'no-etnicheskaia struktura rabotnikov," 67.

29. Iskhakovna interview, May 20, 1997.

as in other large cities, such as Nizhnekamsk. The group also attempted to organize a strike among the KamAZ workforce.[30]

Nationalist leaders continued to tell the same story about discrimination against Tatars seven years later. For example, the cochairman of the Naberezhnye Chelny branch of TOTs, Nailiia Ildanovna Iskhakovna, explained to me, "Tatars are fired more often than Russians. People come to me and tell me stories of how their husband was fired because the enterprise said it had to lay off workers, and then they find out that a Russian was appointed to that job."[31] In the words of one of the more radical nationalist sympathizers, a member of the cultural-political organization Bulgar Club: "At Kamaz, there are seventeen directors, only one of them was a Tatar. The Tatars are disappearing. The people in power all still have a communist orientation. There is discrimination here."[32]

The Naberezhnye Chelny branch of the Tatar Public Center articulated a position that was more ethnically exclusivist than that of TOTs in Kazan. Whereas the latter vacillated between describing its goal as creating a national state (Tatarstan for Tatars) and a multinational state in which all ethnic groups shared equal rights, TOTs in Naberezhnye Chelny was more exclusivist or properly nationalist. The group frequently described the issue of Tatar underrepresentation at KamAZ and the subordinate position of Tatars compared with Russians as unjust and unfair. In its founding program, it articulated several solutions to rectify the injustice. First, because most of the managing directors at KamAZ were ethnic Russians who had come from outside Tatarstan to work in the factory, the group stated that other major enterprises in the republic should not be allowed to hire non-Tatar directors from beyond the republic's borders. It also argued that new jobs at local enterprises should be given only to ethnic Tatars from outside Tatarstan who were migrating to live in the republic (the so-called Tatar diaspora). Beyond the factory in the city at large, TOTs supported ethnic privileges for Tatars through the creation of special zones where Tatar-owned businesses would be established and employ only ethnic Tatars. The group also called for the creation of Tatar-only work brigades in factories. Finally, TOTs' founding document stated that all people holding leading positions in the republic, including enterprise directors, deputies to local soviets, and government workers, should learn the Tatar language.[33]

---

30. Interview with Rashid Zakirov, public relations specialist, KamAZ and former TOTs member, Naberezhnye Chelny, May 19, 1997.

31. Iskhakovna interview, May 20, 1997.

32. Interview with Rashid Kamarovi Khafizov, Naberezhnye Chelny, May 17, 1997.

33. TOTs also called for renaming streets in Tatar, something that ultimately occurred in many cities in the republic. See "Primary Goals of National Reform in Naberezhnye Chelny" *Azatlyk* 5 (1990) cited in Gorenburg, *Minority Ethnic Mobilization,* 2003, 91.

Even after the campaign for nationalist separatism ended and TOTs had lost the popular support it enjoyed in the early 1990s, the group continued to address its appeals to workers at KamAZ to try to turn them against the Russian factory management. For example, it held a demonstration in 1996 where it tried to convince workers that according to the Russian government's rules concerning the privatization of large enterprises they should own 51 percent of the shares of Kamaz but were being cheated by Tatarstan's government, which actually owned the factory. They also claimed that KamAZ had funding available but was reneging on its agreement to build new housing, pools, and cultural centers and to provide social services. This anti-KamAZ demonstration had an ethnic element, according to the nationalists, because of the factory's "special situation in which the management is Russian and the assembly-line workers are Tatar."[34]

Popular Support for Nationalism

The Tatar Public Center established political cells at KamAZ early on in an effort to garner worker support. Instead of conducting its demonstrations in the Tatar language only, it was careful to use both Russian and Tatar. Azatlyk also organized cells at factories.[35] However, in 1991, TOTs, along with other political organizations, was expelled from KamAZ when Boris Yeltsin passed a decree banning the Communist Party and all political organizations from the workplace.[36] Some nationalist leaders maintained that if TOTs had been allowed to continue to operate, the group would have been even more influential than it was.[37] Nonetheless, by the time TOTs was ejected from KamAZ, it had won support among a significant segment of workers at the factory.[38] A September 1991 survey conducted by the KamAZ Center for Sociological Research indicates that 33.2 percent of workers supported TOTs, while another survey conducted a year and half later showed 44.6 percent of workers backing the group. Observing the group's growing authority with workers during the period between the two surveys—which overlapped with the critical period in republican politics—a KamAZ report noted that 55 percent of Tatars "support one or another idea and

---

34. Field notes, January 1997; interview with Damir Iskhakov, Kazan, January 1997.

35. Amadishin interview, May 24, 1997.

36. Political organizations were expelled according to Order N-347, *O vyvedenie organizatsii i struktur politicheskikh partii i massovykh dvizhenie iz A. O. Kamaza.* [On the removal of organizations, political parties and mass movements from KamAZ] Kulakova interview, May 27, 1997.

37. Iskhakovna interview, May 20, 1997.

38. In comparison with Kazan, a significantly larger portion of Chelny's population was of working age or younger: 92 percent compared with Kazan's 79.7 percent. Data from Goskomstat.

initiative of TOTs"[39] and that TOTs significantly influenced worker support of republican sovereignty.[40]

The survey of Tatars in Naberezhnye Chelny conducted by Gibadullin in 1991 and 1992 found many "TOTs-ovites" in the city: 57 percent of Tatar workers supported the group, while 49 percent of specialists (*spetsialisty*) and white-collar workers (*sluzhashii*) did.[41] A higher percentage of respondents (72 percent) supported the goal of republican sovereignty. Of this category, 61 percent understood sovereignty to mean independent statehood, and 12 percent understood it to mean a certain degree of administrative territorial independence.[42]

Finally, popular support for nationalism is shown by the results of the 1992 Referendum on Tatarstan State Sovereignty. First, the KamAZ survey conducted right before the referendum found that 83.3 percent of Tatars would vote for sovereignty.[43] Next, although voting results of KamAZ employees do not exist, the results from the city in general show that 61 percent of city residents voted in favor of sovereignty. By comparison, in Kazan, 47 percent of the city's population voted for it.[44]

Popular Perceptions of Ethnic Economic Inequality

KamAZ reports and survey research conducted by local scholars indicate that workers at KamAZ were concerned with professional mobility. As Yagfar Garipov noted in a study of KamAZ employees, "As a rule, people are very attentive to, and sensitive about the question of professional advancement."[45] This does not mean that they viewed it as an ethnic issue. Tatars and Russians worked together in each tier of the workforce (except upper management) and therefore interacted on a daily basis. In fact, it was explicit KamAZ policy for work collectives to be composed of members of different ethnic groups.[46]

---

39. Platonov and Kulakova, *Otchet po resul'tatam oprosa*, KamAZ Center for Sociological Research, 1992.

40. Taslima Islamshina and Guzel Khamzina, "V molodykh gorodakh sklonny k radikalizmu" [In Young Cities Prone to Radicalism] *Tatarstan*, no. 9 (1993): 22–23.

41. Note that Gibadullin's survey was conducted independently of KamAZ. Gibadullin, *Tatarskoe naselenie*, 88.

42. Ibid., 60.

43. *Otchet po resul'tatam*, 1992.

44. *Dokumenty (protokoly, informatsiia, itogovye rezul'taty)*.

45. Garipov, "Sotsial'no-etnicheskaia struktura," 67.

46. The factory had previously organized monoethnic collectives but had decided to do away with them. Kulakova interview, May 27, 1997.

Did framing of issues of ethnic economic inequality by nationalist leaders convince people that Tatars faced less mobility than Russians or discrimination in general? Although surveys were not conducted before the period of national revival, there is evidence from the early 1990s that people were developing an awareness of imbalanced representation at KamAZ. For example, the assistant director of the KamAZ Center for Sociological Research stated that the managers often complained to her that there were fewer Tatar than Russian specialists, a charge that prompted her to organize a survey at KamAZ.[47] The survey found that more than half of Tatar managers thought that there were insufficient numbers of Tatar managers in the city.[48] Gibadullin's 1991 survey of Tatars in Naberezhnye Chelny found that a majority (56 percent) thought that there were insufficient numbers of Tatar managers and bosses (*rukovodiashchie kadry*) in the city. Only 10 percent of Tatars reported that they viewed representation of Tatars among leadership cadres in a positive light.[49] These two studies, both conducted around the time when support for the nationalist movement was peaking, indicate that a significant, though not overwhelming, percentage of ethnic Tatars believed members of their group were underrepresented in high-status professions.

Could Tatars' perception of blocked Tatar mobility have been caused by the interethnic tension they experienced personally? Although this is possible, evidence from a 1990 survey at KamAZ conducted by the KamAZ Center for Sociological Research suggests it is unlikely. When KamAZ employees were asked to rate interethnic relations within their work collective, a clear majority of both Russians (84 percent) and Tatars (86 percent) described those relations as "completely normal." Interestingly, when respondents were asked to rate interethnic relations at KamAZ in general, significantly fewer respondents—43 percent of Russians and 54 percent of Tatars—considered them normal. This fact suggests that workers' perceptions of interethnic tension may have been related to the general political situation during national revival rather than to personal experiences with members of the other nationality.[50]

Results from the same survey also suggest that considerable percentages of Tatars were concerned with equalization of opportunity. The survey asked respondents to rank a series of factors that they thought would improve interethnic

---

47. Ibid.
48. Platonov and Kulakova, *Otchet po resul'tatam oprosa,* 7.
49. Gibadullin, *Tatarskoe naselenie,* 38.
50. This 1990 study surveyed 1,538 KamAZ employees; 45 percent were Russian and 42.3 percent were Tatar. Two-thirds were blue-collar workers and one-third were white-collar workers. This was the first survey conducted by KamAZ's Center for Sociological Research that asked respondents explicitly about ethnicity. Earlier studies had asked only about plan fulfillment and workers' issues. Garipov, "Sotsial'no-etnicheskaia struktura," 65.

relations at KamAZ. Forty-six percent of Tatars believed that relations would be improved by "raising the skills and educational level of Tatar cadres" (compared with only 19 percent of Russians), and 29 percent of Tatars reported that relations would be improved if the nationality of individual supervisors were taken into account when individuals were being hired or promoted. Only 11 percent of Russians held this view. Finally, slightly more Tatars than Russians (35 percent vs. 30 percent) believed that another way to improve interethnic relations would be to ensure that members of all nationalities were appointed to leadership positions in public organizations (*obshchestvennye organizatsii*).[51] The data indicate that more Tatars than Russians linked education and training for Tatars, as well as Tatar professional representation and mobility, to the amelioration of relations between Tatars and Russians.

Finally, almost no KamAZ employees reported experiencing discrimination on the basis of their ethnic identity, a fact suggesting that the nationalist claim of blocked labor mobility and limited opportunity was more rhetoric than fact. In response to a question about whether they had encountered discrimination while finding a job, rising through the professional ranks at work, or petitioning the government bureaucracy over a personal matter, more Tatars (5–7 percent) than Russians (2.5–3 percent) answered affirmatively. For these respondents, the KamAZ workplace was not the most common site of ethnic discrimination; they were three to four times more likely to have experienced discrimination outside the factory walls, in everyday social situations such as on buses, in stores, waiting in line, or on the street.[52] However, Tatar respondents in Gibadullin's survey reported experiencing more moderate forms of negative behavior by non-Tatars in the city at large. In response to the question "How often do you encounter cases of 'disrespectful' [*neuvazhitel'nii*] or 'scornful' [*prenebrezhitel'nii*] reactions to your nationality?" 40 percent of Tatars answered "rather often," and 43 percent answered "it occurs, but rarely."[53]

Interethnic tension was perceived by city residents to be higher in Naberezhnye Chelny than in Kazan (table 5.2). A 1990 survey found that twice as many respondents in Chelny as in Kazan reported that interethnic tension in their city

---

51. Interestingly, many Tatars (61 percent) answered that achieving state sovereignty would improve interethnic relations. Also, many Tatars (58 percent) and Russians (66 percent) answered that "improving living conditions and raising the welfare [*blagosostoianie*] of the population" would improve relations. Garipov, "Sotsial'no-etnicheskaia struktura," 75–76. *Obshchestvennye organizatsii* here means trade unions, sports groups, women's organizations, hunting organizations, etc.

52. Garipov explains this discrimination as caused by stress over lack of goods and by "the absence of basic courtesy" rather than as an expression of nationalism. "Sotsial'no-etnicheskaia struktura," 78.

53. Gibadullin, *Tatarskoe naselenie*, 54.

was on the rise.[54] Gibadullin also found that the majority of Tatars believed that inter-ethnic relations had worsened since Tatarstan's declaration of sovereignty in 1990.[55] Anecdotal evidence reinforces the statistical evidence. A journalist described instances of interethnic tension on public transportation and between Tatar sales clerks and Russian customers,[56] and a young Kodak store clerk reported that such tension on the street, on public transportation, and in interethnic marriages had become worse during the late 1980s.[57] Another nationalist reminisced, "Although it didn't really exist during the Soviet era...there was a strong anti-Russian sentiment among Tatars in Naberezhnye Chelny. It was on the rise and then it dropped off."[58]

These results suggest that although large numbers of Tatars reported that they did not directly experience discrimination at KamAZ or in terethnic problems in their own work collectives, they did perceive an increase in interethnic tension both at KamAZ and in the city at large. Moreover, the perception of this tension among Tatars was correlated with support for the nationalists. According to Gibadullin's survey, more Tatar supporters of TOTs than either Tatar supporters of the Democratic Party of Russia or Tatar opponents of TOTs believed that instances of "disrespect" toward the Tatar nationality occurred frequently.[59]

Popular perceptions of Tatar underrepresentation and discrimination played an important role in generating support for the nationalist movement in Naberezhnye Chelny. Tatars there felt more disrespected than in other parts of Tatarstan.[60] Although it is difficult to know the precise degree of concern with these issues among Tatars, some observers have claimed that highly educated, white-collar workers appeared more concerned with ethnic representation and discrimination than did blue-collar workers. The leader of Azatlyk, for example, stated that KamAZ workers joined his organization because of their experience of discrimination but also that intellectuals at KamAZ thought about ethnic representation more than workers did.[61] The comments of Farida

---

54. Roza Musina, "Etnokulturnye orientatsii i mezhnatsional'nye otnosheniia," 54.

55. Thirty-five percent of Tatars reported that interethnic relations had worsened; 29 percent thought they hadn't changed and 17 percent thought they had improved. Ibid., 57.

56. Interview with Akhtiam Sabitov, journalist, Naberezhnye Chelny, May 30, 1997. Respondent's name has been changed.

57. Interview with Kodak store clerk, Naberezhnye Chelny, May 26, 1997.

58. Amadishin interview, May 24, 1997.

59. Fifty-five percent of TOTs supporters believed disrespect toward Tatars occurred frequently, compared with 38 percent of DPR supporters and 24 percent of TOTs opponents. Gibadullin, "Tatarskoe naselenie," 87.

60. Zakirov interview, May 19, 1997.

61. Amadishin interview, May 24, 1997.

Table 5.2 Perceptions of change in interethnic relations in Tatarstan, 1990 (%)

	KAZAN		NABEREZHNYE CHELNY	
	TATARS	RUSSIANS	TATARS	RUSSIANS
Worsened	21	22	42	49
Stayed the same	56	55	28	28
Improved	6	3	6	3
Difficult to say	18	20	25	20

Source: Roza Musina, "Etnokul'turnye orientatsii i mezhnatsional'nye otnosheniia," in *Sovremennye natsional'nye protsessy v Respublike Tatarstan*, Vol. II (Kazan: Tatarstan Academy of Sciences, 1994), 54.

Orlova, a high-level manager at KamAZ, suggest the way in which some Tatars understood the connection between their ethnicity and professional mobility:

> During the USSR, one was ashamed to be a Tatar, one was ashamed to be a Jew, one was ashamed to be anything but a Russian. To get a good job, you had to be a party member, and you had to be a Russian. People often tried to change their nationality. For example, I'm a Tatar but I married a Russian man and I took his last name. I was only able to achieve my high position [at KamAZ] because I had a Russian surname. This all began to change when democracy appeared.[62]

Orlova expressed the belief that Tatars were blocked professionally because of their ethnic identity and that she had obtained a good position only by "passing" as a Russian. Yet this is the same informant who, in her role as a specialist in the personnel department at KamAZ, carefully explained to me the policies the factory had set up to provide assistance and advantages to ethnic Tatars. Thus, like other Tatars, Farida discounted the fact that preference policies instituted by the Soviet state had contributed to professional advancement of Tatars at the factory. Instead, she perceived preferences for Russians and discrimination against Tatars and linked these phenomena to the Soviet system. However, she believed that this inequity and unfairness had ended with the dissolution of the Soviet Union and the introduction of democracy.

The case of Naberezhnye Chelny demonstrates that people dependent on the state for their livelihoods, residence, and services may nevertheless mobilize against that state to establish a new national order. Popular support for nationalist renewal developed when group grievances emerged from the interaction of macroeconomic conditions and issue framings by nationalist leaders. When

---

62. Orlova interview, May 23, 1997.

the Soviet Union's economic crisis during perestroika caused decreased production of cars and trucks at KamAZ, people experienced a tightening of economic
opportunity and fear of unemployment. Nationalist entrepreneurs emerged to
convey to people with Tatar identities that their coethnics were underrepresented
in white-collar jobs at the factory by comparison with Russians and were unfairly
victimized by current societal conditions. This contributed to a climate in which
nationalist discourse about ethnic economic inequality convinced people to
understand their personal professional trajectories as tied to others who shared
their ethnic identity. The best way for people to improve their own position and
the position of others who were part of the Tatar nation, the nationalists argued,
would be to support a new national order. The first step toward that order was
achieving republican sovereignty. Thus the particular issue framings by Tatar
nationalists—which focused on rectifying ethnic underrepresentation by achieving state sovereignty—translated into considerable mass support for opposition
nationalist organizations in Naberezhnye Chelny.

6

ETHNIC ENTREPRENEURS AND THE CONSTRUCTION OF GROUP GRIEVANCE

Tuva, Mari El, and Komi Compared

It is generally thought that people support programs of nationalist renewal as a result of long-standing cultural, political, or economic grievances. If people maintain a grievance—a feeling of having been wronged—over the course of many years, that grievance, it is assumed, will be deeply felt and therefore likely to shape political attitudes and motivate political action. Though people may have grievances that persist over time, grievances may also develop rapidly, as a result of the actions and discourse of political entrepreneurs. Nationalist entrepreneurs in particular play a key role in constructing grievances swiftly as part of a contingent process of political mobilization. Nationalist leaders are interested in establishing a nation-state; thus they try to convince ordinary people that they should challenge the existing order. In order for people to act against the status quo, they must have a strong sense that some aspect of current conditions causes them injury. Nationalist leaders try to create that sense by convincing ordinary people that they form a group or a nation and that their nation has been deeply wronged. Nationalists therefore describe social conditions as unjustly subjugating people with a particular ethnic identity. In other words, they try to convince people that they have a grievance (or grievances) that can be resolved only through the establishment of a nation-state. This means that in nationalist politics, the longevity of a grievance among a population, often seen as an indication of intensity, is immaterial. What matters is how political entrepreneurs infuse ethnonational meaning into people's experience of current conditions and connect that meaning to the need to overturn existing political authority.

Thus it is not the mere presence of structural inequalities among people that produces popular support for nationalism. Economic and political inequalities are ubiquitous in political systems around the world. Hierarchy among collectivities is commonplace. The critical question is, do people living in those societies perceive conditions in their societies as unequal? The presence of structural inequalities alone does not mean that aggrieved groups exist. In Russia's republics various kinds of inequalities were present between different collectivities. Rural versus urban populations, educated versus uneducated people, Communist Party members versus non-party members, and titular nationalities versus nontitular nationalities all faced some kind of inequality. Yet people's experiences were not determined solely by their membership in one of these collectivities. As I demonstrate in chapter 3, structural conditions in republican labor markets alone—whether titulars lagged behind or were equivalent to Russians socioeconomically—cannot explain why ethnic populations in certain republics supported opposition nationalist movements while those in other republics did not.

Ordinary people in a given society do not necessarily have an automatic, unmediated understanding of economic conditions in that society; there are multiple ways in which they can understand those conditions. Nationalist leaders put forward one interpretation—a narrative of ethnic economic inequality—in order to construct a grievance about ethnic discrimination in local labor markets. Thus the way in which nationalist leaders framed issues was a critical variable in creating ethnic grievances in the Russian republics where mass nationalist mobilization developed.

The fact that nationalist leaders articulate a particular framing of an issue, however, does not mean that people mechanically accept it. The way in which issues are framed must be commensurate with experiences that are central to their lives. In Russia's republics in the late Soviet period, people were primarily concerned with finding and keeping jobs in the midst of rapid economic contraction and achieving mobility and social status. When ethnic entrepreneurs framed issues of ethnic discrimination in ways that addressed these concerns, people responded by supporting nationalism.

Ethnic grievances in Russia's republics developed as part of a contingent political process. Grievances were not long-standing beliefs that some ethnic groups had and others did not. Rather, ethnic grievances formed out of an interaction between existing social, political, economic, and cultural conditions and the meaning imparted to those conditions by nationalist entrepreneurs through a process of issue framing. According to the social movements literature, issue frames must speak in an empirically credible way to people's existing values, cultural narratives, and beliefs. Social movement theorists identify three dimensions of issue framing. First, political entrepreneurs define the meaning of an event or a social condition as "unjust, intolerable and deserving of corrective action"; second, they attribute blame for that unjust situation to someone or to a set of social processes; and finally, they suggest a solution to the problem and assign responsibility to someone or something for executing that solution.[1]

In Russia's republics in which mass nationalism developed, ethnic entrepreneurs articulated issues about unequal access to resources such as higher education and desirable jobs.[2] They claimed, for example, that Russians dominated management positions at top enterprises while titulars worked in blue-collar jobs at those enterprises. They argued that titular ethnic groups worked in agrarian jobs in the countryside, while Russians occupied prestigious positions in the city. The best jobs requiring the best educations were given to Russians, and titulars were condemned to a subordinate social status. According to the nationalists, the fact of titulars' blocked access to the republic's modern economy hampered the general development of the nation.

The issue frame of ethnic economic inequality resonated because it plausibly described conditions in local labor markets and addressed people's fears and frustration amid rising job insecurity in the Soviet Union's state-controlled economy. As discussed in chapter 3, the years of transition from Soviet rule were marked by a macrolevel crisis in economic production that brought about shortages and the beginnings of unemployment. Soviet citizens, however, continued to expect that the state would provide them with educations, jobs, and occupational security. Instead of identifying rising demand in a shrinking economy as the source of the problem, nationalists decried the putative fact that titular populations had limited access to resources and jobs within the region that they considered their homeland. They alleged that titulars' socioeconomic subordination vis-à-vis Russians kept them from full participation in the republic's modern, industrialized economy—a serious injustice and one they blamed on Soviet authorities in Moscow, the republic, or both.

As we have seen, the nationalists' issue frame of ethnic economic inequality contradicted the fact that titulars had been making significant educational and professional gains. However, the nationalists could not delegitimize Soviet rule by expressing gratitude toward the Soviet state for sponsoring titular mobility. Instead, they painted titulars as victims of the Soviet—and ethnically Russian—state. By claiming victim status and blaming the current state, they could make

---

1. Snow and Benford, "Master Frames," and "Framing Processes and Social Movements: An Overview and Assessment," *Annual Review of Sociology* 26 (2000): 611–39.

2. In some cases, such as Tuva, nationalists also emphasized unequal access to apartments and slots in nursery schools. I describe this later in the chapter.

a persuasive case that titulars were subjects of Russians within their own home-lands, a situation violating the basic nationalist principle that "the political and national unit be congruent."[3] To rectify this injustice, the nationalists called for republican sovereignty and the establishment of a nation-state controlled by members of the titular nationality, in particular, the leaders of the nationalist movement.

Moreover, the nationalists' message underscored Soviet values about what it meant to be a successful person: obtaining an education and a good job and, ironically for a communist workers' state, achieving a respectable social status. The nationalists invoked a norm of proportionality commonly asserted by Soviet authorities: that subcommunities of the Soviet population—whether women, workers, or ethnic minorities—should enjoy proportional representation in various institutions. Nationalists argued not only that ethnic proportional repre-sentation was necessary in political institutions (something that already existed in the republics since titulars held top leadership posts) but that titulars should enjoy special rights and access to desirable resources and opportunities within their own republics. Such special rights were justified, according to the national-ists, because the republic was the group's homeland and because previous in-justices demanded rectification. Thus, both the norms of ethnic proportional representation invoked by nationalists and the commensurability of the logic of ethnic inequality with people's lived experiences in late Soviet-era labor markets, increased the likelihood that ordinary people, who had not previously perceived that ethnic boundaries between themselves and other citizens mattered politi-cally—would become convinced by the nationalists' message.

Ordinary people began to understand their experiences and fears concerning job insecurity as an issue of ethnic injustice. They started to perceive limits to their opportunities and life chances because of their non-Russian ethnicity. As the nationalists repeated how unfair this situation was inside their own republic, people for whom ethnicity was one of several identities, began to connect their personal material interests to the fate of their ethnic community. Nationalist leaders, then, attracted popular support not simply by picking up on preexisting attitudes among aggrieved ethnic populations but by actively creating grievances that interpreted economic information in ethnic terms.

Why did nationalist leaders choose to frame issues in this way? The nation-alists' attention to issues of equality of representation in the economy and in political leadership reveals just how much they were products of the Soviet state whose authority they were trying to undermine. Their focus on pragmatic issues

---

3. Gellner, *Nations and Nationalism,* 1.

of professional mobility, equal ethnic group representation, and individual advancement reproduced typical late Soviet-era ideals, which shows that nationalists had bought into the Soviet value system that viewed modernization as an absolute good. Urbanization, higher education, prestigious employment—in short, marks of high social status in late Soviet society—were the standards by which nationalists in the republics measured their group's value and success. They saw no contradiction in asserting the right to a nation-state in order to realize the goods of modernity as defined by the Soviet state. Like all nationalists, they drew on a range of extant beliefs and practices to construct an idea of national community deserving control of the state.

Most nationalist leaders were not strategic actors, in the manner of the many communist nomenklatura leaders who reinvented themselves as nationalists to retain power. They did not consciously choose the frame of economic inequality after evaluating the costs and benefits of various alternative issue framings. The nationalists acted more sincerely than strategically, though naturally their expectations about their leading roles in a future national state played an important part in shaping their interests. But the particular issues nationalist opposition leaders chose to focus on involved a good deal of contingency. As highly educated members of the titular intelligentsia, they perceived economic information as indicating the presence of interethnic inequalities. Their identities and personal experiences (or those of their parents or grandparents) during the decades of Soviet rule shaped the way in which they perceived economic conditions in the late 1980s.

This chapter presents a comparative analysis of nationalist politics in Russia's republics. I show that in the highly nationalist republics, nationalist leaders framed issues concerning ethnic economic inequality. Conversely, in republics with low levels of mass support for nationalism, leaders failed to articulate these issues and focused instead on other issues like the revival of culture and language and republican economic sovereignty vis-à-vis Moscow. Evidence for this argument is based on (1) a systematic comparison of case studies I compiled of nationalist politics in all of Russia's republics, including a comparison of the founding charters and official resolutions of nationalist organizations[4] and (2) a cross-case comparative analysis of nationalist discourse found in local newspaper articles. The discourse analysis is based on an original data set of newspaper articles published in Russia's republics during 1989–94.

---

4. I compiled the case studies using documents published by nationalist organizations in each republic, a combination of monographs and articles published by Russian and Western scholars, and a systematic reading of news reports from *Radio Free Europe/Radio Liberty Research Reports* and *Current Digest of the Soviet Press* during 1988–93.

The first section of the chapter presents a comparison of all the issues in the founding documents of nationalist movements in all the high-mobilization republics: Tatarstan, Tuva, Chechnya, Yakutia, and Bashkortostan, as well as in the two lowest-mobilization republics: Mordovia and Mari El. I then provide a more in-depth discussion of the issues involved in the founding of the Chechen nationalist movement in Chechnya—one of Russia's most nationalist republics. After that I present a cross-case comparative analysis of nationalist politics and of the discourse nationalists employed in three republics: Tuva, Mari El, and Komi. I find that leaders of the nationalist movement in Tuva, as in Tatarstan, framed issues of ethnic economic inequality so as to ethnify economic issues and create a grievance among people with Tuvan identities. Conversely, leaders in Mari El and Komi rarely mentioned the issue of socioeconomic inequality between titulars and Russians.

I selected these cases for several reasons. First, they maximize variation on the dependent variable of mass support for nationalism: Tuva and Tatarstan (the latter discussed in chapters 4 and 5) had high mass support for nationalism, while Mari El and Komi had low mass nationalist support. These four republics provide a set of cases typical of the variation in mass nationalism across Russia's republics.[5] Second, this case selection also permits a test of two other variables of theoretical interest throughout this book: republican wealth and an ethnic division of labor within republican labor markets. I use the diverse-case method to control first for the variable of republican wealth by selecting cases of high mass nationalism that vary on this dimension. Thus I compare Tuva, a relatively poor republic, with Tatarstan, a relatively wealthy one. Among the nonnationalist republics, I compare the relatively wealthy republic of Komi with the relatively poor republic of Mari El (table 6.1). Next I control for the variable of an ethnic division of labor by comparing republics that vary on this dimension. Because, as discussed in chapter 3, it is not possible to identify whether an EDL was present or absent in the republics, I use one indicator of an EDL: the ratio of titular to Russian representation in the white-collar workforce.[6] The two nationalist republics of Tatarstan and Tuva differ on this dimension—Tatarstan had relatively high levels of titular versus Russian representation in the white-collar workforce, whereas Tuva had relatively low levels. The two nonnationalist republics of Mari

---

5. Thus I use the typical-case method to select these cases, according to John Gerring's typology. Note that although the cases of Tatarstan and Tuva on the one hand and Mari El on the other may lie at the extreme ends of the high-low range of nationalist mobilization in Russia's republics, these cases typify the causal relationship between elite issue framing and nationalist mobilization. See Gerring, *Case Study Research: Principles and Practices* (New York: Cambridge University Press, 2007), 93.

6. See figure 3.1.

Table 6.1 Case selection for discourse analysis

		NATIONALIST REPUBLIC	NONNATIONALIST REPUBLIC
Wealthy	High titular/Russian representation in white-collar workforce	Tatarstan	Komi
Poor	Low titular/Russian representation in white-collar workforce	Tuva	Mari El

El and Komi also differ: Mari in Mari El were underrepresented by comparison with Russians, whereas Komi and Russians were nearly equally represented in white-collar jobs in Komi.[7]

Nationalist Discourse in Founding Documents

When nationalist organizations formed in Russia's republics, they publicized statements concerning their purpose and goals. At founding congresses (*s"ezdi*) they adopted charters encapsulating their programs. Although the programs of the nationalist organizations evolved over time, it is useful to compare them to observe the kinds of issues that the organizations articulated when they first formed and during the critical first several years in which they sought popular support. Therefore, I collected the founding charters of nationalist organizations in each republic and recorded the issues described in the documents. Because some of the charters focused primarily on financial and organizational questions, I also examined the resolutions each organization adopted at its founding congress. Together these documents provide evidence of the official positions of all the organizations when they first formed during a period that ranged from 1989 to 1991. The issues are reported in table 6.2.

It was in the republics with the highest level of nationalist mobilization in Russia—Tuva, Tatarstan, Chechnya, Bashkortostan, and Yakutia—that nationalist organizations articulated issues concerning titular representation in republican economies, as the first line of table 6.2 indicates. Nationalists in the low-mobilization republics of Mari El and Mordovia, by contrast, did not articulate this kind of issue. Nationalist leaders in the five nationalist republics declared, at the moment of their founding, that their goal was attaining political sovereignty—a goal that went unmentioned in the low-mobilization republics.

---

7. Because the titular-to-Russian ratio is a continuous variable (see figure 3.1 in chapter 3), the selection of diverse cases is somewhat more difficult than if it were a categorical variable. I selected two cases with ratio values on the relatively low end of the scale (Mari El and Tuva) and two cases on the relatively higher end of the scale (Komi and Tatarstan). See Gerring, *Case Study Research*, 98.

Table 6.2   Issues in the founding charters of nationalist organizations

	TUVA[a]	TATARSTAN[b]	CHECHNYA[c]	BASHKORTOSTAN[d]	YAKUTIA[e]	MARI EL[f]	MORDOVIA[g]
Titular representation in economy	X	X	X	X	X		
Political sovereignty	X	X	X	X	X	X	
Quotas for titulars in higher education			X	X			
Titular representation in government		X	X	X	X		
Economic sovereignty	X	X		X	X		
Demographic revival		X		X	X	X	X
Language and cultural revival	X	X	X	X		X	X
Assisting ethnic diaspora		X		X			X
Religious/spiritual revival	X	X			X		X
Environmental degradation	X			X	X		
Rewriting official history of the nation			X				
Fighting drugs, alcohol, prostitution	X			X	X		
Anti-ethnic out-migration				X			X
Replacing individual administrators	X	X	X	X			

a. Z. V. Anaibin, M N. Guboglo, and M. S. Kozlov, *Formirovanie etnopoliticheskoi situatsii: Ocherki po istorii postsovetskoi Tuvy* [Formation of the Ethnopolitical Situation: An Essay on the History of Post-Soviet Tuva] (Moscow: RAN 1999).

b. Iskhakov, Damir. "Neformal'nye ob"edineniia," in *Sovremennye natsional'nye protsessy v respublike Tatarstan* [Current Ethnic Processes in the Republic of Tatarstan] (Kazan: Russian Academy of Sciences, Kazan Scientific Center, 1992), 14; and "Programma Naberezhno-Chelninskogo otdeleniia Tatarskogo obshchestvennogo tsentra" [Program of the Naberezhnye Chelny Branch of the Tatar Public Center], 4; "Rezoliutsiia mitinga TOTs" [Resolution of TOTs Demonstration], *Vecherniaia Kazan,* March 19, 1991, 1, and "Programma (platforma) Vsesoyuznogo Tatarskogo obshchestvennogo tsentra—Proekt" [Program (platform) of the Tatar Public Center—Legislation], in *Suverennyi Tatarstan* [Sovereign Tatarstan], Vol. 2., ed. D. M. Iskhakov and M. N. Guboglo (Moscow: Russian Academy of Sciences, 1998).

c. "Resolution of the National Congress of the Chechen People," November 25, 1990, cited in Tishkov, *Ethnicity, Nationalism and Conflict,* 199; Muzaev, *Chechenskaia respublika,* 157; Muzaev, *Etnicheskii separatizm,* 34.

d. Ustav Bashkirskogo narodnogo tsentra (BNTs) "Ural" [Charter of the Bashkir National Center 'Ural'], 1989; "Rezoliutsii s"ezda Bashkirskogo narodnogo tsentra 'Ural.'" [Resolutions of the Congress of the Bashkir National Center "Ural"] in M. N. Guboglo, *Etnopoliticheskaia mozaika Bashkortostana Tom II* [Ethnopolitical Mosaic of Bashkortostan, Vol. 2] (Moscow: Russian Academy of Sciences, 1992), 93–105.

e. Ustav, Soyuz Yakutskikh obshchestvennykh ob"edinenii i grazhdan "Sakha omuk" [Charter of the Union of Yakut Social and Civic Associations 'Sakha omuk'], August 10, 1990; unpublished document personally provided by Marjorie Balzer. Drobizheva, *Natsional'noe Samosoznanie.*

f. S. M. Chervonnaia, M. N. Guboglo, Ustav demokraticheskogo obshchestvennogo ob'edineniia "Marii ushem" [Charter of the Democratic Public Association "Marii ushem"] in *Probuzhdenie Finno-ugorskogo Severa: Opyt Marii El,* Tom I [The Awakening of the Finno-Ugric North: The Experience of Mari El, Vol. I], (Moscow: IEA-RAN, 1996); Sharov, *Etnopoliticheskaia situatsiia v Respublike Marii El,* 5.

g. Ustav, Erziansko-mokshanskogo obshchestvennogo dvizheniia Mastorava, g. Saransk, [Charter of the Erzyan-Mokshan Popular Movement Mastorava], 1989.

The founding charters in Chechnya and Bashkortostan went so far as to advocate quotas for titulars in higher education. For example, at the first congress of the Bashkir nationalist organization Ural, one of the group's resolutions both defined the problem of Bashkir underrepresentation and offered a solution, stating, "The percentage of Bashkir cadres [employees] among top workers and highly qualified specialists in republican organs, city and district organizations, and local and central enterprises, is insignificant. Special measures must be adopted to correct this problem. It is necessary for party and Soviet organs in the republic to develop an entire system of educating Bashkir cadres."[8] In Yakutia, both the moderate nationalist group Sakha Omuk (the Sakha People) and the radical nationalist group Sakha Keskile (Sakha Perspective) mentioned the need to equalize Yakut representation in the republican economy. Sakha Omuk focused on the upper echelon of the economy, stating that Yakuts should have greater representation in enterprise management and greater representation in government. Sakha Keskile targeted a different audience by advocating a cadre policy (i.e., quotas) for Yakut youth in republican industry.[9]

In addition to the issue of ethnic economic inequality, the founding platforms of these nationalist organizations raised issues such as obtaining economic sovereignty, which meant greater control over local natural resources and enterprises situated on republican territory, as well as the right to collect and redistribute tax revenues locally; demographic revival, or stemming the demographic decline of the titular nationality; and language and cultural revival. Nationalists in almost all republics were very concerned about the declining use of titular language and in some republics advocated granting it official state status, increasing language education, and requiring republican political leaders to learn the national language. Related issues that might be categorized as cultural concerns include religious or spiritual revival and the need to rewrite and learn national histories. Nationalist movements in several republics also included planks vowing to assist the ethnic diaspora, fight environmental degradation, and halt the spread of drugs, alcohol, and prostitution.

A brief discussion of nationalist politics in Chechnya provides a more indepth look at how nationalists articulated issues of perceived inequity between

---

8. "Rezoliutsiia s"ezda Bashkirskogo narodnogo tsentra 'Ural,'" in M. N. Guboglo, *Bashkiriia i Tatarstan: Parallely etnopoliticheskogo razvitiia* [Bashkiria and Tatarstan: Parallels in Ethnopolitical Development] (Moscow: Russian Academy of Sciences, Institute of Ethnography and Anthropology, 1994), 105.

9. A. M. Ivanov, *Etnopoliticheskaia situatsiia v Respublike Sakha (Yakutia)* [Ethnopolitical Situation in the Republic of Sakha (Yakutia)] (Moscow: Institute of Ethnography and Anthropology, Russian Academy of Sciences, 1994); Drobizheva, "Natsional'noe samoznanie"; Muzaev, *Etnicheskii separatizm*, 206–10.

Chechens and Russians, placed blame for that inequity on Soviet leaders in both Moscow and the republic, and identified sovereignty and then full independence as the solution to problems facing the Chechen nation.

Nationalist Discourse in Chechnya

In Chechnya, opposition nationalist organizations were concerned from their inception with the status of Chechens in the republican economy and in government administration. According to Timur Muzaev, a specialist on Chechen politics, one of the three main concerns of the nationalist movement was to abolish discrimination against Chechens in appointments to leadership posts, especially in the republic's oil industry, as well as in the Communist Party and organs of state security and justice (i.e., the procurator, the internal police, or MVD, and the state security apparatus, or KGB).[10]

The nationalist group Unity (Bart) formed in 1989 and at first supported the republic's communist leaders, welcoming the appointment of Doku Zavgaev as first party secretary—the first ethnic Chechen ever appointed to that post. From the beginning, Bart advocated republican sovereignty. It spoke about raising the republic's status to that of a union republic within the USSR and renaming it the Vanaikh Republic, a term that refers to both the Chechen and Ingush people.[11] The following year, some of the more radical Bart members (including Zelimkhan Yandarbiev) founded the Vainakh Democratic Party (Vainakhskaia Demokraticheskaia Partiia, or VDP), which became the main organization in the nationalist movement. Initially the VDP maintained a moderate nationalist position supporting democratic reform, multiparty elections, and Zavgaev and the party leadership.

One of the key points in the platform of the VDP stated that the indigenous nations of the republic (Chechens and Ingush) should be given preferences in hiring, or *"prioritet predstavitelei korennoi natsii v rasstanovke kadrov."*[12] John

---

10. The other two main concerns were abolishing the official conceptions in the republic's history in which Checheno-Ingushetia was "voluntarily joined" to Russia and in which Chechen intellectuals were repressed because they were guilty of nationalism. The third main concern was expanding the spheres in which the Chechen language was spoken and taught in middle schools. Muzaev, *Etnicheskii separatizm,* 34.

11. Checheno-Ingushetia was a single republic until Ingushetia split off from it in 1992 after the USSR collapse. Timur Muzaev, *Chechenskaya respublika: Organy vlasti i politicheskie sily.* [The Chechen Republic: Organs of Power and Political Forces] (Moscow: Panorama, 1995), 34.

12. Literally translated as "priority in the job placement of cadres of representatives of the indigenous nation" in ibid., 159.

Dunlop describes this as "affirmative action for ethnic Chechens and Ingush."[13] The VDP started to speak out against the Party, advocated raising the republic's status to that of a UR, and started holding mass rallies in Grozny's central square. Early in the period of national revival, Ingush nationalists broke off from the VDP to form the Congress of the Ingush People.

The Chechen nationalist movement began to acquire momentum when, in summer 1990, the Dosh Society, which included leading members of the Chechen intelligentsia, together with the VDP, decided to organize the National Congress of the Chechen People (ChNS). The congress was carefully planned. District committees, staffed by members of the nationalist groups, composed lists of delegates according to the population size of districts throughout the republic. The one thousand delegates who ultimately attended the congress in November were fairly representative of society in general and included industrial and professional workers, kolkhoz farmers, intelligentsia, Muslim clergy, and *te'ip* (clan or tribal) elders, most of whom opposed the local ruling regime.[14] Yet the congress took place with the agreement of Zavgaev's administration. It was led by the moderate leaders Lechi Umkhaev, Yusip Soslambekov, and Zelimkhan Yanderbiev, with Djokar Dudaev invited as a guest speaker. The congress focused on the need for Chechnya to obtain republican sovereignty.[15] Resolutions adopted delineated a series of problems facing the Chechen people "which must be resolved to secure Chechnya's further development as a nation." Among these problems, a key issue concerned "the elimination of the Chechens' unequal position, 'discrimination against them even in their own country.'" Discrimination, according to the resolutions, was evident in the fact that "Chechen representation in the *organs of state power and administration of the economy* as well as in culture and public life did not correspond to their share in the population of the republic" (italics added). The congress closed with delegates adopting a declaration of state sovereignty.[16]

Soon after the congress concluded, the VDP and other nationalists began to sponsor mass demonstrations in Grozny. From December 1990 to February 1991, thousands of people participated in rallies and demonstrations organized by the nationalists. Activists at the demonstrations began to place blame for current problems on Zavgaev's administration, despite the fact that he was becoming responsive to the nationalist movement. Most important, nationalists at the

---

13. Dunlop, *Russia Confronts Chechnya*, 90.

14. A te'ip is a Chechen and Ingush social organization based on common descent and geographic location. Alexei Kudriavtsev, "Democratic Values and Political Reality in Chechnya, 1991–1999," in *Democracy and Pluralism in Muslim Eurasia,* edited by Yaacov Ro'i (New York: Frank Cass, 2004).

15. Muzaev, *Etnicheskii separatizm,* 35.

16. Resolution of the National Congress of the Chechen People, November 25, 1990, cited in Tishkov, *Ethnicity, Nationalism and Conflict,* 199.

demonstrations began to call for independence for Chechnya. Only later did the Chechen National Congress turn into a more radical organization when, after a power struggle, the moderate leaders on the executive committee were replaced with radical leaders from the VDP and other extremist nationalist groups, including Dudaev.[17] At its second session in early June 1991, activists at the congress described the Soviet Union as a colonial empire that had "robbed the Chechen nation of its religion, language, education, science, culture, national resources, ideology, mass media, leadership cadres, and right to freedom and life."[18]

As this brief discussion shows, Chechen nationalists raised issues of ethnic underrepresentation and discrimination and described these problems as affecting all people with ethnic Chechen identities. They claimed that these problems would inhibit the future development of the Chechen nation. The nationalists placed blame for the present state of affairs on the Soviet state and then later, as the movement became more radical, began to blame current Chechen leadership as well. Although the nationalists had at first identified republican sovereignty as a solution to the problems that constrained the Chechen nation, their goals later shifted from sovereignty to full independence. These issues, furthermore, were articulated very early in the evolution of the movement and inspired considerable mass support before Dudaev took power in the 1991 "coup"—an event that moved nationalist politics in Chechnya in a very different direction from that of Russia's other republics.

Nationalist Politics and Discourse Analysis in Tuva, Mari El, and Komi

The following section relies on various original sources, including newspaper articles, to demonstrate how nationalist entrepreneurs framed issues about economic inequity among titular populations during the period of national revival. Newspapers are a particularly appropriate source for investigating nationalist discourse because they were an influential source of information. The Soviet population—a "literate population of avid readers," in the words of Valery Tishkov[19]—read newspapers voraciously during glasnost, taking advantage of new opportunities to learn about formerly forbidden topics. In most republics new newspapers were founded, and existing mainstream newspapers replaced

17. Muzaev, *Etnicheskii separatizm*, 35.
18. Kudriavtsev, "Democratic Values," 362.
19. Tishkov, *Ethnicity, Nationalism, and Conflict*, 188.

editors conforming to the party line with those who welcomed the expression of alternative viewpoints.

My analysis is based primarily on an original set of newspaper articles I collected in Moscow, as well as on various studies by local and Moscow scholars. For the newspaper analysis, I selected two or three papers published in each of Russia's republics and skimmed through all available issues from the years 1989 to 1993 in order to identify all articles that mentioned any kind of ethnic issue. When possible, I chose to examine newspapers representing different viewpoints, including a democratically oriented paper and the paper that served as the official voice of the republican administration.[20] I collected 40–100 newspaper articles from each republic (and more than 200 in the case of Tuva); these included news reports, editorials, letters to the editor written by ordinary people, statements by administration officials, and statements by nationalist organizations and leaders. Because the nationalist movement in Tuva played a central role in Tuvan politics, there were many more articles published in newspapers there addressing ethnic issues than there were in Mari El and Komi. This fact, together with the sometimes spotty availability of republican newspapers in Moscow libraries, accounts for the lower number of articles I analyzed in Mari El and Komi.

Only a subset of the articles I collected from each republic, it should be noted, specifically contains information about nationalist movements. All together I analyzed over four hundred newspaper articles from newspapers published in Tatarstan, Tuva, Yakutia, Bashkortostan, Mordovia, Mari El, and Komi. However, I present here only the results of my analysis for the high-mobilization republic of Tuva and the low-mobilization republics of Komi and Mari El. I developed a standard coding form in order to record consistent summaries of each article and to analyze the three dimensions of issue framing identified as critical to mobilization in the social movements literature: (1) the definition of social conditions as unjust, (2) the attribution of blame, and (3) the identification of a solution to unjust social conditions.

I found that, as in Chechnya and Tatarstan, nationalists in the high-mobilization republic of Tuva articulated issues of ethnic economic inequality, specifically identifying Russians living there as more privileged than Tuvans. They blamed political authorities in both Tuva and Moscow for this situation. Tuvan nationalists also identified republican sovereignty as a solution to the problems facing

---

20. My choice of which republican newspapers to examine was highly constrained by the holdings of the Moscow libraries containing regional newspapers: the Russian State Historical Library (Istorichka) and Khimki. Furthermore, certain issues of a given newspaper were never deposited in Moscow libraries. (Regional newspapers from the period 1989–93 are not available online.) I therefore culled through as many issues from these years as were available.

Tuvans and steadily articulated demands for sovereignty. Conversely, in the low-mobilization republics of Mari El and Komi, these issues were largely absent. Nationalists there instead emphasized issues such as culture, language, and economic sovereignty vis-à-vis Moscow. As we have seen, socioeconomic inequality between Russians and titulars existed to some degree in all of Russia's republics since all had larger titular than Russian populations living in rural areas and working in low-status occupations. Thus the nationalists in all republics could have identified this issue as a serious one requiring rectification through republican sovereignty. We observe, however, that they did not. Objective economic conditions, though they informed nationalist discourse, did not determine in an unmediated way the specific issues nationalists chose to articulate or the specific manner in which they did so. Each of the three case studies describes the presence or absence of popular support for nationalist opposition movements in the republics and then discusses the discourse of nationalist elites.

The Republic of Tuva

Tuva, a tiny Siberian republic of only 309,000 people in 1989, was one of Russia's most nationalist republics. It was also one of the poorest republics in Russia with an economy based primarily on agriculture and livestock herding as well as on mining of small quantities of coal, asbestos, gold, cobalt, uranium, and rare metals. As with all of Russia's regions, Moscow appropriated most of the resources mined there but also developed the territory by establishing industry, infrastructure, and collective farms.[21] In fact, Tuva experienced a sharp rise in economic development during the 1960s after Moscow upgraded its status from autonomous oblast to autonomous republic.[22] Although ethnic Tuvans outnumbered Russians 65 percent to 32 percent, Russians had been living in Tuva since gold was discovered in the 1800s. Most of them, however, had moved to the republic after it joined the Soviet Union in 1944 in order to build roads, set up mining facilities, and construct schools.[23] However, despite Russian migration and some

---

21. The scholar Zoia Anaibin labeled the republic a "raw materials appendage of Moscow" in "Ethnic Relations in Tuva," in *Culture Incarnate*, ed. Marjorie Balzer (Armonk, N.Y.: M.E. Sharpe, 1995), 102–112. Also see Nelli Moskalenko, *Respublika Tyva [Tuva]—Spravochnik [The Republic of Tyva (Tuva): Reference Book]* (Moscow: Panorama, 1994).

22. Anaibin, *Respublika Tuva.*

23. Tuva is one of the few Russian republics with experience of independent statehood, albeit a brief and highly constrained one. The independent republic of Tannu-Tuva was established in 1921 and lasted until 1944. Prior to 1921, the region was a Russian protectorate. See Marjorie Mandelstam Balzer, "From Ethnicity to Nationalism: Turmoil in the Russian Mini-Empire," in *The Social Legacy of Communism*, ed. James R. Millar and Sharon L. Wolchik (Cambridge: Cambridge University Press,

economic progress, Tuva's economy remained severely underdeveloped at the end of the Soviet era.

Tuva exhibited an ethnic division of labor to a greater extent than most other Russian republics. Tuvans had been nomadic herders of sheep, cattle, camels, and horses who settled into pastoral herding by 1950. Therefore, as of the 1980s, a majority of them still lived in the countryside. Russians, on the other hand, dominated most of the cities, including the capital of Kyzyl, though some also lived in rural areas and worked in agriculture. Tuvans generally lagged behind Russians in educational and occupational achievement. The ratio of Tuvan to Russian representation in the white-collar workforce was 0.64, higher than in Chechnya and Mari El but still the third-lowest among Russia's republics.[24] More Russians than Tuvans worked in industry, whereas Tuvans outnumbered Russians in unskilled labor and agriculture.[25]

The nationalists in Tuva seized on these facts and made the issue of socioeconomic inequality between Tuvans and Russians a central part of their discourse. Perhaps more than in any other republic, the subject received widespread attention. Tuvan nationalists described specific industrial enterprises and state farms where all the directors were ethnic Russians but none were Tuvan. The nationalists also emphasized the backwardness of Tuvans in rural areas, especially among youth, who formed a very large percentage of the republic's population. They claimed that procedures for entering the CPSU favored Russians over Tuvans, and thus, as everyone recognized, the professional advancement of Tuvans was limited. In addition, Tuvan nationalists articulated the related claim that the state distributed key public goods—apartments and spots in nursery schools—to Russians more often than to Tuvans. All of this indicated, they argued, that Tuvans suffered from social inequality.[26] Zoia Anaibin, a local scholar in Tuva, reported that political candidates called attention to these issues in order to win popular support from 1989 to 1992 and especially during the first semifree elections to the Tuvan and federal Supreme Soviet in 1990. They claimed that the Russian-speaking population, when compared with the indigenous population (i.e. Tuvans), was "more fully provided for in material everyday things." Anaibin emphasized, however, that these conditions did not "appear unsatisfactory" to

---

1994), 56–88; Ronald McMullen, "Tuva: Russia's Tibet or the Next Lithuania?" *European Security* 2, no. 3 (Autumn 1993): 451–460.

24. I demonstrate this in figure 3.1 in chapter 3.

25. Anaibin describes these conditions as an ethnic division of labor in *Respublika Tuva*.

26. Similarly, many Yakuts in Yakutia believed that Russian workers were better paid and given better housing and privileges, according to Marjorie Balzer. See Balzer, "A State within a State," 143.

anyone until politicians began to discuss them prior to the 1990 elections, exacerbating Tuvan-Russian tension.[27]

Like nationalists in other republics, Tuvan nationalist leaders discounted Tuvan social mobility and the role of the Soviet state in facilitating it. From the beginning of Soviet rule, Moscow implemented educational and affirmative action policies for Tuvans. For example, the state established boarding schools for Tuvan children from rural areas during the early phase of industrialization.[28] As with KamAZ in Tatarstan, the state set up professional and technical training programs for Tuvans at factories as well as in institutes of higher education, where, local scholars reported, national cadres (i.e., Tuvans) were accepted "under conditions of noncompetitive entrance."[29] Taking advantage of these opportunities, many Tuvans obtained secondary and higher educations, urbanized at high rates, and assumed white-collar jobs in desirable occupations and in the republic's party and administrative leadership. Yet the nationalists did not compare the socioeconomic position of Tuvans at the end of the Soviet era to the position of Tuvans in 1944. Rather, they compared Tuvans with Russians in order to construct a narrative about ethnic group disadvantage and an unfair economic and political system. To be sure, the nationalists' claims of Tuvan inequality were rooted in structural inequalities more stark than those in Tatarstan. Yet by comparing Tuvans with Russians in the way that they did, the nationalists created a particular notion of Tuvans as subordinate within the republic they considered their homeland. The blame for these conditions, claimed the nationalists, rested squarely on the Soviet state.

This issue framing resonated widely in Tuva, winning the nationalist movement considerable popular support. The program of the Popular Front, according to one Russian journalist, "generated in the local population a feeling that its *national rights* had been infringed and dissatisfaction with *its place in society*"(italics added).[30] As one Tuvan woman complained, "The Russians have got the best places…they get enormous wages and multi-room apartments before everyone else. While I, the owner of this land, have to play second fiddle."[31]

---

27. Anaibin, *Respublika Tuva,* 74–75.

28. Boarding schools, however, were heavily criticized for separating Tuvans from their natural heritage and producing uncultured, uneducated students prone to criminal behavior.

29. A. Kuzhuget and M. Tatarintseva, *Etnopoliticheskaia situatsiia v Respublike Tyva* [The Ethnopolitical Situation in the Republic of Tuva] (Moscow: Institute of Ethnography and Anthropology, Russian Academy of Sciences, 1994), 45–46.

30. V. Khrebtov, "Ekonomika s aktsentom," *Ekonomika i zhizn',* no. 31 (1990): 4, quoted in Ann Sheehy, "Russians the Target of Interethnic Violence in Tuva," *RFE-RL Research Report,* September 14, 1990, 13–17.

31. *Komsomol'skaia pravda,* August 3, 1990, quoted in Sheehy, "Russians the Target of Interethnic Violence."

The American anthropologist Marjorie Balzer described the situation in Tuva at this time as one in which "newcomer Russian professionals lived better (or were perceived to live better) than indigenous Tuvans."[32]

NATIONALIST POLITICS IN TUVA

Tuva's first nationalist organization, the Popular Front of Tuva (NFT), was formed in 1989 by scholars at the Institute of Language and Literature. Its founding congress was attended by 258 Tuvans and 31 Russians. From its inception, the stated goal of the front was achieving republican sovereignty. As in other republics, the group initially sought sovereignty through raising Tuva's status from autonomous to union.[33] Though the front shared the concerns of Tuvan cultural groups about the need to renew Tuvan culture—through, for example, shamanism, the unique Tuvan musical practice of "throat singing," and Tuvan language revival—it quickly raised issues concerning the relative position of Russians and Tuvans and made political demands on republican authorities. It criticized the low level of Tuvan language knowledge among Russians in Tuva (only 0.6 percent of the Russian-speaking population knew Tuvan),[34] prompting the republic's communist leadership to pass a language law creating opportunities for Russians to study Tuvan.[35] Tuva's very conservative communist leadership tried desperately but in vain to keep national issues confined to the sphere of culture and language. However, with the moderate wing of the front promoting republican sovereignty and the radical wing advocating secession from the USSR, republican leaders again responded. They issued a sovereignty declaration in the fall of 1990.

The leader of the front, an orientalist named Kaadyr-ool Bicheldei, although a moderate, made the radical claim that parts of Mongolia and Krasnoyarsk *krai* belonged to Tuva.[36] His popularity grew, and he won election to the RSFSR Congress of People's Deputies in 1990. The same year, ten members of the Popular Front were elected deputies to Tuva's supreme soviet in the first semicompetitive elections. Despite this relatively low formal representation, the front represented a serious force in republican politics because of its mass popular support.[37]

Nationalist discourse, in its explicit comparison of Russians and Tuvans, contributed to a worsening of interethnic relations and to a development not found

---

32. Marjorie Balzer, "Dilemmas of Federalism in Siberia," in *Center-Periphery Conflict in Post-Soviet Russia: A Federation Imperiled*, ed. M. A. Alexseev (New York: St. Martin's, 1999), 139.

33. Sheehy, Russians the Target of Interethnic Violence."

34. Anaibin, *Respublika Tuva*, 61, 62.

35. Balzer, "Dilemmas of Federalism in Siberia," 136.

36. Thus Tuva's Popular Front was one of the few nationalist organizations in Russia to question the validity of current republican borders. Sheehy, "Russians the Target of Interethnic Violence."

37. Muzaev, *Etnicheskii separatizm*, 186–89.

in Russia's other republics: interethnic violence or, more accurately, the *perception* of interethnic violence. When several unconnected violent crimes occurred in 1990, many Russians interpreted them as acts of Tuvan aggression against Russians. First, a fight occurred between young (allegedly Tuvan and Russian) "public order volunteers" at a disco in the industrial town of Khovu-Aksy, after which Tuvan youth gangs fanned through the town destroying property, intimidating the population, and clashing with police. Then, in Kyzyl, members of Tuvan gangs shot several Russians, supposedly for not knowing how to speak Tuvan. In another city, Tuvans burned and raided Russians' homes, leaving notes urging them to get out of town. Finally, two Russian fishermen and a schoolboy were killed at a remote mountain lake by a local Tuvan.[38] As a local scholar noted, "Nobody paid attention to the fact that the crime was committed on the grounds of mutual drunkenness and the victim could have turned out to be any of the participants."[39] Other authors reported that much of the violence was Tuvan on Tuvan rather than between Tuvans and Russians.[40] Nevertheless, these and other incidents were perceived by most people as interethnic violence. Some Russians began to fear for their lives. Others grew concerned that they would lose their jobs if (or when) Tuvan nationalists privatized enterprises in the republic. These rumors were picked up and spread by the Russian language press. Ultimately, despite the best efforts of republican leaders, ethnic Russians began to leave Tuva. An estimated ten thousand Russians, including highly skilled engineers, teachers, and doctors, had moved out by the mid-1990s.

Tuva's communist leadership, which had been trying to discredit the Popular Front in order to dispel its growing influence, used the crime wave as an opportunity. The Communist Party first secretary, Gregorii Shirshin, an ethnic Tuvan and the republic's last surviving official from the Brezhnev era, claimed that the front was inciting pogroms against Russians. After the killing of the Russian fishermen, Shirshin called in Black Beret MVD troops from Moscow to calm the situation. However, their presence further polarized the Russian-speaking and Tuvan communities and angered some young Tuvans who felt they were being targeted.[41] The reputation of the Popular Front became severely damaged. Although Bicheldei protested vehemently and appealed to the KGB to clear the group's name, he decided to formally dissolve the organization.[42]

---

38. See Toomas Alatalu, "Tuva—A State Reawakens," *Soviet Studies* 44 (1992): 881–895.

39. Anaibin, *Respublika Tuva*, 75.

40. Stefan Sullivan, "Interethnic Relations in Post-Soviet Tuva," *Ethnic and Racial Studies* 18 (1995): 65–88.

41. See Alatalu "Tuva."

42. Balzer, "From Ethnicity to Nationalism."

Bicheldei remained popular, however, and after the Soviet Union collapsed, was elected chairman of the Tuvan supreme soviet, the only leader of a nationalist organization to be elected to the top post in any of the republics. His rise to the pinnacle of power followed the population's rejection of the communist supreme soviet chairman, D. Ondar, for his strong support of the attempted coup against Gorbachev. After the coup attempt, several nationalists embarked on a sustained hunger strike while residents of Kyzyl participated in a series of mass demonstrations to protest the antidemocratic actions of the nomenklatura leaders during the attempted coup. Hunger strikers successfully demanded the resignation of Ondar and Shirshin—a show of popular opposition that led to a new phase in Tuvan politics in which nationalists and nationalist sympathizers assumed leadership positions.

Two new nationalist organizations were formed to replace the disbanded Popular Front: the People's Front Khostug Tuva (Free Tuva) and the National Party of Sovereign Tuva (NPST). Like the Popular Front before it, Khostug Tuva focused on strengthening republican sovereignty. The group served as an umbrella organization for Tuva's numerous new informal organizations, including Buddhist religious societies, the Society of Homeless, the Union of Cultural Workers of Tuva, the Foundation of Free Trade Unions, and the Society of Former Prisoners.[43] More radical than the Popular Front, Khostug Tuva was composed exclusively of ethnic Tuvans and included young, unemployed migrants from the republic's rural regions. Beginning in 1992, Khostug Tuva employed various strategies to advance its agenda, ranging from appeals to parliament to "mass initiatives" and "direct appeal to the people."[44] It organized rallies for the defense of the homeless, the unemployed, and former prisoners, many of whom belonged to groups operating under the group's umbrella. One of Khostug Tuva's first activities was to defend the activity of one of its member organizations, the Society of the Homeless, which had seized three empty apartments in Kyzyl and demanded that the city's housing stock be divided according to ethnic group membership. The government condemned the society's behavior as illegal, but after meeting with Khostug Tuva, agreed to provide members of the society with their own apartments.[45] According to Drobizheva, the group's impulsive behavior alienated many potential supporters and especially the Russian-speaking

---

43. The republic's Ministry of Justice reported that forty-eight social movements and groups officially registered in the republic during the 1990s. Anaibin, "Ethnic Relations in Tuva," 1995, 105.

44. A. Kuzhuget and M. Tatarintseva, *Etnopoliticheskaia situatsiia v Respublike Tyva* [The Ethnopolitical Situation in the Republic of Tuva] (Moscow: Institute of Anthropology and Ethnography, Russian Academy of Sciences, 1994), 12.

45. Many people in Tuva and many ethnic Tuvans lived in communal apartments. Muzeev, *Etnicheskii separatizm*, 188.

population.[46] However, Khostug Tuva's leader, a well-known television journalist named Vyacheslav Salchak, was elected to the republic's supreme soviet.

The other new nationalist group, the NPST, advocated a liberal program of economic reform and business development. More moderate than Khostug Tuva, it organized as a political party after deciding it could best achieve its goals by participating in institutionalized politics. Its members were mainly professional politicians and representatives of the intelligentsia. The program of the NPST was dedicated to defending Tuva's sovereignty and the supremacy of republican laws over those of the Russian Federation.

The NPST fared better than Khostug Tuva in terms of attracting popular support. The group established local organizations throughout the republic and actively campaigned in the 1993 elections to the renamed supreme soviet—the supreme khural. The party's growing authority among Tuvans translated into electoral success: it won 62.9 percent of the popular vote and three out of five seats in the khural reserved for political parties. In the same elections, a leading NPST member and scientist at the Tuvan branch of the Russian Academy of Sciences, Kara-Kyz Dongakovny Arakchaa, won a seat in the Russian Duma. Together, these two organizations formed the opposition nationalist movement in Tuva and played an influential role until approximately 1994.

NATIONALIST DISCOURSE IN TUVA, 1989–92

Nationalist discourse in Tuva shifted over the course of just a few years. Nationalists articulated issues of Tuvan economic inequality during the years of national revival before the Soviet Union collapsed, from 1989 to early 1992. After the collapse, the nationalists virtually stopped raising these issues and began to discuss new ones. This shift can be explained by the dramatic change in politics in Tuva. First, the Popular Front was dissolved and replaced by Khostug Tuva and the NPST. The ethnic violence that had erupted in 1990 ended but remained a threat that could reemerge. Most actors in Tuva wanted to avoid more violence. Second, by contrast with other republics, the collapse of the Soviet Union was accompanied by a relatively sharp change of leadership in which nationalists (such as Bicheldei and the new president, Sherig-ool Oorzhak) replaced the conservative nomenklatura administration of Shirshin and Ondar. In analyzing Tuvan newspaper articles, I found that the discourse of Tuvan nationalists reflected these changed conditions.

I collected and analyzed newspaper articles from three Tuvan newspapers: *Tuvinskaia pravda, Respublika Tuva,* and *Sodeistvie. Tuvinskaia pravda*—the

---

46. Drobizheva, *Natsional'noe samosoznanie,* 117–34.

official publication of Tuva's communist administration—was the only newspaper available in Moscow libraries for the early years of national revival. Because
Tuva's administration was highly conservative, the paper provided little space to
representatives of the nationalist movement, unlike the main newspapers in the
other republics I examined. Thus nationalist issues and discourse are underre-
ported in articles published in *Tuvinskaia pravda* before the collapse of the Soviet
Union. Also, because so many Tuvans spoke Tuvan, nationalists used the Tuvan-
language press to communicate with them to a greater degree than in Tatarstan
and other republics. Despite these facts, it was during the early years of national
revival that we observe the most discussion about the issue of ethnic economic
inequality. Approximately 25 out of the 110 articles I analyzed from 1989 to February 1992 mention the issue of unequal representation in Tuva's labor market
and inegalitarian resource distribution between Tuvans and Russians. Table 6.3
lists the issues articulated by Tuvan nationalists.[47]

After the Soviet collapse, however, NPST and Khostug Tuva deemphasized
these issues so as to reduce interethnic tension, forestall another outbreak of ethnic violence and Russian out-migration, and preempt the allegations that had
been made against the NFT that they were inciting ethnic violence. Thus most
articles published during the second period emphasize interethnic cooperation.
After 1991 the nationalists also focused more on Tuva's relationship with the new
Russian Federation and on the movement's goal of upholding republican sovereignty by adopting a Tuvan constitution. In terms of the framing dimension of
blame attribution, whereas before 1991 the nationalists placed blame for Tuva's
problems on the republic's communist leadership (as well as on Moscow), after
1991 they shifted blame onto Moscow exclusively. When it came to identifying
solutions to social conditions and problems, however, the nationalist focus on
the goal of achieving republican sovereignty remained constant across the two
periods.

It makes sense that the Popular Front of Tuva concentrated initially on the
issue of Tuvan versus Russian socioeconomic inequality because, as a new organization, it was trying to build a sense of national identity among ethnic Tuvans by identifying them as victims of the existing political order dominated by
Russians. The nationalists were attempting to attract support to their program
by linking the Tuvan nation to the immediate and important goal of replacing

---

47. Note that though the number of times an issue is mentioned in the set of articles I collected
is an indicator of the degree of nationalist concern with the issue, bias may exist in the number and
kinds of articles that were available for me to select in Moscow libraries. Also, I did not examine the
titular-language press in Tuva, in which nationalists steadily presented their message to readers; thus
the results here most likely underreport the frequency with which Tuvan nationalists articulated
certain issues.

Table 6.3 Discourse analysis of Tuvan newspapers

	NUMBER OF ARTICLES MENTIONING THE ISSUE	
ISSUE ARTICULATED BY TUVAN NATIONALISTS	1989–92 (OUT OF 110 ARTICLES)	1993–94 (OUT OF 45 ARTICLES)
Tuvan professional underrepresentation	25	2
Republican sovereignty	30	13
Tuvan language	20	0
No private land	0	8
Relations with Russia/Yeltsin	0	8
Establishment of constitution	0	7
Constitution with right to secede	0	5
Economic sovereignty	14	7
Rebirth of Tuvan culture	21	4
UN norms of self-determination	0	3
Protection of environment	11	2
Respect for Russians in Tuva	10	3
Commission of crimes by Russians	0	1
Economic problems	17	3
Tuvan diaspora	1	1
Political representation of Tuvans	1	1

the status quo with a new national order in which Tuva would be a sovereign republic.

For example, the nationalist leader K. Kuzhuget, who was associated with the Popular Front stated, "The educational and cultural level of Tuvan rural youth lags behind that of Russian urban youth. The reason for this is unequal social conditions." In the article, in which Kuzhuget discussed his candidacy for the Tuvan supreme soviet, he blamed both the republican leaders and the party for "working with old stereotypes" and also called for republican sovereignty.[48] In another article two years later, Kuzhuget, who had by then become chairman of the NPST, complained that he had been accused of "nationalism" when he stated that "a Tuvan man in the countryside lags behind his Russian-speaking peer living in the city, in terms of his educational level." He lamented the fact that in Tuva "our multinational and much-suffering country, almost any utterance in defense of a small nation made by a representative of that nation is taken as an expression of nationalism." Kuzhuget then discussed the particular problems confronting Tuvan youth in the rural countryside who were tempted by crime and alcohol. He identified a solution to the problem by stating that the NPST

48. "K iyudiam idu ne s frontami" [I Walk with People, Not with Fronts], *Tuvinskaia pravda*, February 24, 1990.

advocated passing laws that would "guarantee education, jobs, housing, etc." to rural Tuvan youths.[49]

The author of another article emphasized the unequal representation of Tuvans and Russians in Tuva's industrial sector:

> Right now in our republic there are very large enterprises like TuvaAsbest and TuvaKobalt [flagship enterprises in Tuva]. They are led by representatives of the Russian nationality, who I'm sure are hard-working and moral people of the highest qualifications. However, there are no people with indigenous nationality among the managerial staff at these enterprises. I agree that the reason for this is that as yet there are not enough qualified specialists among Tuvans. But measures should be taken by the leaders of the enterprises to provide help to them.[50]

The nationalist sympathizer Oorzhak, who later became president of Tuva, also discussed this problem by relaying a statement supposedly made by rank-and-file Russian workers at the asbestos factory TuvaAsbest: "In our section...there are mainly representatives of the Russian-speaking population while in the dustiest jobs with the most menial work, there are Tuvans. Our professional trade, our skills, and our knowledge is no better than theirs." The journalist reporting the story stated that he doubted these words were ever actually uttered by Russian factory workers and noted that Oorzhak's statement was published in a Tuvan-language newspaper, implying that his comments were nothing more than nationalist propaganda.[51]

The issue of job representation was not the only way in which nationalists described socioeconomic ethnic inequality. They also argued that Tuvans suffered more than Russians because of the way in which the state allocated resources in short supply. For example, an article by a group of "concerned republican citizens" in *Tuvinskaia pravda* reported that V. S. Salchak, the leader of Khostug Tuva, had published an article in a Tuvan-language newspaper that identified several ethnic Russian government officials by name and criticized them for skirting the law to obtain high-quality apartments for themselves. In the article Salchak described another instance of corruption among ethnic Russian officials and claimed that these cases illustrated the oppression of the Tuvan nation. The authors of the *Tuvinskaia pravda* article castigated Salchak for "trying to turn one part of the population of Tuva against another" and also denounced the media

---

49. Kuzhuget, "Za nadezhnuiu bazu suvereniteta" [Is Sovereignty Based on Hope?] *Tuvinskaia pravda*, February 15, 1992, 2.

50. S. Sagaan, "Predlagaiu obsuzhdat'" [Let's Discuss], *Tuvinskaia pravda*, September 13, 1989.

51. "Idti vmeste" [Moving Forward Together], *Tuvinskaia pravda*, February 13, 1990.

for providing him with a pulpit from which he could proclaim his "unobjective" point of view.[52]

The fact that Tuva's communist administration discussed the nationalist claims of occupational underrepresentation and took them seriously suggests the centrality of (and publicity given to) the issue in the discourse of Tuvan nationalists. During the first few years of national revival, the communist administration tried desperately to counter these kinds of claims, more than did their counterparts in other republics. *Tuvinskaia pravda* expressed the view that Tuvan cultural and language revival was a legitimate goal, but it consistently criticized the idea of Tuvan occupational subordination. The paper's articles either directly asserted that claims of Tuvan occupational underrepresentation were false or tried to shift the blame for the situation away from republican administrators. As Supreme Soviet Chairman Ondar stated in an interview, "People complain that there are not enough Tuvans at TuvaAsbest. But whose fault is this? The director of the factory wouldn't listen to me."[53]

Overall, the discourse on ethnic issues in Tuvan newspapers from 1989 to 1992 indicates that Tuvan economic inequality was a key issue for Tuvan nationalists. In addition, Tuvan nationalists assigned blame for the problem primarily to local republican authorities, pointing out in some cases that these authorities were ethnic Russians. Finally, the nationalists advocated providing education and jobs to ethnic Tuvans and strongly supported the goal of republican sovereignty.

NATIONALIST DISCOURSE IN TUVA, 1993–1994

I analyzed forty-five articles published in 1993 and 1994 in Tuva's three newspapers. Of these, twenty contain information about the nationalist NPST and Khostug Tuva. Twelve articles present the views of republican government officials, including President Oorzhak, his minister of nationalities, and the chair of the supreme soviet Bicheldei.[54] Republican sovereignty was mentioned more frequently than any other issue (see table 6.3). The second-most-common subject was the need to create a constitution for the republic of Tuva affirming the republic's sovereignty. The republican administration and supreme soviet shared this goal and worked on a draft constitution throughout 1993. Tuvan nationalist organizations played a big role in pushing for a constitution and also supported

---

52. "Vozmushcheny! I eto-zashchita spravedlivosti?" [We are Outraged! Is this Defending Justice?], *Tuvinskaia pravda*, 1992.

53. "Krepnut' nashei druzhbe" [Strengthening Our Friendship], *Tuvinskaia pravda*, December 7, 1989.

54. Of the remaining articles, one was written by the leader of the democratic opposition group in Tuva affiliated with the Moscow-centered party Democratic Russia. Three articles reflect the opinions of local journalists, and three present the views of ordinary citizens.

the inclusion of a clause guaranteeing Tuva the right to secede. Tuvan nationalists also described economic conditions in Tuva as inhibiting the republic's ability to develop economically and achieve sovereignty. Because Tuva received significant subsidies from Moscow, some nationalists advocated reducing this dependence by ending central subsidies and transfers, introducing privatization, and establishing manufacturing plants. Others favored the promotion of "traditional" (i.e., Tuvan) forms of economic activity, such as livestock herding. Government officials were more likely than nationalists to express support for the continuation of central economic subsidies.

In many articles, nationalist leaders articulated their opposition to the private ownership of land. Land should belong to those who cultivate it, they said. This issue, which represented a position antithetical to the nationalists' generally strong support for free markets and privatization, was based on their stated fear that entrepreneurs would buy and sell the land out from under the people who lived and worked on it—the ethnic Tuvans living in the countryside.[55] The issue of private land ownership was connected to the broader issue of the distribution of republican resources along ethnic lines, which was a central concern of Khostug Tuva.

Finally, nationalists discussed various issues connected to federal relations and development in Moscow, expressing, for example, both support for Yeltsin before the 1993 April referendum on his leadership and opposition to his shelling of the federal parliament, and then, in 1994, opposition to the reformulated Russian Constitution with a watered-down federation treaty that reduced the autonomy of the republics.

The analysis of blame attribution in newspaper articles published in Tuva between 1993 and 1994 presents a very clear finding: Tuvan nationalists most often blamed the federal government in Moscow for the republic's problems. They also placed blame on Tuva's leaders, albeit less frequently than on the federal government. In addition, Soviet policies and legacies were identified as the source of social, political, and economic problems, as were local politicians representing centrist views, the poor state of the economy, the Russian mass media, and ethnic Russians. Only two of the articles containing nationalist discourse explicitly blamed ethnic Russians; in both cases, it was the extremist group Khostug Tuva that did so. As described above, the reasons that Tuvan nationalists more generally took care to avoid scapegoating or even mentioning Russians in negative terms were the interethnic violence that occurred in 1990 and the allegations that

---

55. The local scholar Nelli Moskalenko also views the nationalist position against the private ownership of land as rooted in Tuvans' opposition to the Soviet collectivization campaign of the 1930s. See *Respublika Tyva [Tuva]*.

nationalist groups had caused interethnic tension and Russian out-migration. Finally, during 1993 and 1994, as mentioned above, Tuvan nationalists consistently invoked republican sovereignty as the ultimate solution to problems and as the only way to develop a future for the Tuvan nation. As Khostug Tuva stated, "The peoples [*narodi*] of Russia in the final analysis will become independent in the interests of rights and free individuality....The leaders of Khostug Tuva... demand recognition of the illegal annexation of the Tuvan Republic to the SSSR in 1944."[56]

Nationalist discourse in Tuva was similar to that in Tatarstan and Chechnya. Tuvan nationalists bemoaned ethnic inequality caused by occupational underrepresentation and socioeconomic subordination; they placed primary blame for the inequity on local and federal political authorities; and finally, they saw republican sovereignty as the solution to the problems inhibiting the Tuvan nation. The case of Tuva may be directly contrasted with the republics of Komi and Mari El, which experienced very low mass nationalist mobilization.

The Republic of Mari El

The Mari ASSR, situated in the Middle Volga region, had one of the lowest levels of mass nationalism among all of Russia's republics. The Mari nationalist movement—composed of a moderate and radical wing, as in other republics—focused its program on cultural and language issues and the deprived status of the ethnic Mari diaspora. Nationalists infrequently mentioned the underrepresentation of ethnic Mari in the republic, and when they did, they failed to frame the issue as one of an ethnic injustice that denied rights to the people within their own territory. Nor did the nationalists connect the problem of Mari underrepresentation to the goal of republican sovereignty. As a result, the nationalist movement failed to win popular support, attracting followers only among a narrow layer of the Mari intelligentsia. The low level of mass nationalism is indicated in part by a lack of demonstrations and meager electoral success in republican and federal elections.

The economy of Mari El was based primarily on machine building and metallurgy, with approximately 80 percent of its enterprises engaged in defense production. As a result, it was highly economically dependent on the central government; 60 percent of Mari El's economy was financed by the Russian budget.[57]

---

56. Ibid., 11.

57. V. D. Sharov, *Etnopoliticheskaia situatsiia v Respublike Marii El* [The Ethnopolitical Situation in the Republic of Mari El] (Moscow: Institute of Ethnography and Anthropology, Russian Academy of Sciences, 1994), 5.

Also, Mari El was one of the few republics (along with Chechnya) with labor conditions that approximated an ethnic division of labor. Large numbers of ethnic Mari continued to live in rural regions and work in agriculture at the end of the Soviet era. Although the republic was almost evenly split between Russians, who formed a 47.5 percent majority, and Mari, who comprised a 43.3 percent minority, Mari made up only 26 percent of the urban population.[58] In addition, the republic's capital city, Ioshkar-Ola, was dominated by Russians, with Mari comprising only 15 percent of its population.[59] In terms of ethnic representation in the workforce, Mari were proportionally underrepresented in desirable occupations: the ratio of Mari to Russian representation in the white-collar workforce was .54, the second-lowest among all the republics.[60]

If structural economic conditions alone determined political outcomes, we might observe mass nationalist mobilization in Mari El instead of quiescence. Enterprises in the republic were reliant on the center for defense contracts at a time when Moscow was cutting defense spending. At the same time, Mari lagged behind Russians in the urban economy. Structuralist arguments would say that an exogenous shock like Russia's economic crisis would have caused Mari to realize that they were oppressed by current economic conditions. They would then have decided to throw their support behind politicians advocating overthrow of the unfavorable status quo by a new national order. The lack of nationalist mobilization in Mari El shows that this was not the case.

The argument of this book is that mass mobilization develops when nationalist entrepreneurs create a narrative of ethnic disadvantage and blocked opportunity and blame the current political authority for their predicament—something the Mari nationalists could have done. However, they concentrated instead on the loss of Mari culture and language and the rebirth of national consciousness. As a result, the nationalist movement there failed to win support among the general population.

The nationalist movement in Mari El was composed of two main organizations: the radical nationalist Kugeze Mlande (Land of our Ancestors) and the moderate Mari Ushem (Mari Union). Kugeze Mlande advocated secession from Russia and exclusivist laws on migration. Despite the fact that the majority of Mari were Orthodox Christian, the group also supported a return to

---

58. M. N. Guboglo and S. M. Chervonnaia, *Probuzhdenie finno-ugorskogo severa. Opyt Marii El* [Awakening of the Finno-Ugric North. The Experience of Mari El] (Moscow: Institute of Ethnography and Anthropology, Russian Academy of Sciences, 1996), 252.

59. Valery Tishkov, "Materialy po problemam mezhnatsionalnykh otnoshenii v Rossiiskoi Federatsii" [Material on Issues of inter-ethnic relations in the Russian Federation], in *Rossiiskii Etnograf* (Moscow: Institute of Ethnography and Anthropology, Russian Academy of Sciences, 1993), 18.

60. See figure 3.1 in chapter 3.

paganism—the putative beliefs of native Mari—and helped a new pro-pagan organization obtain official recognition. The provocative statements and rallies of Kugeze Mlande brought the group attention, but it never became popular or succeeded in taking control of the nationalist movement.[61] The main nationalist organization in the republic, Mari Ushem, developed in a manner similar to that of movements in other republics. It formed in 1989 on the initiative of young members of the Mari creative intelligentsia and was backed by part of the republican elite. The group's first program supported a declaration on state sovereignty, advocated official state status for the Mari language, and espoused Mari cultural revival and the end of Russification. Mari Ushem, however, was unique in its decision not to become an oppositional movement. Rather, the organization decided from its inception to cooperate with official leaders of the republic, including the CPSU.

Mari Ushem's influence on public opinion was insignificant, despite the fact that the population, especially ethnic Mari, was well informed about the group.[62] Results from the 1993 elections to the federal Duma and the parliament of Mari El indicate this fact: only one representative from Mari Ushem won a seat in the Duma, while the radical Kugeze Mlande failed to win any seats at all. In addition, none of the five candidates from Mari Ushem was elected to the Mari El parliament. The group's lack of popular influence is also demonstrated by the fact that they backed the losing candidate in the republic's first presidential election.[63] Ultimately, the movement was embraced by only a small portion of the republican intelligentsia.

NATIONALIST ISSUE FRAMING: DEFINING SOCIAL CONDITIONS

I coded thirty newspaper articles published in Mari El's main newspaper from 1990 to 1992, examining the three dimensions of nationalist framing in each article. In terms of the first dimension, Mari Ushem focused primarily on defining three kinds of issues or social conditions: (1) a need for the rebirth of national consciousness and of the Mari nation (*narod*), which was mentioned in six articles by nationalist leaders; (2) the status of the Mari language, which was discussed in eight articles; and (3) the loss of culture and language among the ethnic Mari diaspora, which was mentioned in seven (see table 6.4).[64] Notably,

---

61. Muzaev, *Etnicheskii separatizm,* 159–63; Sharov, *Etnopoliticheskaia situatsiia v Respublike Marii El,* 5.

62. Sharov, *Etnopoliticheskaia situatsiia,* 15.

63. Muzaev, *Etnicheskii separatizm,* 160.

64. Nationalist leaders wrote or were interviewed in fifteen out of the thirty articles I analyzed on ethnic politics. Other articles included news reports written by journalists or letters to the editor.

Table 6.4   Discourse analysis of Mari El newspapers

ISSUE ARTICULATED BY MARI NATIONALISTS	NUMBER OF ARTICLES MENTIONING THE ISSUE (OUT OF 30 ARTICLES)
Rebirth of Mari national consciousness	6
Mari language	8
Loss of culture/language among Mari diaspora	7
Improving representation of Maris in technical/ scientific spheres	3

in three articles, nationalists mentioned improving the representation of ethnic Mari in the technical and scientific spheres of the economy. However, this issue was framed as a result not of the Mari people's unequal status but of contingent circumstances that could change. Thus a critical attribution of blame is missing from the way in which Mari nationalists framed these issues.

NATIONALIST ISSUE FRAMING: ATTRIBUTING BLAME

There was not a single instance in any of the fifteen articles in which the nationalists assigned blame to ethnic Russians for any problem or inequity facing the Mari nation. In fact, in most articles nationalist leaders specifically singled out Russians for praise or stated their warm feelings for all peoples living in the republic. In nine of the fifteen articles, the author expressed a positive feeling toward Russians. Around the time Mari Ushem held its second congress in 1992, each article in which nationalists expressed their positions contained the tolerant phrases "We do not infringe on the interests of any nations living in the republic" and "We do not aspire to a special position or special privileges."[65] Newspapers published statements demonstrating that ethnic Mari in the republic did not harbor negative attitudes toward ethnic Russians. As one man stated in a letter to the editor, "I, for one, have never felt resentful of Russians, those who taught me in school and with whom I live."[66]

Mari Ushem could have placed blame on Moscow, as nationalists in Tatarstan did. However, here again, not a single article condemned the Russian government for infringing on the general rights of Mari or for causing any of the problems the group enumerated as important. One article offered mild criticism of Russia's lack of a structure to propagate a unified state policy on cultural development of its ethnic minorities,[67] while another criticized Russia for not protecting

---

65. "Iz istorii Mariiskogo natsional'nogo dvizheniia" [The History of the Mari National Movement], *Mariskaia pravda*, October 30, 1992, 1.

66. *Mariiskaia Pravda*, 12 March 1990.

67. A. Trishina, "Chem zhivet 'Mari ushem,'" [On What Is Mari Ushem Living?] *Mariiskaia pravda*, April 18, 1992, 1–2.

the Mari diaspora. Two articles attributed blame for loss of the Mari language to an internal rather than external source: the Mari themselves. For example, one nationalist denounced "national nihilism" among the "ersatz national intelligentsia" (i.e., Mari) who used the republic's privileges to become educated but now "deny their roots."[68]

The Mari nationalists placed most blame on either imperial Russia (two articles) or the Soviet system (five articles) under Stalin (four of the five articles) and under Brezhnev (three of the five). Several articles also placed blame on Soviet state policies of Russification, assimilation of ethnic groups into a single identity (*sliianie*), and urbanization (two articles). By the early 1990s, criticism of past Soviet leaders or policies did not constitute a challenge to the current political system and therefore did not represent a call for drastic change in the direction of state sovereignty or a new, nationalist leadership in the republic.

NATIONALIST ISSUE FRAMING: IDENTIFYING SOLUTIONS

Mari Ushem suggested various solutions to problems facing the Mari population and the republic. Strikingly, the issue that was emphasized by each of the nationalist movements in the republics with mass nationalist mobilization—that of achieving republican sovereignty—was rarely mentioned by Mari Ushem leaders. In fact, Mari Ushem advocated state sovereignty for Mari El in only two out of the fifteen articles. In the first of three articles that mentioned Mari underrepresentation in the industrial sphere, the author stated that Mari Ushem supported "adopting a series of measures to form a national [i.e., Mari] working class and technical intelligentsia in an urban ethnic cultural milieu." The author's solutions to this problem were a program for talented Mari school children to study physics and math and making Mari State University "a center" for educating Mari.[69] Though the author offered solutions, it is important to note that the issue of Mari representation was not framed as an instance of ethnic injustice to be remedied via state sovereignty. The solutions to the problem identified by Mari nationalists were far less comprehensive than the Tatar and Tuvan nationalists' call for state sovereignty and for ethnic quotas in education and the job market.

In another article in which a Mari Ushem leader criticized the small number of Mari industrial workers and enterprise managers, the problem was blamed on what he called "demographic policies"—the poor quality of rural schooling and

---

68. Eleva Malofeeva, "Put' k vzaimoponimaniiu" [Path to Mutual Understanding], *Mariskaia pravda,* March 7, 1990. Other articles mentioned the fact of Mari language loss as a tragedy but did not place blame on anything in particular.

69. "Po puti vozrozhdeniia" [On the Path to Rebirth], *Mariiskaia pravda,* March 12, 1990, 2.

the lack of available housing in the cities for young specialists from the village. No solution to this problem was mentioned. Near the end of the article, the journalist reporting on Mari Ushem's statements critiqued the group in general for failing to offer concrete suggestions about how to implement its goals.[70]

Two years later, another Mari Ushem leader stated again that Mari El needed technical-scientific intelligentsia, engineers, and physicists but that it had enough cultural workers. He went on to say that recent events were improving the prospects for the development of a technical intelligentsia, since a specialized grade school had been established in Ioshkar-Ola. The school would make it possible, he stated, for the republic to send "our students" to study in universities in Moscow, or even Estonia and Finland.[71] That a nationalist leader perceived the establishment of a single grade school as a positive step toward eradicating the subordinate professional position of ethnic Mari in the republic suggests that, for Mari Ushem, the issue of Mari underrepresentation fell far short of an intolerable problem that sovereignty would eradicate.[72]

Thus, unlike that in Tatarstan, the nationalist movement in Mari El weakly and ineffectually framed the issue of ethnic economic inequality as an injustice. As a result, the movement's framing of other issues found little resonance among the population in the republic. Only a small segment of the republican intelligentsia supported nationalism. After 1993, Mari Ushem began to concern itself more and more with the issue of Mari language education,[73] and the activity of both nationalist organizations significantly decreased. The nationalists stopped participating in elections, and many group members migrated to other voting blocs.[74]

The Republic of Komi

The population in the Komi Republic—located in the remote, northern part of European Russia—gave very little support to the opposition nationalist

---

70. A. Trishina, "Vnachale vybrat' put'—Zametki s"ezda Mari Ushem" [Beginning to Choose a Path—Notes from the Mari Ushem Congress], April 13, 1990, 2.

71. A. Trishina, "Chem zhivet 'Mari ushem.'"

72. Other solutions to unjust social conditions identified by Mari Ushem consisted of increasing Mari presence in republican government organs, adopting Mari as a state language, demanding that a cultural mission in Moscow be established of the kind that existed during the 1920s, encouraging Mari intellectuals to conduct studies and surveys, rebuilding the national consciousness of the Mari diaspora by setting up radio and television stations, publishing Mari language periodicals, and supplying Mari with language education.

73. Allen Frank and Ronald Wixman, "The Middle Volga: Exploring the Limits of Sovereignty," in *New States New Politics: Building the Post-Soviet Nations,* ed. Ian Bremmer and Ray Taras (Cambridge: Cambridge University Press, 1997), 177.

74. Muzaev, *Etnicheskii separatizm,* 162.

movement.[75] This fact cannot be attributed to a lack of commitment or effort on the part of Komi nationalists. Composed of both a moderate and a radical wing, the Komi nationalist movement was as assertive as nationalist movements in other republics. It was also highly visible; the group Komi Kotyr (Komi Nation) had an office in the building of the republic's supreme soviet and held a series of Komi national congresses that received wide public attention. Nor can the low level of nationalist mobilization be attributed to an absence of problems in the republic or a lack of issues that nationalists usually care about. First, the economic crisis unfolding throughout the USSR in the late 1980s also hit Komi, prompting Communist Party first secretary Yuri Spiridonov to introduce food rationing and to command enterprises to surrender 15 percent of their output in order to barter for food—a common practice among regions at the time.[76] Second, in terms of ethnic demography, the share of ethnic Komi in the republican population fell during the Soviet era by approximately 65 percent—the largest drop among all of Russia's titular nationalities. By 1989, Komi formed only 23.3 percent and Russians 57.7 percent of the population. The Russian population in Komi had expanded as a result of two separate developments. First, Moscow decided in the 1920s to situate gulags (labor camps) on Komi's territory and use prison labor to extract the natural resources located there. Second, Moscow constructed coal, gas, and oil enterprises in the republic's northern cities after World War II. In the 1920s, prisoners, administrative migrants (*administrativnye ssyl'nye*) and special migrants (*spetspereselentsy*) streamed into Komi from throughout the Soviet Union to work as miners. By 1932 these groups already composed 40 percent of the republican population.[77] Though these and other issues (discussed below) provided grist for nationalist leaders, they did not elicit automatic concern among ethnic Komi and did not produce support for the nationalist movement.

Nor can labor market conditions in Komi during perestroika explain the lack of nationalist mobilization there. Although almost all ethnic Komi were rural at the start of the Soviet era—only 1.5 percent lived in cities in 1926—they had become primarily urban by 1989. Through education and linguistic

---

75. Culturally, ethnic Komi are very similar to Russians—they are Orthodox Christian, physically undifferentiated, and fluent in the Russian language. Although a majority of Komi (71 percent), according to the 1989 Soviet census, considered the Komi language (which belongs to the Finno-Ugric group) their native language, this figure represented a drop from the 99 percent of Komi who did so in the 1930 census.

76. Residents of Syktyvar were allowed one chicken and five hundred grams of sausage every three months. *RFE-RL,* 3, no. 14, April 5, 1991.

77. The mining industry was controlled by the NKVD and later the MVD in Moscow V. Il'in, *Respublika Komi: Etnos i politika,* (Moscow: Institute of Ethnography and Anthropology, Russian Academy of Sciences, 1994).

Russification,[78] the Komi achieved near occupational equivalence with Russians.[79] As reported in chapter 3, the ratio of Komi to Russian representation in the white-collar workforce was 0.9, the fourth-highest among all of Russia's republics. If ethnic Komi did not lag behind Russians socioeconomically, the logic of the ethnic division of labor model predicts that they would have had no grievance and thus no reason to support nationalism. But occupational equivalence was also the case in Tatarstan between Tatars and Russians, and it did not stop Tatars from supporting nationalism there. In fact, despite Tatars' impressive occupational achievements, Tatar nationalist leaders lamented their socioeconomic subordination to Russians. In Komi, on the other hand, the relative socioeconomic positions of Komi and Russians were rarely mentioned. This was not because there were more blue-collar Tatars in Tatarstan than blue-collar Komi in Komi. As in Tatarstan, many Komi continued to live in rural areas and work in agriculture and forestry, while Russians (and other Russian-speaking nationalities) worked in the coal, oil, and gas extraction industries. Thus, just like Tatarstan, the Republic of Komi had elements of an EDL as well as a general occupational equivalence between its ethnic groups.

NATIONALIST POLITICS IN KOMI

When national revival began to develop in the late 1980s, Komi Kotyr was formed as a cultural organization. It promoted new initiatives such as teaching Komi language, history, and culture—initiatives that coexisted for a while with Soviet traditions like singing Komi national songs to honor Lenin's birthday.[80] Then the group began to focus on political issues. In early 1991, it organized the first extraordinary national congress of the Komi nation (*S"ezd Komi naroda*), which proclaimed itself to be the highest representative organ of the indigenous people. In the words of one journalist describing the congress, "All the pains and problems of the Komi people…came 'flooding out.'"[81] Three national congresses would be held before the decline of the nationalist movement in the mid-1990s.

---

78. According to a survey by local scholars, a majority of Komi (91 percent) reported that they spoke Russian fluently. See Il'in, *Respublika Komi*, 7.

79. A small but significant number of ethnic Komis were highly educated even before World War II, including Pitirim Sorokin, the famous sociologist who became chair of Harvard University's Department of Sociology in the 1930s. Sorokin claimed that the Komi were among the most educated of Russia's nationalities. Iurii Shabaev, "Peculiarities of Nation-Building in the Republic of Komi," in *Nation-Building and Common Values in Russia*, ed. Pal Kolsto and Helge Blakkisrud (Lanham, Md.: Rowman & Littlefield, 2004.)

80. Komarova, *Khronika zhizni natsional'nostei nakanune raspada SSSR*.

81. A. Smirnov, "Po puti vozrozhdeniia [On the Path to Rebirth] *Krasnoe Znamya*, January 16, 1991, 1.

The Komi congress elected an executive body called the Committee for the Rebirth of the Komi Nation (Komitet Vozrozhdeniia Komi Naroda, or KVKN), which became the primary nationalist group in the republic. The committee was led by V. P. Markov, a physicist who had decided to enter politics so that his "children and grandchildren could live on this land and see it as it was when I was a child."[82] Markov was a moderate who carefully navigated among the party apparatus and democrats. The Komi congress outlined a position encompassing two approaches: to defend the general regional interests of the entire population of the republic and to promote the specific interests of the Komi nation. The congress identified the *source* of republican sovereignty as the "multicentury development of the Komi ethnos...on the territory of its historical homeland" but also identified the *bearers* of sovereignty as the "multinational society of people" living on republican territory. The main and most radical goal of the Komi congress was to establish a new, bicameral supreme soviet in which one chamber would be reserved exclusively for ethnic Komi deputies.

A more radical group—Asshor Olom (Party of Komi Independence)—formed in 1991, calling for separation from Russia and for the creation of a presidency and citizenship in the republic. Another radical Komi organization, Doryaem as'nymos (Let's Defend Ourselves), formed at the beginning of 1993. The radical wing was more openly nationalist—advocating the creation of an ethnic Komi government and the creation of an independent Komi state. The group accused the KVKN of appeasing republican officials. The radicals believed that the republic was run in the interests of Russians who had a monopoly in the supreme soviet.

Despite the presence of radical groups and the high visibility of the main moderate nationalist organization through their Komi national congresses, the nationalist movement received negligible popular support. This fact allowed Komi's government to pay little more than lip service to the group's goals. As a result, KVKN became more radical at its second national congress in 1992, demanding that the supreme soviet adopt all its resolutions and criticizing the republican leadership for "having ignored the interests of the Komi people." As a concession to the nationalists, the republican government then passed symbolic legislation, "On the Status of the Congress of the Komi People," that described the congress as the highest representative assembly of the Komi people. Nevertheless, by 1994, the nationalist movement had been weakened by its split into a radical and a moderate wing.

---

82. I Murygina, "Kak ukhodiat v politiki" [How to Go into Politics] *Respublika*, June 21, 1991, 2.

NATIONALIST DISCOURSE IN KOMI

In analyzing nationalist discourse in Komi, it is striking to find that not a single newspaper article mentioned the issue of ethnic representation in the republic's economy. In fact, the entire subject of educational and professional opportunity among Komi was absent, with the exception of a single letter to the editor.[83] The nationalists in Komi also did not mention the subject of the proper distribution of resources among Komi and Russians living in the republic.

My discourse analysis of newspapers published in the republic of Komi examined a total of forty-eight articles, selected from two local newspapers, *Krasnoe znamia* and *Respublika*. Of all the articles, twenty-one were written either by or about Komi nationalists. I identified eleven principal issues, reported in table 6.5, as well as several minor ones. The issue most commonly discussed by Komi nationalists concerned general economic problems in the republic, including the current economic crisis,[84] the republic's low level of economic development,[85] and concerns about privatization.[86] Other issues raised by Komi nationalists included language and education (the declining use of Komi, the argument that the president should be required to speak Komi and the lack of Komi education available in the republic); the lack of state sovereignty; poverty in the Komi village; the need for economic sovereignty, meaning that Moscow should cede to Komi the right to control the natural resources located on republican territory;[87] the rebirth of national consciousness among the Komi; political institutions within the republic, such as the presidency and legislature; ecological devastation; Komi culture and history (such as the purging of the Komi intelligentsia

---

83. The letter's author argued that graduates of Komi language schools should be given priority in admittance to higher education and that people working in service professions should be required to speak Komi. He also advocated complete sovereignty: i.e. Komi should leave the RSFSR. V. Sazhin, "Prekratit kolonialnyi grabezh" [Put an End to Colonial Plunder], *Krasnoe znamia*, May 16, 1991, 3.

84. A. Smirnov, "Po puti vozrozhdeniia." Sazhina, "Dvukhpalatnyi parlament pod trekhtsvetnym flagom" [A Bicameral Parliament under a Tricolor Flag], *Respublika*, December 8, 1993, 1; V. Timin, "Posle s'ezda" [After the congress] *Respublika*, May 9, 1991. "Ia realist" [I'm a realist] *Respublika*, March 1, 1991, 2.

85. "Priniaty rezoliutsii" [Resolutions passed] Krasnoe Znamia, January 15, 1991, 1.

86. V. Kanev, "Ne replikami a delom nuzhno reshat' mezhnatsional'niye voprosy" [Not through Retorts but through Deeds Should We Decide Interethnic Questions], *Respublika*, November 22, 1991, 2. O. Sazhina, "Na III s'ezde Komi naroda [At the third congress of the Komi nation], *Respublika*, December 6, 1993, 1.

87. Viktor Makarov, "Tsentr ne skryvayet svoikh pritiazanie" [The Center Is Not Hiding Its Claims], *Respublika*; "Osnovnye polozheniia predvybornoi programmy" [The Main Positions of the Election Program], *Respublika*, December 3, 1993, 2.; V. Kanev, "Ne replikami a delom nyzhno re-shat', 2; "Ne zakhvat vlasti a iziavlenie voli Komi naroda" [Not a Power Grab but the Expression of the Will of the Komi people], *Respublika*, November 29, 1991, 1, 2. One nationalist also advocated the nationalization of all enterprises located in the republic in V. Osipov, "V odinochku vyzhit' trudnee" [It's Harder to Survive on Your Own], *Respublika*, January 1, 1991, 1, 3.

under Stalin); establishing a Komi presidency; and demographic decline among
the Komi population, as well as several others.[88] As this long list suggests, Komi
nationalists did not suffer a lack of imagination in identifying and discussing
the various problems in the republic. Yet, as stated above, no articles mentioned
the unequal representation of Komi in the republican workforce by comparison
with Russians. The closest the nationalists came to discussing the idea of Komi
economic underrepresentation and blocked life chances was their reference to
poverty in Komi villages.

Nationalists discussed the problem of the "Komi village" fairly frequently, in
nine articles. Indigenous rural dwellers, according to the nationalists, experienced a drop in "quality of life" during the Soviet era,[89] as a lower standard of
living existed there than in the republic's urban areas.[90] According to the nationalists, Komi's rural regions suffered not only from economic shortages brought
on by the collapsing Soviet economy but from poverty more generally, as well as
from environmental degradation caused by Soviet industrialization. The leader
of Komi Kotyr stated the need to "revive the Komi village"[91] and the KVKN
passed a resolution at the first national congress calling for the protection of the
rural indigenous population.[92]

What is interesting about the nationalists' focus on problems of Komi villages
is that they did not ethnify the problem, though it would have been relatively easy
for them to do so. No articles, for example, compared Komi villagers to Russians
by describing an ethnic division of labor. In discussing the subject, the nationalists
depicted the Komi as victims in two articles but also depicted both the republic as
a whole as a victim (two articles) and the entire republican population as victim
(one article). None of the articles, furthermore, assigned blame for the poverty of
the village to Russians. Instead, the nationalists blamed the Soviet system (three
articles), the republican government (two articles), and the central state (one article). They alleged, for example, that the administration was not doing anything to
protect the impoverished rural population, which was sure to suffer from market

88. Other nationalist issues included the privatization of land, the establishment of a nationalities agency, and a short-lived separatist movement among Russian miners in the city of Vorkuta, an
important industrial site in Komi among Russian miners. "Otkazalis' ot deklaratsii" [(We've) Abandoned the Declaration], *Respublika*, March 15, 1991, 3.

89. K. Korolev and E. Tsypanov, "Chtoby ne ushla 'tikhaia radost'" [So That a Calm Happiness
Remains] *Respublika*, October 4, 1991.

90. V. Osipov, "V odinochku vyzhit' trudnee" 1991; Gennady Ushkov, "Segodnia otkryvaetsia
pervyi s"ezd Komi naroda" [The First Congress of the Komi People Opens Today], *Krasnoe Znamia*,
January 11, 1991.

91. Ibid.

92. V. Kiselev, "K s"ezdu—Za polnomochiyem" [To Congress—For Full Powers], *Respublika*, October 18, 1991, 4.

Table 6.5 Discourse analysis of Komi newspapers

ISSUE ARTICULATED BY KOMI NATIONALISTS	NUMBER OF ARTICLES MENTIONING THE ISSUE (OUT OF 48 ARTICLES)
Economic problems/crisis	14
Language/education	13
Lack of state sovereignty	9
Impoverished Komi village	9
Lack of economic sovereignty	7
Rebirth of national consciousness	6
Political institutions	6
Ecological devastation	6
Culture/Komi history	2
Republican presidency	3
Demographic decline	3
Other	3

reform,[93] and they criticized the supreme soviet for focusing on the energy sector instead of the village. The nationalists did a very poor job of identifying solutions to the problem of poverty in the village. In only two articles did they present a concrete plan of action: one advocated a return to the kolkhoz farming structure, but with private ownership instead of leasing the land from the state, and another recommended giving, rather than selling, land to the peasants. Neither of those articles assigned responsibility, though the former criticized the republican government for not implementing this solution.

ISSUE FRAMING: ATTRIBUTION OF BLAME

As in Mari El, Komi nationalists were very reluctant to place blame for the republic's problems on ethnic Russians. The founder of Komi Kotyr and chairman of the Komi Writers' Union, Gennady Ushkov, even specifically stated that it was the system and not Russians who were to blame,[94] while other nationalists repeatedly emphasized ethnic inclusiveness.[95] Many articles, for example, mentioned that the nationalist movement was open to all nationalities and that the problems of the republic must be solved by all of them. Several repeated that the nationalist groups were not pursuing "narrowly national goals" (*uzkonatsional'nye tseli*) and that the charter of Komi Kotyr stipulated that members could be of any nationality.[96] In only a single article did Komi nationalists place blame on Russians.

---

93. Ibid.

94. Ushkov, "Segodnia otkryvaietsia pervyii s"ezd komi naroda," 1.

95. However, the authors of several letters to the editor did attribute blame to Russians.

96. This ethnic inclusivism may have been due to the nationalists' recognition that they needed to attract a larger portion of the republic's population than just ethnic Komis, who made up only 23 percent of the total. Osipov, "V odinochku vyzhit' trudnee."

In general, Komi nationalists spread around the blame for problems facing the Komi, assigning it most often to republican political authorities (seven articles) and to the central state (six articles). They castigated the central state for failing to grant the republic control over its economy, its natural resources, and its mining enterprises. For example, a leader of the KVKN argued that the republic should win control of "strategic raw materials" away from Russia so that it would not be "deprived of the right to use its own natural resources."[97] Two years later the nationalists argued that despite the declaration of sovereignty, the Russian Federation still managed and set the prices for the raw materials in the energy sector extracted in Komi. If Moscow did not grant economic sovereignty to the republic, they said, "we will continue to live in poverty."[98] The nationalists sometimes blamed the central state along with the republican government, as when the KVKN criticized the supreme soviet for allowing some "higher-ups to maneuver behind closed doors…to promote the colonial interests of the center." The committee also criticized Komi's government for simply duplicating laws passed by the RSFSR, which, they said, expropriated property from the people.[99]

Komi nationalists also blamed the Soviet system and its policies (four articles)—such as the in-migration of Russian speakers and industrialization for environmental degradation, the end of native language education, and the decline of traditional Komi livelihoods like hunting, fishing, animal husbandry, and agriculture. Some nationalists attributed the drop in the standard of living among Komi living in the countryside to Soviet industrialization.[100] Two articles specifically blamed the Stalin era for repression of the Komi intelligentsia.[101] Nationalist discourse directed blame most often to political authorities, holding them responsible for the issue that concerned the nationalists the most: the republic's economy. One journalist described delegates and resolutions passed at the Komi national congresses as blaming everyone, including "the federal government, the party, the republic's supreme soviet and the monopolies who steal the national wealth."[102]

ISSUE FRAMING: IDENTIFYING A SOLUTION

My analysis of Komi nationalist discourse identified ten different solutions to the various problems and issues in Komi articulated by the nationalists. Strikingly,

---

97. Kanev, "Ne replikami a delom,"
98. Makarov, "Tsentr ne skryvayet."
99. Ibid.
100. Korolev and Tsypanov, "Chtoby ne ushla."
101. Ibid.; A. Beznosikov "Zemlia—bogova, no rodina—nasha," [The land belongs to God, but the homeland is ours] *Krasnoe Znamia. January 3, 1992, 2.*
102. "Po puti vozrozhdeniia."

only one article presented republican sovereignty as a solution. More often (in three articles), the nationalists identified economic sovereignty—i.e., winning control of natural resources on Komi's territory away from Moscow—as a solution. Other ideas varied widely and included greater cooperation with the Komi administration (three articles); adopting a bilateral treaty with Russia (two articles); raising recognition that the territory of the republic belonged to ethnic Komis (one article); creating a state agency, or Goskomnats, in charge of nationalities issues (two articles); establishing a chamber in Komi's parliament made up exclusively of ethnic Komi deputies (one article); and appealing to the United Nations in the event that it adopted a declaration on the rights of indigenous people (two articles).[103] Thus, in comparison with the nationalist republics, the issue of republican sovereignty did not form a central goal of the movement.

Overall, Komi nationalists failed to articulate any claims concerning the underrepresentation of Komi in the republic's economy but focused instead on issues of macroeconomic crisis and language and education. Nor did the nationalists place blame on ethnic Russians; they directed blame toward republican and central authority. Finally, nationalists did not identify achieving sovereignty as the solution to the republic's various problems. Rather, they recommended various types of solutions, emphasizing greater economic autonomy in which Moscow would grant the republic increased control over the natural resources on its territory.

This chapter has argued that historical, economic, and social events that occur in a multiethnic society do not automatically engender ethnic grievances. Instead, political entrepreneurs intentionally construct grievances by framing events or social conditions as unjust, intolerable, and in dire need of rectification. In Russia's republics, ethnic entrepreneurs infused meaning into people's experience of events and economic conditions in order to establish a link between the supposed subordinate position of titular ethnic groups and the need to acquire political sovereignty. The way in which nationalist leaders framed issues of ethnic economic inequality created such a link. When they articulated issues that emphasized culture, history, religion, and language, they were not as successful in attracting mass support.

Evidence from a comparative case study analysis, including a comparison of nationalist founding documents and a discourse analysis of newspaper articles in Russia's republics, demonstrates that populations in the republics did not automatically throw their support behind nationalist leaders. They did not reflexively

---

103. "Ne zakhvat vlasti."

respond to nationalists who articulated language and cultural issues or economic issues concerning expropriation of natural resources by a redistributing central state. This was the case in the republics of Mari El and Komi. I demonstrate instead that mass publics backed nationalism when nationalists framed issues of ethnic underrepresentation in local economies vis-à-vis Russians, attributed blame for the problem to ethnic Russians and the political authorities supposedly representing those Russians, and identified the solution as wholesale transformation of the status quo through achieving state sovereignty. In the republics of Tatarstan, Tuva, Chechnya, Yakutia, and Bashkortostan, where nationalist discourse about ethnic economic inequality was present, mass populations mobilized behind opposition nationalist movements in the early 1990s.

SECESSIONISM FROM THE BOTTOM UP

Democratization, Nationalism, and Local Accountability in Russia

This chapter addresses secessionist campaigns mounted by Russia's republics vis-à-vis Moscow in the early 1990s. It asks why some republics made strong demands on Moscow for increased autonomy, sovereignty, or even independence while other republics did not. In contrast to existing explanations that see republican wealth as the motivating force behind secession, the approach developed here brings politics back into the study of secessionism. I argue that disintegration of the Soviet Union's centralized, single-party system produced a contest for political control inside Russia's republics and that that contest determined the strength of separatist demands the republics made on Moscow. With the massive transformations of late perestroika, communist leaders in the republics suddenly found themselves accountable to local constituencies rather than to Moscow. Three key aspects of democratization at the center produced this shift in accountability. First, the dissolution of the Communist Party ended the nomenklatura system in which regional leaders were appointed according to party lists maintained by Moscow. Second, the first semicompetitive elections to republican parliaments were held in 1990, introducing new representatives with new ideas into what had been rubber-stamp legislatures. Third, Gorbachev's glasnost policies allowed informal organizations to emerge and employ grassroots tactics such as mass demonstrations. In certain republics the most popular, visible, and vocal of these organizations became ethnonationalist movements, which developed into a critical yet commonly overlooked variable in Russia's transition. These three aspects of liberalization transformed Russia's republics within a very short time from hollow administrative units into new competitive arenas or, in the words of Carol Leff, "separate and distinct political marketplaces."[1]

Once we recognize that change in the center restructured the incentives of republican leaders by creating a contest for local control, it is possible to theorize how relations among subfederal actors—nomenklatura leaders, opposition nationalist movements, and mass publics—influenced secessionism vis-à-vis Moscow. In those republics where nationalist movements were gaining popularity, the very visible fact of growing crowds at rallies and the rising status of opposition leaders on the street and in local parliaments represented a palpable threat to incumbents. Communist leaders were pressured into addressing nationalist programs and petitioning Moscow for autonomy. In other republics, nationalists replaced nomenklatura leaders and led campaigns for sovereignty themselves. These scenarios occurred in republics that mounted the strongest challenges to federal authority: Tatarstan, Tuva, Chechnya, Yakutia, and Bashkortostan. Conversely, in republics where nationalist movements failed to attract support, incumbents could ignore nationalist appeals with impunity and remain safely in office. This variation in popular support for nationalism can explain the level of republican secessionism toward Moscow.

In the first section of the chapter, I briefly describe republican campaigns for sovereignty vis-à-vis Moscow and then introduce a coding of republican secessionism based on actions initiated by the republics as well as their responses to policies initiated by Moscow. Then I analyze how a shift in political accountability facing republican leaders allowed mass nationalist mobilization to exert a significant influence on republican separatist campaigns. In the third section I present evidence for my arguments using data showing correlations between secessionism on the one hand and ethnic demonstrations and ethnic violent events in the republics on the other. Finally, brief case studies of three republics demonstrate that mass nationalism in Tuva and Yakutia influenced republican demands on Moscow at key moments in their sovereignty campaigns, whereas low mass nationalism in Mari El resulted in low secessionism there. I maximize variation on the independent variable of mass nationalism by comparing two cases that are representative of Russia's secessionist republics, Tuva and Yakutia, with Mari El, a typical low-secession republic.[2] In addition, the comparison of Tuva and Yakutia undermines the wealth hypothesis because the republics differed in terms of republican wealth but exhibited a common outcome of secessionism. The fact that separatism emerged in the territorially tiny, economically underdeveloped,

---

1. Leff, "Democracy and Disintegration," 210.

2. I use the diverse-case method and the typical-case method to select cases, according to John Gerring's typology in *Case Study Research*.

and resource-poor republic of Tuva and also in the enormous and resource-rich republic of Yakutia suggests that the variable of wealth provides scant causal leverage. Finally, the republics of Tuva, Yakutia, and Mari El are neglected in most studies of nationalism in Russia, which generally examine the high-profile republics of Chechnya and Tatarstan and ignore republics with low nationalism.

Campaigns for Sovereignty in Russia's Republics, 1990–94

To determine levels of secessionism among Russia's republics, I use a fourteen-point coding index based on actions initiated by the republics as well as their responses to Moscow's policies during the years 1989 to 1994. My coding captures the main ways in which the republics challenged Moscow and improves upon previous codings that have relied on a single indicator, omitted key developments in center-periphery relations, and miscoded the critical case of Tuva.[3] The indicators (discussed below) show that the republics that made the strongest secessionist demands on Moscow were Tatarstan, Tuva, Chechnya, Yakutia, and Bashkortostan (see table 7.1).

In the earliest separatist act, all the autonomous republics issued declarations of sovereignty following the RSFSR's momentous decision to do so in June 1990 (indicator 1). For the next year and a half, Gorbachev tried to preserve the Soviet Union and undermine the growing power of Boris Yeltsin by offering more rights to the autonomous republics, even suggesting that their status in a "renewed federation" would match that of the union republics.[4] Yeltsin also promised the ARs greater recognition within a sovereign Russia, but despite his efforts, fewer voters in the republics than in the rest of the RSFSR voted to create a Russian (i.e., Yeltsin) presidency in a March 1991 referendum. Tatarstan, Tuva, Chechnya, and North Ossetia even refused to hold the referendum (indicator 2).[5]

---

3. See Emizet and Hesli's use of the timing of supreme soviets' sovereignty declarations as a single indicator of secessionism in "The Disposition to Secede," 500, and Treisman's miscoding of Tuva in "Russia's Ethnic Revival," in 224–25.

4. Thus a majority of the electorate in the ARs (82.6 percent) voted to preserve the USSR in the March 1991 referendum. See Edward Walker, *Dissolution: Sovereignty and the Breakup of the Soviet Union* (Lanham, Md.: Rowman & Littlefield, 2003), 96, 102, 117; Vladimir Shlapentokh, Roman Levita, and Mikhail Loiberg, *From Submission to Rebellion: The Provinces versus the Center in Russia* (Boulder: Westview, 1997), 91; and Yurii Baturin, "Shakhmatnaia diplomatia v Novo-Ogarevo," *Demokratizatsiia* 2 (Spring 1994): 212–21.

5. Sheehy, "The All-Union and RSFSR Referendums of March 17," 22. Results of the presidential election in June 1991 indicate the same pattern: Yeltsin won 50.6 percent of the votes in the autonomies compared with 58.4 percent in the RSFSR as a whole. Walker, *Dissolution,* 117, 123–24.

Table 7.1   Index of secessionism in Russia's republics, 1989–94

	TATARSTAN	TUVA	CHECHNYA	YAKUTIA	BASHKORTOSTAN	KALMYKIA	KARELIA	BURYATIA	N. OSSETIA	KOMI	KABARDINO-BALKARIA	CHUVASHIA	UDMURTIA	DAGESTAN	MARI EL	MORDOVIA
1) Declared sovereignty	1	1	1	1	1	1	1	1	1	1	1	1	1	1	1	1
2) Boycotted RSFSR presidency referendum, 1991	1	1	1						1							
3) Established presidency	1	1	1	1	1	1	1	1		1	1	1			1	
4) Passed language law	1	1		1				1			1	1				
5) Titular language sole language		1														
6) Set own tax policy/stopped paying taxes	1	1	1	1	1				1							
7) Refused to sign Yeltsin's federation treaty, 1992	1		1													
8) Held sovereignty referendum	1				1											
9) Adopted constitution	1	1	1	1	1	1	1		1	1			1	1		
10) Before new RF constitution?	1	1		1												
11) With right to secede?		1		1												
12) Republic law supreme?	1	1	1	1	1	1	1	1								
13) Boycotted/invalidated referendum on Yeltsin, April 1993	1		1													
14) Boycotted referendum on RF constitution, December 1993	1		1													
Index of secessionism	12	10	9	8	6	4	4	4	4	3	3	3	2	2	2	1

After the Soviet collapse, the republics' behavior diverged. Some scaled back their separatist activity. Others took advantage of central state weakness by establishing presidencies (indicator 3), drafting constitutions, and passing language laws (indicator 4), some of which named the titular language as the sole official state language (indicator 5). When Yeltsin's economic shock therapy reforms led to rampant inflation and reduced central financing of regional budgets, a few republics began to withhold tax revenue and/or set their own tax policy.[6] Tatarstan, Tuva, and Chechnya, for example, nearly stopped paying taxes to Moscow in 1993, while Yakutia and Bashkortostan regularly delayed their tax payments (indicator 6).[7]

---

6. Elizabeth Teague, "Center-Periphery Relations in the Russian Federation," in *National Identity and Ethnicity in Russia and the New States of Eurasia,* ed. Roman Szporluk (Armonk, N.Y.: M.E. Sharpe, 1994), 42; and Darrel Slider, "Federalism, Discord, and Accommodation: Intergovernmental Relations in Post-Soviet Russia," in *Local Power and Post-Soviet Politics,* ed. Theodore Friedgut and Jeffrey Hahn (Armonk, N.Y.: M.E. Sharpe, 1994), 249.

7. North Ossetia declared bankruptcy and also reduced tax payments to Moscow. Shlapentokh, Levita, and Loiberg, *From Submission to Rebellion,* 169. Also see Jeremy Azrael and Emil Payin, eds., *Conflict and Consensus in Ethno-Political and Center-Periphery Relations in Russia* (Santa Monica: Rand Conference Proceedings, 1998), 29.

A constitutional crisis cum power struggle between the executive and legislative branches of Russia's federal government developed, prompting Yeltsin to try to secure the republics' support by drafting a federation treaty, which was to become part of the new Russian constitution. The treaty acknowledged republican sovereignty and granted special rights to ethnic regions. Though most republics voted the treaty into law in March 1992, Tatarstan and Chechnya refused to sign, and Bashkortostan signed only after Moscow added an appendix recognizing its independence. Yakutia also took an oppositional stance throughout the negotiations and signed after obtaining an agreement allowing it to retain part of the revenue from diamonds and gold on its territory (indicator 7).[8]

Around the same time, certain republics initiated highly destabilizing acts. In Tatarstan, 61 percent of the population voted yes in a referendum on state sovereignty that many interpreted as a vote for independence.[9] Bashkortostan held a similar but less radical referendum a year later (indicator 8). In another series of challenges, most republics adopted constitutions (indicator 9). Tatarstan, Tuva, and Yakutia did so prior to the December 1993 referendum on Russia's federal constitution organized by Yeltsin (indicator 10).[10] The boldest republican constitutions contested Moscow's authority by stipulating that republican law took supremacy over federal law and, in the case of Tuva and Yakutia, specified the right to secede (indicators 11 and 12).[11]

In a critical event in April 1993, Yeltsin held a national referendum on his leadership and reformist policies in order to delegitimize the antireform federal legislature. A majority of Russia's population voted for Yeltsin, but support varied in the republics, with six of the sixteen voting against him.[12] Two republics,

---

8. Teague, "Center-Periphery Relations in the Russian Federation," in *National Identity and Ethnicity in Russia and the New States of Eurasia*, ed. Roman Szporluk (Armonk, NY: M.E. Sharpe, 1994); Vera Tolz, "Thorny Road toward Federalism in Russia," *RFE/RL Research Report*, December 3, 1993, 1–8; and Kahn, *Federalism*, 126–32.

9. This perception was reinforced ten days later when Tatarstan refused to sign the federation treaty. Ann Sheehy, "Tatarstan Asserts Its Sovereignty," *RFE/RL Research Report*, April 3, 1992), 1.

10. In fact, the actions of these republics convinced Moscow of the need to replace the federation treaty with a new federal constitution. Tishkov, *Ethnicity, Nationalism and Conflict in and after the Soviet Union* (Thousand Oaks, Calif.: Sage, 1997), 62.

11. Most constitutions asserted control over natural resources and gave both Russian and the titular language official status. See Teague, "Center-Periphery Relations" in Szporluk, ed., 43; Kahn, *Federalism*, 82–84; and Gorenburg, Minority Ethnic Mobilization. For the constitutions' full texts, see Iu. A. Dmitriev and E. L. Malakhova, *Konstitutsii respublik v sostave Rossiiskoi Federatsii* [Republican constitutions of the Russian Federation] (Moscow: Izdatel'skaia Firma Manuscript, 1995).

12. Bashkortostan, Dagestan, Kabardino-Balkaria, Mari El, Chuvashia, and Mordovia voted against Yeltsin. In Tuva, a majority endorsed Yeltsin's reform policies (in questions one and two) but also voted for early presidential elections—signaling a rejection of Yeltsin. Wendy Slater, "No Victors in the Russian Referendum," *RFE/RL Research Report*, May 21, 1993, 10–19. However, an anti-Yeltsin vote was not necessarily a challenge to federal authority since some republics voted against him to signal support for the Supreme Soviet's conservative policies of preserving federal subsidies

Tatarstan and Chechnya, blatantly defied federal rule by refusing to hold the referendum on their territory (indicator 13).[13] The republics maintained the initiative in relations with the center until September 1993, when Russia's constitutional crisis came to a head and Yeltsin rashly passed a decree dissolving parliament. Several republics condemned or ignored his decree during the two-week standoff in which deputies refused to leave the parliament building in Moscow. A majority of republics, however, softened their stance following Yeltsin's drastic decision to shell parliament and arrest the opposition. Most republics complied with his ensuing order to hold new local parliamentary elections, but Tatarstan and Chechnya obdurately boycotted a national referendum on Russia's constitution (indicator 14).[14]

Some analysts believe Yeltsin's dissolution of parliament averted Russia's collapse. Whether or not that belief is accurate, it did permit the central government to consolidate power, beginning with the passage of the Russian constitution. Another important development was Moscow's decision to sign bilateral treaties with several republics. Yet by the time this occurred in the mid-1990s, mass nationalism was fading in even the most assertive republics. Nationalist movements had been losing support, in some cases as early as 1993. This suggests that declining subfederal political competition led to lower levels of secessionism vis-à-vis Moscow. By the mid-1990s, republican separation from Russia had become unlikely. Yeltsin's centralization of power altered Russia's entire institutional environment, shifting power from republican parliaments to executives and eliminating the massive central state weakness that had made possible republican challenges to federal sovereignty in the early 1990s.

Democratization, Shifting Accountability, and Nationalism

During the Soviet era political accountability ran vertically from center to region, with the Communist Party in Moscow appointing republican leaders according to the nomenklatura system. Regional party leaders were selected and

---

to the regions. Ralph Clem and Peter Craumer, "The Geography of the April 25 (1993) Russian Referendum," *Post-Soviet Geography* 34, no. 8 (October 1993): 481–96.

13. Chechnya boycotted the referendum, and Tatarstan's administration discouraged voting, a fact that resulted in a 22.6 percent voter turnout, which invalidated the republic's results.

14. Seven republics voted for the constitution, five voted against it, and voter turnout was under 50 percent in two republics. Lapidus and Walker, "Nationalism, Regionalism, and Federalism," 100–101. On local elections, see Elizabeth Teague, "North-South Divide: Yeltsin and Russia's Provincial Leaders," *RFE/RL Research Report*, November 26, 1993, 7–23.

dismissed on the basis of central party decisions.[15] These nomenklatura leaders in turn controlled the appointment of party and managerial cadres within their republics.[16] But Gorbachev embarked on a strategy of shifting power away from the CPSU and toward central and regional legislatures.[17] In 1988 he undermined the power of the central party apparat and later eliminated article 6 of the Soviet constitution, which had granted the CPSU a monopoly.[18] After the 1991 coup attempt, the party's remaining legitimacy rapidly drained away. The Soviet legislature suspended all party activity, and two months later Yeltsin formally banned the Communist Party in Russia.[19] With the party's collapse, the Soviet Union's main integrative institution disappeared, shattering accountability of local leaders to the center.

Vertical accountability was also eroded by Gorbachev's decision to hold semicompetitive elections in 1990 to replace nomenklatura in federal and local legislatures, or supreme soviets. Nomenklatura maintained a majority of seats, but independent deputies served alongside them in many republics, introducing ideas that would have been unthinkable just a few years earlier. Independents won seats despite the fact that local party nomenklatura were loath to give up control and blocked informal groups from nominating candidates directly.[20] Although supreme soviets in many republics did not experience a significant change in membership, those that did permitted increasingly open debate. Moreover, the presence of new nationalist deputies reshaped the loyalties of other deputies in parliament. In Tatarstan, for example, candidates affiliated with nationalist organizations won in only a handful of electoral districts, but once they were elected to the supreme soviet, they gained the backing of some independent and nomenklatura deputies to form a pronationalist voting bloc. Similarly, Chechnya's supreme soviet had evolved a liberal wing by 1990 that was sympathetic to the emerging nationalist movement.[21] In certain republics, then, both newly elected representatives and "reborn" nomenklatura deputies helped to transform rubber-stamp legislatures into fledgling representative institutions.

---

15. Jeffrey Hahn, "Introduction: Analyzing Parliamentary Development in Russia," in *Democratization in Russia: The Development of Legislative Institutions,* ed. Jeffrey Hahn (Armonk, N.Y.: M.E. Sharpe, 1996).

16. Kryshtanovskaia, "Transformation of the Old Nomenklatura into a New Russian Elite."

17. Stephen Kotkin, *Armageddon Averted: The Soviet Collapse, 1970–2000* (New York: Oxford University Press, 2001).

18. Ibid., 75–85.

19. Stephen White, Graeme Gill, and Darrell Slider, *The Politics of Transition: Shaping of a Post-Soviet Future* (Cambridge: Cambridge University Press, 1993).

20. Slider, "Federalism, Discord, and Accommodation," 296–97.

21. Kudriavtsev, "Democratic Values and Political Reality."

The supreme soviets then elected new chairmen to lead the parliament. The chairman replaced the top post in the republic's governing body—party first secretary of the Obkom. This further reduced the authority of the CPSU. Most of these new chairmen came from the communist nomenklatura, though not, generally, from its old-guard, conservative wing. Some of them, moreover, were reformers sympathetic to nationalist ideas. In Chechnya, for example, the Soviet chairman, Doku Zavgayev, was a reformer and had begun legalizing Islamic activity and replacing party conservatives with members of the Chechen intelligentsia while still serving as Obkom first secretary in 1989.[22] One republic—Tuva—even elected the leader of the nationalist movement as chairman of the republic's supreme soviet. However, in most republics, the new Soviet chairmen, such as Mikhail Nikolaev in Yakutia and Murtaza Rakhimov in Bashkortostan, were moderate, pragmatic politicians interested in retaining or augmenting their personal political power. In general, competitive elections endowed independent deputies as well as local parliaments with a new kind of legitimacy, one that originated in the localities rather than Moscow.[23] Rubber-stamp soviets were transformed into fledgling representative institutions.

Furthermore, Gorbachev's democratization policies allowed opposition nationalist groups to emerge and openly articulate heterodox ideas.[24] Initially, nationalist activists acted cautiously so as to avoid provoking punishment from republican authorities. Sometimes nationalists were fired from their jobs, beaten up, and arrested. But after Gorbachev removed particular corrupt regional leaders who opposed reform, and as the popularity of the nationalists grew, republican leaders adopted a more self-interested approach in dealing with the nationalist opposition.

As opposition movements developed a mass following in Tatarstan, Tuva, Chechnya, Yakutia, and Bashkortostan, leaders there took note. They watched as new constituencies started to seize the political initiative. Incumbents observed rising support for nationalism by looking out their office windows at mass demonstrations held on central squares, by reading impassioned debates in the local press, and by monitoring nationalist group activity. They watched as pillars of the Soviet establishment became targets of organized campaigns against corruption and mismanagement. In Tatarstan, for example, nationalists led a grassroots campaign that resulted in the expulsion of several old-guard communists

22. Ibid., 359.

23. Gavin Helf and Jeffrey Hahn, "Old Dogs and New Tricks: Party Elites in the Russian Regional Elections of 1990," *Slavic Review* 51, no. 3 (Fall 1992): 511–530.

24. See Herrera's discussion on the challenge to orthodox Soviet ideology and institutions in *Imagined Economies*, 98–142.

from the republican Obkom. Opposition groups in Bashkortostan went further, voting no confidence in the republic's entire party leadership and driving it from power.[25]

Another way that the nationalists put pressure on local governments was by establishing national congresses. Nationalist groups formed national congresses in an attempt to supplant republican supreme soviets. The congresses exerted varying levels of influence on the soviets, depending on the degree of popular support for nationalism in the republic. In Komi, for example, where popular support for nationalism was low, the nationalist Second Congress of the Komi People demanded that the republic's supreme soviet adopt all its resolutions. The government ignored the demands.[26] But when the founding meeting of the Chechen National Congress in 1990 passed a resolution on state sovereignty, Chechnya's supreme soviet did the same two days later.[27] Thus, though the congresses were ultimately unsuccessful as alternative parliaments, the demands they raised in the republics with significant mass nationalism prompted supreme soviets to respond.

Most important, nationalist organizations sponsored mass demonstrations, rallies, pickets, and an occasional hunger strike in front of government buildings, where they could attract maximum attention. Tatarstan, as described in chapter 4, was home to 142 nationalist demonstrations with thousands of participants. In Bashkortostan, the nationalist Union of Bashkir Youth marched on the television station and went on air to denounce the supreme soviet's vote to delay presidential elections.[28] These acts stimulated public debate and won massive media attention, while demonstrators risking arrest, job loss, and physical injury sent signals of strong commitment to their cause. All these events increased the power and resources nationalists wielded within the political arena.

For nomenklatura leaders unaccustomed to considering popular opinion, a misstep was potentially fatal. Shaimiev, the president of Tatarstan, learned this lesson after he responded to the attempted coup against Gorbachev by clamping down on opposition forces within the republic. When the coup failed, opposition groups began a grassroots campaign to impeach him. The campaign eventually fizzled out as nationalist groups decided that since Shaimiev was an ethnic

---

25. At this point several Bashkir nationalists joined the republic's interim leadership. "Bashkir Oblast Party Leaders Resign" *RFE/RL Research Report,* February 23, 1990, 47–48; and "Plenary Sessions Held," *Pravda,* February 11, 1990, 2, in *Current Digest of the Soviet Press* 42, no. 6 (1990): 26.

26. Iurii Shabaev, "Peculiarities of Nation-Building in the Republic of Komi," in *Nation-Building and Common Values in Russia,* ed. Pal Kolsto and Helge Blakkisrud, (Lanham, Md.: Rowman & Littlefield, 2004.)

27. Alexei Kudriavtsev, "Democratic Values and Political Reality."

28. "Protest in Bashkiria about Election Postponement," *RFE/RL Research Report,* November 22, 1991.

Tatar, he would ultimately back their interests. Responding to the mass criticism against him, Shaimiev then announced support for republican sovereignty—a position the nationalists had been advocating since glasnost began.[29] The fact that Shaimiev, a good communist apparatchik, supported saving the Soviet Union one moment and demanded state sovereignty the next suggests the impressive political opportunism that produced secessionism in Russia's republics.

Republican leaders could not even necessarily count on enterprise directors to continue to support the status quo. Directors of factories and mines had financial incentives to support the nationalist goal of republican sovereignty, realizing that they could exploit central state weakness to increase ownership of state property under their management. Some directors had already begun to pursue personal profit by forming cooperatives that marketed the products of the state-owned enterprises they managed.[30] In general, perestroika benefited enterprise directors by releasing them from following the economic plan and by reducing monitoring by ministries in Moscow. The increase in local control offered by republican sovereignty could further enlarge these benefits. Ultimately, by the mid-1990s, enterprise directors of lucrative large enterprises in the nationalist republics did profit financially from the increased autonomy their republics won from Moscow.[31]

In addition, the demonstration effect of nationalism in certain union republics served as a warning to leaders in Russia's republics. Together with their populations, they observed how radicalizing nationalist crowds had forced out even the popularly elected presidents Zviad Gamsakhurdia in Georgia and Ayaz Mutalibov in Azerbaijan.[32] Thus, although republican leaders used the threat of ethnic unrest during negotiations with Moscow, they did not foment nationalism simply to strengthen their bargaining position. The risk inherent in such behavior was clear. Popular opinion—instantiated in nationalist rallies, intense public debate, and occasional violence—could turn against them. Like politicians everywhere, republican leaders wanted to satisfy constituents and keep their jobs. Their demands for sovereignty from Moscow were motivated by self-interest.

---

29. Giuliano, "Who Determines the Self?"

30. This began after Gorbachev passed the 1987 Law on Cooperatives. Eric Hanley, Natasha Yershova, and Richard Anderson, "Russia—Old Wine in a New Bottle? The Circulation and Reproduction of Russian Elites, 1983–1993," *Theory and Society* 24 (October 1995): 639–68.

31. So did former nomenklatura political leaders. For example, the oil company Tatneft underwent little restructuring and remained controlled by Tatarstan's Soviet-era managers. See Leo McCann, "Embeddedness, Markets and the State: Observations from Tatarstan," in *Russian Transformations: Challenging the Global Narrative,* ed. Leo McCann (New York: RoutledgeCurzon, 2004), 8: 173–90; and Jozsef Borocz and Akos Rona-Tas, "Small Leap Forward: Emergence of New Economic Elites," *Theory and Society* 24 (October 1995): 751–81.

32. White, Gill, and Slider, *Politics of Transition,* 103.

An alternative hypothesis might argue that the key variable influencing secessionism was whether republican incumbents repressed or co-opted nationalist groups soon after they formed, denying them the ability to win popular support and pressure local leaders. Yet comparing the republics, we observe no correlation between repression/co-optation and weak nationalist movements or between nonrepression/non-co-optation and popular nationalist movements. Party leaderships in most republics were changing as a result of personnel reforms in 1989, supreme soviet elections in 1990, and the anti-Gorbachev coup in 1991 and were therefore either unable to repress or uninterested in doing so. For example, Chuvashia's leadership was under fire from the democratic opposition for corruption, failed to control the 1990 parliamentary elections, and was ultimately deposed for supporting the coup.[33] This gave Chuvashia's nationalists an opening to attract support, which they nonetheless failed to do. Even conservative party leaderships did not co-opt or repress nationalist movements in republics where they retained power. In Mari El, a conservative supreme soviet chairman replaced a conservative Obkom leader, yet the nationalist group Mari Ushem was able to field a presidential candidate. Despite this, Mari Ushem attracted minimal popular support.[34] Finally, in Tatarstan, nationalist groups won support even when authorities used repressive tactics early on to dilute their influence. In short, republican leadership was contested during this time, and executives did not control republican politics.[35] By the mid-1990s, however, when popular support for nationalism had dwindled, republican presidents were able to disregard the weakened opposition and consolidate power.

Mass Nationalism and Republican Sovereignty Campaigns

Popular support for nationalism influenced republican secessionism both directly, by electing nationalist candidates to republican legislatures, and indirectly, by pressuring incumbent leaders concerned with self-preservation. I provide two types of evidence of the effect of mass nationalism on republican secession. First, I show that both the number of ethnic demonstrations and the instances of ethnic violence in the republics are correlated with the level, or index, of republican secessionism presented above. Three graphs below depict the relationship between these variables. Second, case study evidence from Tuva and Yakutia

33. Gorenburg, *Minority Ethnic Mobilization*, 62–3, 72.
34. Muzaev, *Etnicheskii separatizm*, 159–63.
35. White, Gill, and Slider, *Politics of Transition*, 101.

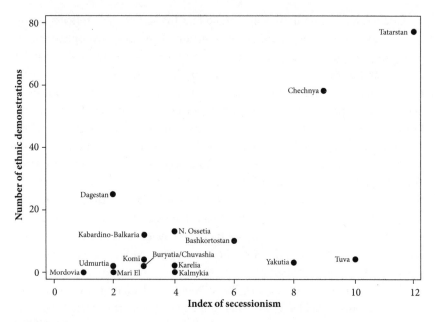

FIGURE 7.1   Number of ethnic demonstrations in Russia's republics versus index of secessionism

shows how mass nationalism increased those republics' secessionist demands on Moscow, while evidence from Mari El indicates that low mass nationalism kept secessionism to a minimum there.

In Figure 7.1, we observe a relationship between the number of demonstrations and the republics with the highest secessionism scores. These two variables are significantly correlated (.661; p≤.005).[36] For example, the highly secessionist Tatarstan and Checheno-Ingushetia had 77 and 58 demonstrations, respectively, while the minimally secessionist republics of Mordovia and Mari El had none. However, in other secessionist republics, there were few demonstrations: Bashkortostan (10), Tuva (4), and Yakutia (3).

The late Soviet and early post-Soviet years generated much popular protest by many groups on a variety of issues. Examining ethnic demonstrations as a percentage of total demonstrations, we see in figure 7.2 that this variable is also correlated with republican secessionism (.518; p≤.05). In the highly secessionist republics of Tatarstan, Tuva, and Checheno-Ingushetia, a majority of demonstrations (between 60 percent and 100 percent) concerned ethnic issues. In

---

36. The variables of ethnic demonstrations and ethnic violence are from Mark Beissinger's dataset of mobilization events in the Soviet Union, as described in chapter 2. Codebook, "Non-Violent Demonstrations," 4, 6.

the secessionist republics of Yakutia and Bashkortostan between 40 percent and 50 percent of demonstrations concerned ethnic issues. Note that the three North Caucasian republics of Dagestan, Kabardino-Balkaria, and North Ossetia have low secessionism scores yet a high number of ethnic demonstrations. This can be explained by the fact that most demonstrations in these republics concerned issues other than ethnonational sovereignty including the repatriation of ethnic groups deported by Stalin and expressions of sympathy with the neighboring republics of Abkhazia and South Ossetia in their violent conflicts with the Georgian central state.[37] Ethnic demonstrations in Dagestan, Kabardino-Balkaria, and North Ossetia did not develop into secessionism.

Several republics experienced ethnic violence during the years 1987–92. Ethnic violence or violence that republican residents *perceived* to be related to ethnic identity indicated a deterioration of relations between titulars and Russians. In some republics interethnic relations worsened as nationalist mobilization progressed, leading to isolated instances of inter-ethnic violence. In such places, the ethnic violence was related to campaigns for sovereignty. In other republics, ethnic violence had nothing to do with sovereignty campaigns. As shown in figure 7.3, the largest number of ethnic violent events occurred in the secessionist republics of Checheno-Ingushetia (21), Tatarstan (6), Tuva (7), and Yakutia (2). In contrast, the low-secession republics witnessed little to no ethnic violence during this period. North Ossetia is again an outlier because of the violent conflict that took place between Ingush and Ossetians in the fall of 1992, which was not related to a campaign for sovereignty.[38] Thus mass violent events and secessionism were statistically correlated but less strongly so than the variables of ethnic demonstrations and secessionism (.438; p≤.10).

Though suggestive, demonstrations and ethnic violence are not comprehensive indicators of popular support for nationalism. Case study evidence more accurately captures how mass nationalism influenced republican campaigns for sovereignty at critical junctures. Below I compare the republics of Tuva, Yakutia, and Mari El, which differed in terms of popular support for nationalism. Tuva and Yakutia are representative of republics where mass nationalism pressured incumbent leaders into adopting nationalist policies and making secessionist

---

37. Concerning repatriation issues, Akkintsy clashed with neighboring ethnic groups in Dagestan; Balkars challenged Kabardins in Kabardino-Balkaria, and Ingush made claims in the Prigorodnii region of North Ossetia. In terms of the violent conflicts, North Ossetia supported South Ossetia against Georgia by taking Ossetian refugees and sending aid and volunteer fighters, while Kabardino-Balkaria took the side of Abkhazia against Georgia. See Jane Omrod, "The North Caucasus: Confederation in Conflict," in *New States, New Politics,* ed. Ian Bremmer and Ray Taras, 96–107 (Cambridge: Cambridge University Press, 1997).

38. Tomila Lankina discusses ethnic conflict and mobilization in North Ossetia in *Governing the Locals,* ch. 5.

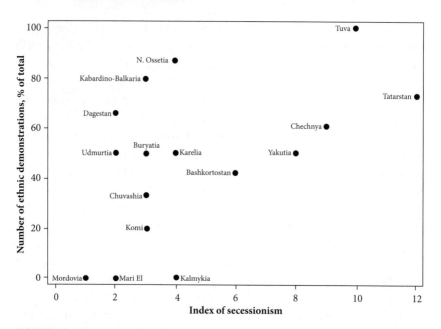

FIGURE 7.2   Number of ethnic demonstrations as a percentage of total demonstrations in Russia's republics versus index of secessionism

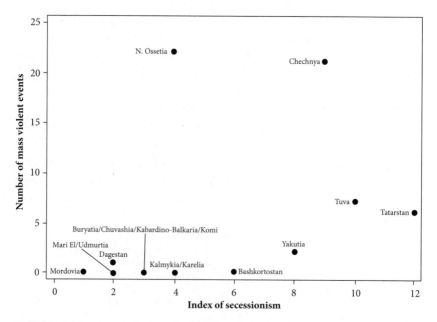

FIGURE 7.3   Number of ethnic mass violent events in Russia's republics versus index of secessionism.

demands. Mari El, conversely, is typical of those republics where low levels of mass nationalism allowed incumbents to ignore opposition nationalist movements and remain in office.

Case Studies

The Republic of Tuva

Tuva made strong secessionist demands on Moscow and offers solid evidence that popular support for nationalism influenced republican campaigns for sovereignty. As discussed in chapter 6, the nationalist movement in Tuva found significant popular support among the population. Several members of nationalist organizations were elected to Tuva's supreme soviet in 1990 and 1993, and the leader of the nationalist movement, Kaadyr-ool Bicheldei, served in the highest post in the republic—chairman of the supreme soviet. The republic experienced very high levels of ethnic violence in the early 1990s as rising Russian-Tuvan tension caused people to perceive violent crimes as ethnically motivated.

Popular support for nationalism exerted the greatest pressure on republican policy during the crafting and adoption of Tuva's constitution in 1993. Two issues defined public debate: Tuva's new constitution and the republic's right to secede from Russia. After a popular referendum, both NPST and Khostug Tuva actively lobbied for a constitutional amendment allowing Tuva the right to secede. The issue of secession was widely debated in the media and among the general population in "kitchen conversations." According to a local (Russian) analyst whose husband served in Tuva's parliament during the debate, the drafting of the constitution elicited high concern among the population, with most people coming to agree by 1992 that the constitution should include a right to secede.

Khostug Tuva took a more aggressive stance than the NPST, calling for the republic to hold an immediate referendum on secession from Russia. The group constructed a protest "yurt" on Kyzyl's main square to stimulate mass support for the referendum. However, Tuva's supreme soviet, by then renamed the supreme khural, voted against holding a referendum, stating that Tuva was still too economically dependent on Russia to survive independent statehood.[39] Nevertheless, parliamentary deputies heeded general popular opinion on the issue and voted in favor of including a secession amendment in the constitution. The amendment was to serve as a warning to Moscow that Tuva would consider secession if its sovereignty were infringed upon. Because nationalist groups had

---

39. Drobizheva, *Natsional'noe samosoznanie,* 125.

been lobbying for the right to secede since their inception, they considered the amendment's inclusion a victory for their movement.[40] When the constitution was officially adopted several weeks later, it included this key nationalist goal. It also included another amendment backed by the nationalists—a ban on private land ownership—along with a statement that republican law took primacy over federal law.

Another of the NPST's major initiatives consisted of its opposition to the Russian constitution. It sponsored demonstrations protesting the adoption of the federal constitution as part of its electoral campaign in the fall of 1993. The campaign was successful. When both the federal and Tuvan constitutions were put to a popular vote on the same day, December 12, 1993, a majority of Tuva's population voted for Tuva's constitution (53.9 percent) but against the federal constitution. Only 29.8 percent voted to approve the federal constitution.[41] The results of these votes indicate that Tuva's population supported key elements in the program of the Tuvan nationalist movement. The republic's Supreme Khural responded to their preferences.[42]

Despite the influence of the Popular Front in republican politics, by the mid-1990s, popular support for nationalism in Tuva was declining. This decline, together with Yeltsin's consolidation of central state control, began to shift political power away from the parliament led by Bichildei and toward the executive branch. As had been done in other republics, Tuva's new president, Shegir-Ool Oorzhak, co-opted nationalist leaders by offering them government positions. Nevertheless, during the autonomy campaign in the early 1990s, the nationalist movement attracted extensive levels of support among the general population and was able to significantly influence republican policy.

The Republic of Yakutia

Yakutia was another of Russia's secessionist republics, demanding the right from Moscow to control its economy, including the sale of natural resources located on its territory. According to the conventional wisdom, the existence of diamonds, gold, and coal motivated Yakutia's leaders to make secessionist

---

40. Anaibin, "Ethnic Relations in Tuva" in *Culture Incarnate*, ed. Marjorie Balzer (Armonk, N.Y.: M.E. Sharpe, 1995), 104, 110.

41. Tuva's supreme khural had voted to adopt Tuva's constitution earlier that fall, in October, while Yeltsin was busy bombing the federal parliament. Kuzhuget and Tatarintseva, *Etnopoliticheskaia situatsiia v Respublike Tyva*, 9.

42. Ann Sheehy, "Tuva Adopts New Constitution," *RFE/RL Daily Report*, 26 October 1993, 2.

demands.[43] I argue, however, that the key determinant of separatism was the presence of popular support for the Yakut nationalist movement, which was able to exert influence on republican policy. Evidence for this view consists of (1) the election of nationalist candidates to republican legislatures; (2) a moderate level of mass activity, including demonstrations, strikes, and instances of ethnic violence; and (3) popular pressure on the republic's supreme soviet for the adoption of Yakutia's constitution.

The two main nationalist groups in Yakutia were the moderate umbrella organization Sakha Omuk and the more radical Sakha Keskile. Sakha Keskile advocated union republic status for Yakutia and actively supported republican sovereignty. Its founder, the linguist Lazar Afanas'ev, pithily summarized the group's stance as "our sharp politics against those in power." In fact, some Sakha Keskile members were fired from their jobs in provincial cities in Yakutia after the group supported Boris Yeltsin in the 1991 coup attempt.[44] Sakha Omuk, the moderate group, advocated cultural rebirth of the Sakha nation and greater Yakut representation in the top tiers of republican administration and enterprise management, and it demanded that Yakutia keep a greater share of the income from its natural resources.

The nationalist opposition began to win popular support. Several Sakha Omuk candidates were elected to local soviets throughout Yakutia and to the supreme soviet in 1990. Though nomenklatura continued to dominate, Yakut nationalists allied with democrats in the supreme soviet to declare sovereignty in 1990.[45] Sakha Omuk lobbied for the election of Mikhail Nikolaev as the republic's first president. Nikolaev, a product of the Soviet establishment, had just been elected chairman of Yakutia's reconstituted supreme soviet in 1990. When the post of republican president was created one year later, he won a majority (76.7 percent) of the popular vote. The nationalists backed Nikolaev because he supported their interest in greater economic sovereignty and because he was an ethnic Yakut who fulfilled the requirement that the president be able to speak Yakut.[46]

---

43. See, for example, Daniel R. Kempton, "The Republic of Sakha (Yakutia): The Evolution of Centre-Periphery Relations in the Russian Federation," *Europe-Asia Studies* 48 (June 1996): 587–613.

44. Marjorie Mandelstam Balzer, "A State Within a State: The Sakha Republic (Yakutia)," in *Rediscovering Russia in Asia,* ed. Stephen Kotkin and David Wolff (Armonk, N.Y.: M.E. Sharpe, 1995), 139–59.

45. Yakutia changed its name to the Sakha Republic (Yakutia) after declaring sovereignty. The titular nationality uses the ethnonym Sakha whereas Russians use the term Yakut.

46. F. M. Zykov, *Etnopoliticheskaia situatsiia v Respublike Sakha do i posle vyborov 12 dekabria 1993 g.* [Ethnopolitical Situation in the Republic of Sakha before and after the Elections of December 1993] (Moscow: Institute of Ethnography and Anthropology, Russian Academy of Sciences, 1994). Anatolii Khazanov writes that Nikolaev "liked to point out [during negotiations with Yeltsin] that he acted under heavy pressure from Sakha Omuk and that some decisions of Yakutia's parliament were made against his will." See *After the USSR,* 183.

In terms of mass activity, there were several isolated instances of interethnic violence in Yakutia. Marjorie Mandelstam Balzer notes that the everyday ethnic tension that existed between Yakuts and Russians erupted into violence at several points in the 1980s and 1990s.[47] In addition, Yakutia's coal, diamond, and gold miners went on strike during the final years of the Soviet Union. For example, in 1990, in the diamond-mining town of Mirny, where most miners were recent ethnic Russian migrants, a short-lived Russian movement developed, advocating secession from Yakutia and the creation of a "Lena Republic." A relatively low number of demonstrations occurred in Yakutia since the nationalist movement chose not to employ the strategy of mass protest rallies. However, a demonstration held in 1992 indicates how a strong display of popular opinion influenced policy at a critical juncture in republican politics: the vote on Yakutia's constitution.

By spring 1992, Yakutia's parliament and population had been considering for some time whether to adopt a constitution—an act that would be the first of its kind among Russia's republics. The general population and Yakuts in particular actively participated in the debate surrounding its adoption. There were two main issues of contention: whether the constitution should be passed before or after the Russian constitution and whether it should include a right to secede. As the supreme soviet opened its session in April, expectations had risen among the population that it would be adopted. When it became apparent that the parliament was leaning toward allowing Moscow to first hold its vote on the federal constitution, nationalist groups organized a mass demonstration in front of the parliament building calling for the constitution's immediate passage with an amendment guaranteeing a right to secede. The rally was well attended, by both the Yakut intelligentsia and youth from the nationalist student organization Eder Saas (Youth). Protesters at the rally threatened to replace the supreme soviet chairman with the vice chairman if the constitutional vote was not held.[48]

The parliament responded to this pressure by voting for immediate adoption of the constitution and for inclusion of the controversial clause on secession. Sakha Keskile's influence on the population prompted the supreme soviet to meet the group's call for a right to secede. Another of Sakha Keskile's demands, however—that the Yakut nation be labeled the "bearers of state sovereignty"—was rejected. Nevertheless, the passage of the constitution represented an enormously important symbolic event in the republic after a year and a half of tense national debate. The constitution asserted the supremacy of republican law over

---

47. Balzer and Vinokurova, "Nationalism, Interethnic Relations and Federalism."

48. Drobizheva notes that this threat indicated a very radical mood among Yakuts since it would have meant replacing a Yakut with an ethnic Russian. See *Natsional'noe samosoznanie*, 135–52.

federal law and provided for the right to secede. The nationalists considered its adoption their victory and organized a national (*vsyenarodnaia*) public celebration in the central square of the city.[49] By the mid-1990s, however, the nationalist movement's popularity had declined. But the considerable popular support it enjoyed in the early 1990s allowed it to influence key republican policy.

The Republic of Mari El

Mari El was perhaps the least secessionist of Russia's republics. Its government advanced very few initiatives and made almost no demands on Moscow after issuing a declaration of sovereignty in August 1990.[50] For example, the Mari El supreme soviet failed to pass a draft language law written in the early 1990s. It finally passed such a law in 1995, after the period of national revival had ended. The soviet did not adopt a new constitution but amended the one it had adopted in the late 1970s. It was not until 1997 that it finally adopted a new one.[51] The absence of mass nationalist mobilization in Mari El meant that republican leaders felt no pressure to mount a separatist campaign vis-à-vis Moscow.

The two nationalist organizations in Mari El—Mari Ushem and Kugeze Mlande—found little popular support among the mass public, as discussed in the previous chapter. There were few mass demonstrations and no ethnic conflict, and the nationalists had little electoral success in either local or federal elections. Mari Ushem, the main nationalist group, attempted its major initiative in spring of 1992 when it organized the First Congress of the Mari Nation in the capital, Ioshkar-Ola. The congress passed resolutions calling for greater Mari representation in government and identifying Maris as "a national minority in their own republic." Yet it remained moderate, opposing secession and supporting Yeltsin's federation treaty, which was to become part of the Russian constitution.

The following fall, the republican administration began to co-opt the nationalists, deciding to legitimize the Mari nationalist movement by making it "the national representative organization of the Mari nation." The administration financed a second congress with the participation of several key government officials, including the president and vice president. Unsurprisingly, the resolutions it passed mirrored those of the earlier congress sponsored by Mari Ushem: greater

---

49. Ibid., 137; see also Muzaev, *Etnicheskii separatizm*, 206–10.

50. See www.notes.society.ru. It took the supreme soviet until 1995 to pass a language law. Iurii P. Shabaev, "National Movements in the Eastern Finnic Republics of Rossiia" *Anthropology and Archeology of Eurasia* 37, no. 2 (Fall 1998): 48–78.

51. Shabaev, "National Movements."

representation for Maris in organs of power, quotas in elections to the republican parliament, and the creation of conditions for the rebirth of the Mari language.[52]

Although some government officials were among the leaders of the Mari congress, several supreme soviet deputies issued a formal protest to President Zotin stating that the resolutions contradicted existing representative organs and laws. In response, Zotin had the resolutions published in the press along with a statement that they were mere recommendations without any legal status and that the government did not share the group's approach to solving problems.

Popular support for Mari nationalism never moved beyond a narrow layer of the Mari intelligentsia. Thus the administration of Mari El had no need to respond to nationalist initiatives or pressure Moscow for greater autonomy. After 1993 Mari Ushem began to concern itself mainly with language and education issues.[53] Both nationalist groups significantly decreased their activity as members stopped participating in elections and migrated to other voting blocs.[54]

These case studies have shown that popular support for nationalism in Tuva and Yakutia contributed to secessionism. In republics that failed to make secessionist demands, such as Mari El, popular nationalism was virtually absent. Political choices made by mass populations, therefore, and the effect of those choices on the competition for power within republics explain variation in secessionism.

Politics within subfederal regions matters for the development of secessionism. Ethnic federations undergoing democratization produce conditions that may encourage regional separatism. Specifically, the transfer of political accountability from center to region shifts the incentives of regional leaders, forcing them to react to local constituencies in order to retain office. If these constituencies desire autonomy, regional leaders must respond, making separatism not merely an opportunistic strategy but a necessary one for their own political survival. Democratization turns administrative territories into electoral arenas. In Russia, the republics became arenas in which popular support for nationalism pressured local leaders into making separatist demands. Thus the contest for political control of subfederal territories is a critical variable driving regional secession.

These findings have implications for other culturally plural societies concerned with preventing secession, such as Iraq and Afghanistan. The fact of destabilizing campaigns for sovereignty in Russia in the early 1990s implies that democratizing, multiethnic states should avoid establishing subfederal territories that

52. Muzaev, *Etnicheskii separatizm*, 161.
53. Wixman and Frank, "The Middle Volga."
54. Muzaev, *Etnicheskii separatizm*, 162.

overlap with socially recognized ethnic or religious communities. On the other hand, varying levels of secessionism among Russia's republics and the ultimate decline of nationalism suggest that secessionism is not inevitable but depends on the presence and degree of mass nationalism within subfederal territories. And mass nationalism is neither a latent attribute of federal regions nor a simple function of natural resource endowments, nor is it summoned into existence by the manipulations of regional leaders. Consequently, attention should be directed toward understanding both the origins of popular nationalism in ethnofederal states and its role in the elite contest for power within those states.

LESSONS FROM RUSSIA

A Critical View of the Relationship between Ethnic
Elite Claims and Mass Interests

It is by now conventional wisdom in social science that ethnic identity is a contingent, socially constructed phenomenon rather than a primordial one. As the hegemony of primordialist explanations of ethnic mobilization fades, rational choice-based as well as other approaches to the formation of ethnicity and its politicization have appeared. However, while recognizing the constructedness of ethnicity, many of these accounts retain essentialist assumptions concerning the preferences of ethnic groups. In an essentialist understanding of ethnic politics, ethnic group members have fixed, uniform preferences that support a nationalist program. These preferences, furthermore, are conflicting and opposing across ethnic groups. Thus there is a direct line from individual identity to preference formation to nationalist political behavior. This approach, however, tends to underestimate the role of politics in determining people's preferences and to overpredict the incidence of ethnic conflict. It also obscures the thorniest questions of all: why people decide to organize along ethnic lines and how ethnicity is mobilized in support of particular political goals. Perhaps most critically, essentialist understandings of ethnic politics prevent us from recognizing the possibility that mobilization in support of nationalism is not necessarily a permanent or even an enduring outcome.

According to the framework presented in this book, people's preferences in favor of nationalist programs do not inhere in individuals with ethnic affiliations as easily and as automatically as many observers assume. People who share ethnic affiliations, in other words, should not be conceptualized as interest groups or coherent political actors. Even when the ethnic group with which an individual is affiliated occupies a particular economic position vis-à-vis other social groups or people in other regions, and even when an ethnic entrepreneur emerges to represent their putative ethnic group, people with those identities do not necessarily respond. A person who maintains an ethnic identity, even a strongly felt one, does not reflexively throw his or her support behind nationalism. Instead, people's preferences in support of nationalism result from the particular *meanings* that develop among a population in response to proximate experiences, events, and conditions. In other words, the process of political mobilization itself transforms the meaning of ethnicity among a given population into a community defined by a belief that it must control its own state. The sense of nationhood that motivates mobilization, however, may be a fleeting phenomenon. People with ethnic affiliations often abandon the shared sense of nationhood that places primacy on the political control of an independent state. When this happens, nationalist mobilization comes to an end.

Processes in Russia's republics during the transition from Soviet rule suggest one way in which this may occur. Vigorous systemic political and economic change in the late Soviet era structured the kinds of experiences people were undergoing in local republican economies. However, the meaning of these experiences and their relationship to politics were not self-evident. Nationalist political entrepreneurs emerged who imbued these experiences and local economic conditions with particular meanings. They communicated particular messages that associated economic conditions with ethnic identity and the political future of the ethnic group. They attempted to construct an ethnic nation—a group that felt dignity could only be achieved if the nation were able to control its own state.

By examining variation in popular support for nationalism in Russia's republics, I have found that the messages put forward by politicians that helped to generate a sense of nationhood among titular populations were those that linked group subordination and victimhood to an aspect of people's present experiences. Though these experiences may vary across contexts, in Russia they involved concerns central to people's lives: professional achievement and social mobility, the same issues that occupied people in the Soviet Union. Individuals in the republics faced a situation of rising competition for education and jobs that had been brought about by economic development and by the Soviet state's affirmative action policies for titular nationalities. Large numbers of people were seeking educations, jobs, and social status in the modern industrial economy as well as in other high-status, white-collar positions. Macroeconomic contraction in the late 1980s exacerbated this competition. However, these economic conditions by themselves did not polarize republican populations along ethnic lines. It took ethnic political entrepreneurs to invest local conditions with ethnic and political meaning for ethnic boundaries to acquire political significance. Nationalist leaders framed issues about ethnic economic inequality in order to establish boundaries between titular and nontitular persons. They claimed that titulars were unfairly limited in their own republics because they lagged behind Russians in terms of urbanization, education, and professional achievement. The current system, the nationalists claimed, unjustly privileged Russians and denied full participation to titulars in the local economy. Using this framing, nationalist leaders defined titulars as victims, placed blame on a discriminatory state, and claimed that obtaining state sovereignty would restore justice to the nation. For many (though not all) people, these messages resonated by emphasizing a connection between individual sense of self-worth, socio-professional status and ethnicity. Moreover, the messages seemed to provide a logical explanation for people's anxieties about unemployment and their experience of rising competition for resources. Thus, in republics where nationalists articulated a message of ethnic economic inequality—in Tatarstan, Chechnya, Tuva, Bashkortostan, and Yakutia—popular support for nationalism rose in the early 1990s. In contrast, in republics where they raised other issues, as I show in Mari El and Komi, popular support for nationalism failed to develop. Nationalist organizations and leaders in these places seemed to a majority of people there to be irrelevant to their personal interests and political concerns.

This book has also shown that, in the republics with mass support for nationalism, the issues and causal claims expressed by nationalists did not necessarily accurately describe local economic conditions at the end of the Soviet era. Whereas people were experiencing rising job competition and fears of unemployment, the nationalists spoke about blocked opportunity, discrimination, and titular economic subordination. Nationalists, as a rule, downplayed the fact of titular mobility during the course of Soviet rule. If they did acknowledge gains made by titulars over the decades, these gains were attributed to personal ability and effort. The nationalists disregarded the fact that affirmative action policies existed for titular nationalities.

Despite the disconnect between the nationalist message of socioeconomic subordination and people's experience of rising socioeconomic equivalence between titulars and Russians, the nationalist message seemed to many to accurately describe the current situation. As a result, a significant segment of the population responded by supporting nationalism. Therefore, the way in which nationalist entrepreneurs frame issues is a critical part of the process by which ethnic categories become invested with social and political meanings. However, this book has shown that issue frames cannot be completely detached from economic and social realities. They must offer a plausible logic describing experiences that are central to people's lives.

Policy Implications

In the process of analyzing the various kinds of material I had collected while researching this book, including demographic and economic statistics and the statements and writings of nationalist leaders, I noticed a discrepancy. Nationalists were talking about socioeconomic disadvantages facing Russia's minorities in the republics, as well as the "fact" that they were underrepresented in desirable professions. Demographic and economic data, however, suggested that titular disadvantage had actually been evaporating over time. When I explored this discrepancy, it became apparent that even though titulars had been moving into high-status jobs and professions in recent decades, nationalist entrepreneurs genuinely perceived socioeconomic conditions and data as indicating that they occupied a position subordinate to that of Russians within their republics. Thus they framed issues and articulated messages in ways that expressed this understanding. The leaders were not simply picking up on preexisting attitudes among ethnic populations and communicating those attitudes back to people. Nor were they merely describing existing economic conditions. Instead, nationalist entrepreneurs actively interpreted economic and demographic data in ethnic terms. This suggests that ethnic entrepreneurs in other countries and contexts construct plausible grievances about ethnic oppression whether or not those grievances accurately reflect existing economic realities.

The idea that people may develop ethnic group grievances concerning structural economic inequalities in the absence or near absence of unequal structures gives one pause. Does this mean that a message of group socioeconomic disadvantage, though not a guaranteed means of dividing populations along ethnonational lines, will often serve to convince them to support nationalism? Throughout this book, I have argued that neither the discourse of elites nor structural economic conditions by themselves lead automatically or easily to mass political mobilization. However, the fact that ordinary people may be convinced by ethnified framings of economic issues that leaders put forward has implications for policymakers and other interested observers.

First, it is important to recognize, as Breuilly argues and as this book has shown, that the power of such elite rhetoric lies in its ability to provide a broader public landscape on which members of the intended target (ethnic) population can project their own personal interests and experiences.[1] But the rhetoric of elites may also exert influence in another way. A discourse about ethnic inequality will often resonate with outsiders, such as journalists, policymakers, and representatives of nongovernmental organizations who are attuned to issues

---

1. Breuilly, *Nationalism and the State,* 13.

of minority rights, inequality, and oppression. Outsiders usually come from democratic societies and international organizations that value egalitarianism and economic opportunity and thus may be predisposed to accept at face value an ethnic leader's description of discrimination against a minority population or, less dramatically, of interethnic inequality. The term "ethnic minority" itself evokes a set of assumptions about ongoing political, economic, and social subordination experienced by an ethnic community. Yet outside observers should recognize the possibility that such subordination could be of a historical character, as in Russia's republics. Although ethnic minorities in some multinational societies continue to face structural disadvantage and oppression by the state, in many cases, state-led policies of economic development and education have altered the former subordinate positions of ethnic minorities, reducing if not effacing their subordinate status. India and Malaysia, for example, have implemented a range of education, language, and economic policies that recognize and advance minority populations.

Outside observers—who are motivated by genuine sympathy for minority rights and issues of inegalitarianism—should nonetheless approach claims made by ethnic entrepreneurs about minority economic victimization and blocked opportunity with a healthy skepticism. If outsiders accept claims made by political entrepreneurs at face value, if they repeat and write about group inequalities or promote policies that recognize ethnic groups as discrete, polarized communities, prior to investigating whether this is actually the case, they may unwittingly assist ethnic entrepreneurs in reifying ethnic boundaries. This can make the politicization of ethnicity in multicultural societies more likely than it otherwise would have been. Such an outcome has the potential to produce ethnic conflict and violence and is currently a concern in authoritarian states such as China or transitioning states such as Iraq.

External Observers and Ethnic Entrepreneurs in China and Iraq

Currently, there is substantial international concern for ethnic minorities in China, such as Tibetans. Tibetan leaders in exile who claim to speak on behalf of Tibetans describe them as wanting independence or regional autonomy to escape religious and political oppression by the Chinese state. Large protests by Buddhist monks and Tibetan rural dwellers in 2008 suggest that support for independence or at least strong opposition to the Chinese government has been widespread among the Tibetan population in recent years. Yet the internal situation in Tibet is more complex than it often appears to outsiders, making it critical to consider whether people living there maintain the political interests ascribed to them.

On the one hand, China's history provides ample evidence of the harsh oppression of the Tibetan population during the Great Leap Forward, under Mao in the 1960s and 1970s, and in the recent repression of Tibetan monks and intellectuals. Yet China has also enacted periods of cultural recovery and economic development in Tibet. During the past two decades, the Chinese government has promoted the region's development through large-scale investment, economic integration with the rest of China, and the migration of non-Tibetan Chinese to the region.[2] In recent years, it has allowed Tibetans to open small shops, which has facilitated the development of a new class of Tibetan entrepreneurs. Tibet has witnessed a developing private sector, the emergence of an imported, Western commercial culture, an influx of Chinese migrants, and an increase in the number of Tibetan parents who send their children to study the Chinese language.[3] What have these changes meant for the experiences, identities, and interests of ordinary Tibetans? How have local and central elites in China interpreted these developments? I do not mean to suggest that these changes have benefited Tibetans or that they have reduced regional opposition to the central state. But given the considerable transformations in China and Tibet, we cannot assume that people with Tibetan identity form a homogeneous interest group with shared economic and political interests. The international community and many in the West, however, tend to think about Tibetans as an economically and culturally oppressed group that supports Tibetan national autonomy—because the discourse of Tibetan leaders in exile have described them as such. How ordinary people in the region understand their identities and interests, whether they have developed economic grievances toward the central state or Han Chinese, and whether people there support campaigns for national autonomy are empirical issues subject to investigation.

It is critical for actors engaged in reporting, analysis, and policymaking to dissect issues articulated by ethnic entrepreneurs and to scrutinize the various forms of evidence they present in making claims about ethnic group subordination. Policymakers have learned in recent years to cross-examine the claims of nationalist leaders concerning supposed national histories of independent statehood and interethnic enmities. Yet they are less aware of the need to question the veracity of elite claims about the economy and socioeconomic subordination. Policymakers, journalists, and academics may be predisposed to accept

---

2. Melvyn C. Goldstein, "The Dalai Lama's Dilemma," *Foreign Affairs* 77, no. 1 (January/February 1998): 83–97.

3. Robert Barnett, "The Issues," 1998. http://www.columbia.edu/cu/weai/tibetan-issues.html.

economic claims at face value for several reasons. First, political entrepreneurs often cite published statistical data to support their claims about the economy and such data are generally considered to be more objective than other forms of information. Next, if political claims about economic inequality are supported by published research by local scholars, outsiders are also likely to trust these publications because they are produced by intellectuals, who are seen as understanding trends and social processes in their own societies.

There are several problems with these assumptions, as we saw in Russia. First, statistical data may not provide a full, objective picture of local economic conditions. In Russia, data from the 1989 Soviet census supported nationalists' claims about an ethnic division of labor in certain places but obscured socioeconomic trends over time indicating educational and professional progress made by titulars. Next, such data may be incomplete, outdated or may not capture new kinds of activities taking place within a country. For example, Goskomstat data in Russia did not include information about unemployment since the Soviet state maintained that unemployment did not exist. Also, Goskomstat did not record the number of people working in new jobs in the private sector and thus failed to provide an accurate picture of ethnic representation in the emerging private-sector economy. Finally, local scholars often are not disinterested observers. As we saw in Tatarstan, intellectuals who were part of the nationalist movement helped to frame the subject of ethnic group underrepresentation in the republican economy. The statistics themselves may have been more or less accurate, but local specialists often interpret them through their own ethnicized cognitive frame.[4]

Instead of accepting economic data at face value, policymakers must direct their efforts toward investigating how elites frame these data. Alternative readings of data should be conceptualized, and the interpretations of academics and intellectuals from that society must be interrogated. This is not to say that local academics and scholars maintain nationalist attitudes or that their analyses consistently present an ethnified framing of various issues. However, this may be the case if they are sympathetic to the claims of ethnic politicians or if they are merely present in a society in which certain ethnic cognitive frames have become naturalized. Ideally, outsiders should identify and challenge ethnified framings of local economic information so that blame for putatively objective economic inequalities will not be convincingly but fallaciously placed on another ethnic group or on the ethnic group in control of the state.

More broadly, outsiders should also carefully evaluate general claims made by ethnic entrepreneurs in multicultural societies about ethnic minority oppression

---

4. This has been a problem in academic studies of national minorities in the Soviet Union that accepted titular underrepresentation as an established social fact.

and the politicization of ethnic and religious groups. This point is directly relevant to present-day Iraq where politics have been developing along ethnic and sectarian lines. Quotas based on ethnicity and sect—the system of *muhasisa*—guide the appointment of government leaders, ambassadors, and top officials in the army.[5] Iraq's government has been led for several years by a Shiite Arab prime minister, a Kurd president, and a Sunni Arab speaker of parliament. Iraqi leaders who benefit from the quota system argue that the number of each group's representatives in leadership posts, as well as the status of the particular offices they occupy, should be proportional to the demographic weight of the group in the population. The critical question in current Iraqi politics is whether future governments will lock in this ethnicized system of political representation.

The politicization of ethnicity and religious sect in Iraq is not a predetermined outcome.[6] Yet U.S. policymakers may have facilitated this outcome when, after the war ended in 2003, U.S. pro-consul Paul Bremer formed an interim Iraqi Governing Council composed of representatives from each group: thirteen Shiites, five Kurds, five Sunnis, one Assyrian Christian, and one Turkoman.[7] Bremer appointed representatives to the Governing Council based largely on the recommendation of leaders of Iraq's exiled former opposition who were themselves persecuted by Saddam Hussein due to their Shiite and Kurd identities. Thus, U.S. policymakers—concerned with redressing the oppression experienced by Shiites and Kurds—were receptive to the advice given by Iraq's exiled former opposition that Sunni Arab privilege under Saddam should be reversed and that the Governing Council should grant proportional representation to Iraq's ethnic and sectarian groups. The way in which the Governing Council was set up in 2003 created shared expectations among Iraqi leaders that representation according to ethnicity and sect was fair and would continue.

Viewing Iraq as divided by sect and ethnicity does not capture the complex reality of personal and social identities, political groups, and individual preferences among the population there. Yet in the absence of information on mass attitudes and interests, U.S. policymakers relied on the statements of ethnic leaders. Convinced that ethnic groups and sects in Iraq existed as bounded, self-aware actors that required political representation, U.S. policymakers may have unintentionally contributed to their reification, moving the country closer to a political system divided along ethnic lines.

5. Salah Hemeid, "Carving Up the Ship of State," Al-Ahram Weekly online, July 1–7, 2010, no. 1005. http://weekly.ahram.org.eg/2010/1005/re4.htm.

6. See Eric Davis, "The New Iraq: The Uses of Historical Memory," *Journal of Democracy* 16, no. 3 (July 2005): 54–68.

7. Anthony Shadid, "Divvying Up the Spoils of Political War," *New York Times,* June 27, 2010, 7.

This book has argued that, on the contrary, people with ethnic affiliations do not form distinct interest groups ready to support nationalist and ethnic leaders. The fact of wavering and ultimately failed popular support for nationalism in Russia's republics underscores this point. As my analysis suggests, greater attention to the variables of how ethnic entrepreneurs frame economic issues and how people's experiences shape their receptivity to those issue framings can help to identify policies that successfully defuse mass nationalism and that avoid politicizing ethnic group boundaries in the first place.

Bibliography

Abdelal, Rawi. *National Purpose in the World Economy: Post-Soviet States in Comparative Perspective.* Ithaca: Cornell University Press, 2001.

Alatalu, Toomas. "Tuva-a State Reawakens." *Soviet Studies* 44 (1992): 881–95.

Akhmetov, R. M. "Elita Tatar" [The Tatar Elite]. In *Sovremennye natsional'nye protsessy v Respublike Tatarstan* [Contemporary Nationality Processes in Tatarstan], 119–27. Kazan: Russian Academy of Sciences, Kazan Scientific Center, 1992.

Akhmetov, R. M. "O problemakh kompleksnogo issledovaniia sotsial'nykh struktur russkikh i Tatar Tatarstan" [Research on the Social Structure of Russians and Tatars in Tatarstan]. In *Sovremennye natsional'nye protsessy v Respublike Tatarstan* [Contemporary Nationality Processes in Tatarstan], 88–95. Kazan: Tatarstan Academy of Sciences, 1994.

Alexseev, Mikhail A. "Asymmetric Russia: Promises and Dangers." In *Center-Periphery Conflict in Post-Soviet Russia: A Federation Imperiled,* edited by Mikhail A. Alexseev, 247–80. New York: St. Martin's Press, 1999.

——. "Decentralization versus State Collapse: Explaining Russia's Endurance." *Journal of Peace Research* 38, no. 1 (January 2001): 101–6.

Anaibin, Z. V. *Respublika Tuva—Model' etnologicheskogo monitoringa* [The Republic of Tuva: A Model of Ethnographical Monitoring]. Moscow: Institute of Ethnography and Anthropology, Russian Academy of Sciences, 1996.

Anaibin, Zoia. "Ethnic Relations in Tuva." In *Culture Incarnate,* edited by Marjorie Balzer, 102–112. Armonk, N.Y.: M.E. Sharpe, 1995.

Anaibin, Z. V., M. N. Guboglo, and M. S. Kozlov. *Formirovanie etnopoliticheskoi situatsii: Ocherki po istorii postsovetskoi Tuvy* [Formation of the Ethnopolitical Situation: An Essay on the History of Post-Soviet Tuva]. Moscow: RAN, 1999.

Analiz i prognoz mezhnatsional'nikh konfliktov v Rossii i SNG Ezhegodnik 1994 [Analysis and Prognosis of Interethnic Conflict in Russia and the CIS: Handbook 1994] (Moscow: Rossiiskii nezavisimyi institut sotsial'nykh problem tsentr sotsiologicheskogo analiza mezhnatsional'nikh konfliktov, 1994.

Anderson, Barbara A., and Brian D. Silver. "Some Factors in the Linguistic and Ethnic Russification of Soviet Nationalities: Is Everyone Becoming Russian?" In *The Nationalities Factor in Soviet Politics and Society,* edited by Lubomyr Hajda and Mark Beissinger, 95–130. Boulder, Colo.: Westview, 1990.

Anderson, Richard. "Russia—Old Wine in a New Bottle? The Circulation and Reproduction of Russian Elites, 1983–1993." *Theory and Society* 24, no. 5 (October 1995): 639–68.

Arutiunian, Iuryi, and Iuryi Bromlei, eds. *Sotsial'no-kul'turnyi oblik sovetskikh natsii* [The Socio-cultural Character of Soviet Nations]. Moscow: Nauka, 1986.

Azrael, Jeremy R., and Emil Payin, eds. *Conflict and Consensus in Ethno-Political and Center-Periphery Relations in Russia.* Santa Monica, CA: Rand, 1998.

Bahl, Roy, and Christine I. Wallich. "Intergovernmental Fiscal Relations in the Russian Federation." In *Decentralization of the Socialist State,* edited by Richard M. Bird, Robert D. Ebel, and Christine I. Wallich, 321–77. Washington, D.C.: World Bank, 1995.

Balakina, G. F. and Z. V. Anaiban. *Sovremennaia Tuva: Sotsiokul'turnye i etnicheskie protsessy* [Modern Tuva: Social and Ethnic Processes]. Novosibirsk: Nauka, 1995.

Balzer, Marjorie, ed., *Culture Incarnate*. Armonk, N.Y.: M.E. Sharpe, 1995.

——. "From Ethnicity to Nationalism: Turmoil in the Russian Mini-Empire." In *The Social Legacy of Communism*, edited by James R. Millar and Sharon L. Wolchik, 56–88. Cambridge: Cambridge University Press, 1994.

——. "A State within a State: The Sakha Republic (Yakutia)." In *Rediscovering Russia in Asia*, edited by Stephen Kotkin and David Wolff, 139–159. Armonk, N.Y.: M.E. Sharpe, 1995.

Balzer, Marjorie Mandelstam, and Uliana Alekseevna Vinokurova. "Nationalism, Interethnic Relations, and Federalism: The Case of the Sakha Republic (Yakutia)." *Europe-Asia Studies* 48 (January 1996): 101–20.

Balzer, Marjorie. "Dilemmas of Federalism in Siberia." In *Center-Periphery Conflict in Post-Soviet Russia: A Federation Imperiled*, edited by Mikhail A. Alexseev. New York: St. Martin's, 1999.

Barnes, Andrew. *Owning Russia: The State Struggle over Factories, Farms, and Power*. Ithaca: Cornell University Press, 2006.

Barnett, Robert. "The Issues." 1998. http://www.columbia.edu/cu/weai/tibetan-issues.html.

Barth, Fredrik, ed. *Ethnic Groups and Boundaries: The Social Organization of Culture Difference*. Boston: Little, Brown, 1969.

Bates, Robert. "Modernization, Ethnic Competition, and the Rationality of Politics in Contemporary Africa." In *State versus Ethnic Claims: African Policy Dilemmas*, edited by Donald Rothchild and Victor Olorunsola, 152–171. Boulder, Colo.: Westview, 1983.

Baturin, Yurii. "Shakhmatnaia diplomatia v Novo-Ogarevo." *Demokratizatsiia* 2 (Spring 1994): 212–21.

Beissinger, Mark R. *Codebook for Disaggregated Event Data: "Mass Demonstrations and Mass Violent Events in the Former USSR, 1987–1992."* http://www.princeton.edu/~mbeissin/research.htm.

——. "Event Analysis in Transitional Societies: Protest Mobilization in the Former Soviet Union." In *Acts of Dissent: New Developments in the Study of Protest*, edited by Dieter Rucht, Ruud Koopmans, and Friedhelm Neidhardt, 284–316. Berlin: Sigma Press, 1998.

——. *Nationalist Mobilization and the Collapse of the Soviet State*. Cambridge: Cambridge University Press, 2002.

——. "Nationalisms That Bark and Nationalisms That Bite: Ernest Gellner and the Substantiation of Nations." In *The State of the Nation: Ernest Gellner and the Theory of Nationalism*, edited by John A. Hall, 169–90. Cambridge: Cambridge University Press, 1998.

Benford, Robert D., and David A. Snow. "Framing Processes and Social Movements: An Overview and Assessment." *Annual Review of Sociology* 26 (2000): 611–39.

Bonacich, Edna. "A Theory of Ethnic Antagonism: The Split Labor Market." *American Sociological Review* 37 (October 1971): 547–59.

Borocz, Jozsef, and Akos Rona-Tas. "Small Leap Forward: Emergence of New Economic Elites." *Theory and Society* 24 (October 1995): 751–81.

Bremmer, Ian, and Ray Taras. *New States, New Politics: Building the Post-Soviet Nations*. Cambridge: Cambridge University Press, 1997.

Breuilly, John. *Nationalism and the State*. Chicago: University of Chicago Press, 1994.

Brown, Michael. "Causes and Implications of Ethnic Conflict." In *Ethnic Conflict and International Security*, edited by Michael Brown, 3–26. Princeton: Princeton University Press, 1993.

Brown, Michael. "The Causes of Internal Conflict: An Overview." In *Nationalism and Ethnic Conflict*, edited by Michael Brown, Owen R. Cote, Jr., Sean M. Lynn-Jones, and Steven E. Miller, 3–25. Cambridge, Mass.: MIT Press, 1997.

Brubaker, Rogers. *Ethnicity without Groups*. Cambridge, Mass.: Harvard University Press, 2004.

———. "Myths and Misconceptions in the Study of Nationalism." In *The State of the Nation: Ernest Gellner and the Theory of Nationalism,* edited by John A. Hall, 272–306. Cambridge: Cambridge University Press, 1998.

———. *Nationalism Reframed: Nationhood and the National Question in the New Europe.* Cambridge: Cambridge University Press, 1996.

Brubaker, Rogers, Margit Feischmidt, Jon Fox, and Liana Grancia. *Nationalist Politics and Everyday Ethnicity in a Transylvanian Town.* Princeton: Princeton University Press, 2006.

Bunce, Valerie. *Subversive Institutions: The Design and the Destruction of Socialism and the State.* Cambridge: Cambridge University Press, 1999.

———. "Subversive Institutions: The End of the Soviet State in Comparative Perspective." *Post-Soviet Affairs* 14, no. 4 (October 1998): 323–54.

Calhoun, Craig. "The Problem of Identity in Collective Action." In *Macro-Micro Linkages in Sociology,* edited by Joan Huber. London: Sage, 1991.

Carrère d'Encausse, Hélène. *The End of the Soviet Empire: The Triumph of the Nations.* New York: Basic Books, 1993.

Chervonnaia, S. M., and M. N. Guboglo. Ustav Demokraticheskogo obshchestvennogo ob'edinenniia "Marii ushem" [Charter of the Democratic Public Association "Marii ushem"] in *Probuzhdenie Finno-ugorskogo Severa. Opyt Marii El. Tom I* [The Awakening of the Finno-Ugric North. The Experience of Mari El. Vol. I]. Moscow: IEA-RAN, 1996.

Clarke, Simon. *The Formation of a Labour Market in Russia.* Cheltenham, U.K.: Edward Elgar, 1999.

Clem, Ralph. *Research Guide to the Russian and Soviet Censuses.* Ithaca: Cornell University Press, 1986.

———. "The Ethnic Dimension, Part II." In *Contemporary Soviet Society,* edited by Jerry G. Pankhurst and Michael Paul Sacks, 33–60. New York: Praeger, 1980.

Clem, Ralph S., and Peter R. Craumer. "The Geography of the April 25 (1993) Russian Referendum." *Post-Soviet Geography* 34, no. 8 (October 1993): 481–96.

Collier, Paul. "Doing Well out of War: An Economic Perspective." In *Greed and Grievance: Economic Agendas in Civil Wars,* edited by Mats R. Berdal and David M. Malone. Boulder, Colo.: Lynne Rienner, 2000.

Collier, Paul, and Anke Hoeffler. "Greed and Grievance in Civil War." *Oxford Economic Papers* 56, no. 4 (October 2004): 563–95.

Colton, Timothy. *Yeltsin: A Life.* New York: Basic Books, 2008.

Connor, Walker. "Beyond Reason: The Nature of the Ethnonational Bond." *Ethnic and Racial Studies* 16, no. 3 (July 1993): 373–89.

Cornell, Svante E. "Autonomy as a Source of Conflict: Caucasian Conflicts in Theoretical Perspective." *World Politics* 54, no. 2 (January 2002): 245–76.

Davis, Eric. "The New Iraq: The Uses of Historical Memory." *Journal of Democracy* 16, no. 3 (July 2005): 54–68.

Derluguian, Georgi M. "Ethnofederalism and Ethnonationalism in the Separatist Politics of Chechnya and Tatarstan: Sources or Resources?" *International Journal of Public Administration* 22 (September/October 1999): 1387–1428.

Despres, Leo A. *Ethnicity and Resource Competition in Plural Societies.* The Hague: Mouton, 1975.

Dmitriev, A., and E. L. Malakhova. *Konstitutsii respublik v sostave Rossiiskoi Federatsii* [Republican Constitutions of the Russian Federation]. Moscow: Izdatel'skaia Firma Manuscript, 1995.

Dmitrieva, Oksana Genrikhovna. *Regional'naia ekonomicheskaia diagnostika* [Regional Economic Diagnostics]. St. Petersburg: Izdatel'stvo Sankt-Peterburgskogo Universiteta Ekonomiki i Finansov, 1992, 128–32.

Dokumenty (protokoly, informatsiia, itogovye rezul'taty) po rezul'tatam golosovaniia na referendume Respubliki Tatarstan ot 21 marta 1992 goda [Documents on the Results of the Referendum of the Republic of Tartarstan, 21 March 1992]. Fond no. P2297, opis no. 2, delo no. 2.

Drobizheva, Leokadia M., A. R. Aklaev, M. C. Kashuba, and V. V. Koroteeva. *Natsional'noe samosoznanie i natsionalizm v Rossiiskoi Federatsii nachala 1990-kh godov* [National Consciousness and Nationalism in the Russian Federation in the early 1990s]. Moscow: Institute of Ethnography and Anthropology-Russian Academy of Sciences, 1994.

——. "Processes of Disintegration in the Russian Federation and the Problem of Russians." In *The New Russian Diaspora: Russian Minorities in the Former Soviet Republics,* edited by Vladimir Shlapentokh, Munir Sendich, and Emil Payin, 44–55. Armonk, N.Y.: M.E. Sharpe, 1994.

Druckman, James N. "The Implications of Framing Effects for Citizen Competence." *Political Behavior* 23, no. 3 (September 2001): 225–56.

Druckman, James N., and Arthur Lupia. "Preference Formation." *American Political Science Review* 3 (2000): 1–24.

Dunlop, John B. *Russia Confronts Chechnya: Roots of a Separatist Conflict.* Cambridge: Cambridge University Press, 1998.

Elster, Jon, Claus Offe, and Ulrich Klaus Preuss. *Institutional Design in Post-Communist Societies: Rebuilding the Ship at Sea.* Cambridge: Cambridge University Press, 1998.

Emizet, Kisangani N., and Vicki L. Hesli. "The Disposition to Secede: An Analysis of the Soviet Case." *Comparative Political Studies* 27, no. 4 (January 1995): 493–536.

Ershova, G. I., N. N. Loginova, V. A. Nezhdanov, and V. N. Presniakov. "Etnodemograficheskie osobennosti rasseleniia na territorii Mordovii" [Ethnodemographic Features of Settlement on the Territory of Mordovia] in *Vozrozhdenie Mordovskogo Naroda* [Rebirth of the Mordvinian Nation]. Saransk: Scientific Research Institute of Regionology at Mordova State University, 1995.

Evangelista, Matthew. *The Chechen Wars.* Washington, D.C.: Brookings Institution Press, 2002.

Faisullina, Guzel. "Tatar Patriots Recall Ivan the Terrible." *CDSP* 53, no. 21 (1991): 24.

Fearon, James D., and David D. Laitin. "Ethnicity, Insurgency, and Civil War." *American Political Science Review* 97, no. 1 (February 2003): 75–90.

——. "Explaining Interethnic Cooperation." *American Political Science Review* 90 (December 1996): 715–35.

Fondahl, Gail. "Siberia: Assimilation and Its Discontents." In *New States New Politics: Building the Post-Soviet Nations,* edited by Ian Bremmer and Ray Taras, 190–232. New York: Cambridge University Press, 1997.

Frank, Allen, and Ronald Wixman. "The Middle Volga: Exploring the Limits of Sovereignty." In *New States, New Politics: Building the Post-Soviet Nations,* edited by Ian Bremmer and Ray Taras, 140–89. Cambridge: Cambridge University Press, 1997.

Gagnon, V. P. *The Myth of Ethnic War: Serbia and Croatia in the 1990s.* Ithaca: Cornell University Press, 2004.

Ganiev, M. N. "Sotsial'no-etnicheskaia struktura nauchnykh kadrov respubliki Tatarstan i nekotorye problemy ee optimizatsii" [Socioethnic Structure of Scientific Cadres in the Republic of Tatarstan and Several Issues in Its Optimization]. In *Sovremennye natsional'nye protsessy v Respublike Tatarstan* Vol. I, edited by D. M. Iskhakov and R. N. Musina, 91–99. Kazan: Russian Academy of Sciences, Kazan Scientific Center, 1992.

Garipov, Yagfar. "Sotsial'no-etnicheskaia struktura rabotnikov i mezhnatsional'nye otnosheniia na KamAZe" [The Socioethnic Structure of Workers and Interethnic Relations at KamAZ]. In *Sovremennye natsional'nye protsessy v Respublike Tatarstan* Vol. I, 65–82. Kazan: Russian Academy of Sciences, Kazan Scientific Center, 1992.

Geertz, Clifford. *Old Societies and New States: The Quest for Modernity in Asia and Africa.* New York: Free Press, 1963.

Gellner, Ernest. *Nations and Nationalism.* Ithaca: Cornell University Press, 1983.

———. *Thought and Change: The Nature of Human Society.* London: Weidenfeld and Nicolson, 1964.

Gerring, John. *Case Study Research: Principles and Practices.* New York: Cambridge University Press, 2007.

Gibadullin, R. M. *Tatarskoe naselenie naberezhnykh chelnov v tsifrakh etnosotsiologii, 1992 g* [The Tatar Population of Naberezhnye Chelny: An Ethnosociology in Numbers, 1992]. Naberezhnye Chelny: Mag'rifat, 1993.

Gimpelson, Vladimir, and Douglas Lippoldt. *The Russian Labour Market: Between Transition and Turmoil.* Lanham, Md.: Rowman & Littlefield, 2001.

Giuliano, Elise. "Secessionism from the Bottom Up: Democratization, Nationalism, and Local Accountability in the Russian Transition." *World Politics* 58 (January 2006): 276–310.

———. "Theorizing Ethno-Nationalist Mobilization in Russia." In *Re-Bounding Identities in Russia and Ukraine,* edited by Blair Ruble and Dominique Arel, 33–61. Baltimore: Johns Hopkins University Press, 2006.

———. "Who Determines the Self in the Politics of Self-Determination?: Identity and Preference Formation in Tatarstan's Nationalist Mobilization." *Comparative Politics* 32, no. 3 (April 2000): 295–316.

Goble, Paul. "Ethnicity and Economic Reform." *RFE/RL Research Report,* February 16, 1990, 23–24.

———. "Gorbachev and the Soviet Nationality Problem." In *Soviet Society under Gorbachev: Current Trends and the Prospects for Reform,* edited by Maurice Friedberg and Heyward Isham, 76–100. Armonk, N.Y.: M.E. Sharpe, 1987.

———. "Moscow's Nationality Problems in 1989." *RFE/RL Research Report,* January 12, 1990, 13–14.

Goldstein, Melvyn C. "The Dalai Lama's Dilemma." *Foreign Affairs* 77, no. 1 (January/February 1998): 83–97.

Gorenburg, Dmitry P. *Minority Ethnic Mobilization in the Russian Federation.* New York: Cambridge University Press, 2003.

———. "Soviet Nationalities Policy and Assimilation." In *Rebounding Identities: The Politics of Identity in Russia and Ukraine,* edited by Dominique Arel and Blair Ruble, 273–303. Baltimore: Johns Hopkins University Press, 2006.

Graney, Katherine. "'Russian Islam' and the Politics of Religious Multiculturalism in Russia." In *Rebounding Identities: The Politics of Identity in Russia and Ukraine,* edited by Dominique Arel and Blair A. Ruble, 89–115. Baltimore: Johns Hopkins University Press, 2006.

Gourevitch, Peter Alexis. *Paris and the Provinces: The Politics of Local Government Reform in France.* Berkeley: University of California Press, 1980.

Guboglo, M. N. *Etnopoliticheskaia mozaika Bashkortostana Tom II* [Ethnopolitical Mosaic of Bashkortostan Vol. 2]. Moscow: Russian Academy of Sciences, 1992.

———. *Sovremennye etnoiazykovye protsessy v SSSR* [Current Ethnolinguistic Processes in the USSR]. Moscow: Nauka, 1984.

——. *Razvitie etnogdemograficheskoi situatsii v stolitsakh avtonomnykh respublik v 1959–1989 gg (po materialam perepisei naseleniia SSSR)* [The Development of the Ethnodemographic situation in the capitals of the autonomous republics from 1959 to 1989 (based on USSR censuses)]. Moscow: IEA-RAN, 1992.

Guboglo, M. N., and S. M. Chervonnaia. *Probuzhdenie finno-ugorskogo severa. Opyt Marii El* [Awakening of the Finno-Ugric North. The Experience of Mari El]. Moscow: Institute of Ethnography and Anthropology, Russian Academy of Sciences, 1996.

Gurr, Ted Robert. *Peoples versus States: Minorities at Risk in the New Century.* Washington, D.C.: United States Institute of Peace Press, 2000.

Gurr, Ted Robert, and United States Institute of Peace. *Minorities at Risk: A Global View of Ethnopolitical Conflicts.* Washington, D.C.: United States Institute of Peace Press, 1993.

Gurr, Ted Robert, and Woodrow Wilson School of Public and International Affairs. Center of International Studies. *Why Men Rebel.* Princeton: Princeton University Press, 1970.

Hahn, Jeffrey. "Introduction: Analyzing Parliamentary Development in Russia." In *Democratization in Russia: The Development of Legislative Institutions,* edited by Jeffrey Hahn, 3–28. Armonk, N.Y.: M.E. Sharpe, 1996.

Hale, Henry. *The Foundations of Ethnic Politics: Separatism of States and Nations in Eurasia and the World.* New York: Cambridge University Press, 2008.

——. "The Makeup and Breakup of Ethnofederal States: Why Russia Survives Where the USSR Fell." *Perspectives on Politics* 3, no. 1 (March 2005): 55–70.

——. "The Parade of Sovereignties: Testing Theories of Secession in the Soviet Setting." *British Journal of Political Science* 30 (January 2000): 31–56.

Hale, Henry, and Rein Taagepera. "Russia: Consolidation or Collapse?" *Europe-Asia Studies* 54, no. 7 (November 2002): 1101–25.

Hall, John A. *The State of the Nation: Ernest Gellner and the Theory of Nationalism.* Cambridge: Cambridge University Press. 1998.

Hanley, Eric, Natasha Yershova, and Richard Anderson. "Russia—Old Wine in a New Bottle? The Circulation and Reproduction of Russian Elites, 1983–1993." *Theory and Society* 24 (October 1995): 639–68.

Hanson, Stephen E. "Ideology, Interests, and Identity: Comparing the Soviet and Russian Secession Crises." In *Center-Periphery Conflict in Post-Soviet Russia,* edited by Mikhail A. Alexseev, 15–46. New York: St. Martin's, 1999.

Hechter, Michael. *Containing Nationalism.* New York: Oxford University Press, 2000.

——. "Group Formation and the Cultural Division of Labor." *American Journal of Sociology* 84 (1978): 293–318.

——. *Internal Colonialism: The Celtic Fringe in British National Development, 1536–1966.* Berkeley: University of California Press, 1975.

——. "Nationalism as Group Solidarity." *Ethnic and Racial Studies* 10 (October 1987): 415–26.

Helf, Gavin, and Jeffrey Hahn. "Old Dogs and New Tricks: Party Elites in the Russian Regional Elections of 1990." *Slavic Review* 51 (Fall 1992): 511–30.

Hemeid, Salah. "Carving Up the Ship of State." *Al-Ahram Weekly* online, no. 1005 (July 1–7, 2010), http://weekly.ahram.org.eg/2010/1005/re4.htm.

Herrera, Yoshiko M. *Imagined Economies: The Sources of Russian Regionalism.* New York: Cambridge University Press, 2005.

Hobsbawm, E. J., and T. O. Ranger, eds. *The Invention of Tradition.* New York: Cambridge University Press, 1992.

Horowitz, Donald L. *Ethnic Groups in Conflict.* Berkeley: University of California Press, 1985.

——. "Patterns of Ethnic Separatism." *Comparative Studies in Society and History* 23 (1981): 165–95.

Hosking, Geoffrey, Jonathan Aves, and Peter J. S. Duncan. *The Road to Post-Communism: Independent Political Movements in the Soviet Union, 1985–1991.* New York: St. Martin's Press, 1992.

Hroch, Miroslav. *Social Preconditions of National Revival in Europe: A Comparative Analysis of the Social Composition of Patriotic Groups among the Smaller European Nations.* Cambridge: Cambridge University Press, 1985.

Huber, Joan. *Macro-Micro Linkages in Sociology.* Newbury Park, Calif.: Sage, 1991.

Hughes, James. "From Federalism to Recentralization." In *Developments in Russian Politics 5,* edited by Stephen White, Alex Pravda, and Zvi Gitelman, 131–34. Durham, N.C.: Duke University Press, 1998.

Humphries, Caroline. "Buryatia and the Buryats," In *The Nationalities Question in the Post-Soviet States,* edited by Graham Smith, 113–125. New York: Longman, 1996.

Huntington, Samuel P. *Political Order in Changing Societies.* New Haven: Yale University Press, 1968.

Iasnyi, Victor Kogan, and Diana Zisserman-Brodsky, "Chechen Separatism." In *Separatism: Democracy and Disintegration,* edited by Metta Spencer, 205–26. Lanham, Md.: Rowman & Littlefield, 1998.

Il'in, V. *Respublika Komi: Etnos i politika* [The Komi Republic: Ethnos and Politics]. Moscow: Institute of Ethnography and Anthropology, Russian Academy of Sciences, 1994.

Iskhakov, Damir. "Etnodemograficheskie protsessi v Respublike Tatarstan 1920–1989gg" [Ethnodemographic Processes in Tatarstan]. In *Mnogonatsional'nyi Tatarstan* [Multiethnic Tatarstan], edited by I. V. Terent'eva and A. S. Alishev, 9–12. Kazan: Tatarstan Presidential Apparat, 1993.

——. "Khronika natsional'nykh dvizhenii (1980-e gody-avgust 1992 g)" [Chronicle of the Nationalist Movement, 1980s to August 1992]. In *Suverennyi Tatarstan* [Sovereign Tatarstan], Vol. 1, edited by D. M. Iskhakov and M. N. Guboglo. Moscow: Russian Academy of Sciences, 1998.

——. "Neformal'nye ob"edineniia v sovremennom tatarskom obshestve" [Informal Associations in Current Tatar Society]. In *Sovremennye natsional'nye protsessy v Respublike Tatarstan,* Vol. I, edited by D. M. Iskhakov and R. N. Musina, 5–52. Kazan: Russian Academy of Sciences, Kazan Scientific Center, 1992.

——. "Programma (platforma) Vsesoyuznogo Tatarskogo Obshchestvennogo tsentra" [Program (platform) of the All-Union Tatar Public Center]. In *Suverennyi Tatarstan* [Sovereign Tatarstan], Vol. 2, edited by D. M. Iskhakov and M. N. Guboglo. Moscow: Russian Academy of Sciences, 1998.

Iskhakov, D. M., and R. N. Musina, eds. *Sovremennye mezhnatsional'nye protsessy v TSSR* [Current Interethnic Processes in the TSSR]. Kazan: Russian Academy of Sciences, Kazan Scientific Center, 1991.

——. *Sovremennye natsional'nye protsessy v Respublike Tatarstan* [Current Ethnic Processes in the Republic of Tatarstan]. Vol. 1. Kazan: Russian Academy of Sciences, Kazan Scientific Center, 1992.

——. *Sovremennye natsional'nye protsessy v Respublike Tatarstan* [Current Ethnic Processes in the Republic of Tatarstan]. Vol. 2. Kazan: Tatarstan Academy of Sciences, 1994.

——. "Sovremennoe Tatarskoe natsional'noe dvizhenie: Pod'em i krizis" [The Current Tatar National Movement: Rise and Crisis]. *Tatarstan* 8 (1993): 25–31.

Iskhakov, D. M., Ia Z. Garipov, and Iu. V. Platonov. "Urbanizatsiia v Tatarstane v XX v.: Osobennosti i posledstviia" [Urbanization in Tatarstan in the 20th Century:

Particularities and Consequences]. In *Tatarstan—Strana gorodov* [Tatarstan—A Country of Cities], edited by D. M. Iskhakov, 6–15. Naberezhnye Chelny: Krona 1993.

Islamshina, Taslima, and Guzel Khamzina. "V molodykh gorodakh sklonny k radikal-izmu" [In Young Cities Prone to Radicalism]. *Tatarstan* 9 (1993): 22–23.

Ivanov, A. M. *Etnopoliticheskaia situatsiia v Respublike Sakha (Yakutia)* [Ethnopolitical Situation in the Republic of Sakha (Yakutia)]. Moscow: Institute of Ethnography and Anthropology, Russian Academy of Sciences, 1994.

Jack, Andrew. *Inside Putin's Russia*. Oxford: Oxford University Press, 2006.

Jenkins, Craig J., and Charles Perrow. "Insurgency of the Powerless: Farm Worker Movements (1964–1972)." *American Sociological Review* 42 (1977): 249–68.

Jones, Ellen, and Fred W. Grupp. "Modernisation and Ethnic Equalisation in the USSR." *Soviet Studies* 36, no. 2 (April 1984): 159–84.

Kahn, Jeffrey. *Federalism, Democratization, and the Rule of Law in Russia*. Oxford: Oxford University Press, 2002.

Kaiser, Robert John. *The Geography of Nationalism in Russia and the USSR*. Princeton: Princeton University Press, 1994.

——. "Nationalizing the Work Force: Ethnic Restratification in the Newly Independent States." *Post-Soviet Geography* 36, no. 2 (February 1995): 87–111.

Kaplan, Robert D. *Balkan Ghosts: A Journey through History*. New York: St. Martin's, 1993.

Karklins, Rasma. "Ethnic Politics and Access to Higher Education: The Soviet Case." *Comparative Politics* 16, no. 3 (April 1984): 277–94.

Kaufman, Stuart J. "Spiraling to Ethnic War: Elites, Masses and Moscow in Moldova's Civil War." *International Security* 21, no. 2 (Fall 1996): 108–38.

Kempton, Daniel R. "The Republic of Sakha (Yakutia): The Evolution of Centre-Periphery Relations in the Russian Federation." *Europe-Asia Studies* 48 (June 1996): 587–613.

Khakimov, Rafael. "Politicheskaia zhizn" [Political Life]. In *Tatary i Tatarstan* [Tatars and Tatarstan]. Kazan: Tatarskoe knizhnoe izdatel'stvo, 1993.

Khazanov, Anatoly M. *After the USSR: Ethnicity, Nationalism and Politics in the Commonwealth of Independent States*. Madison: University of Wisconsin Press, 1995.

Kolstø, Pål. "Nationalism, Ethnic Conflict, and Job Competition: Non-Russian Collective Action in the USSR under Perestroika." *Nations and Nationalism* 14, no. 1 (2008): 151–69.

——. *Russians in the Former Soviet Republics*. Bloomington: Indiana University Press, 1995.

Komarova, G. A. *Khronika mezhnatsional'nykh konfliktov v Rossii: 1991 god* [Chronicle of interethnic conflicts in Russia: 1991]. Moscow: Institute of Ethnography and Anthropology, Russian Academy of Science, 1994.

——. *Khronika zhizni natsional'nostei v SSSR: 1990 god* [Chronicle of the life of nationalities in the USSR: 1990]. Moscow: Institute of Ethnography and Anthropology, Russian Academy of Science, 1996.

——. *Khronika zhizni natsional'nostei nakanune raspada SSSR: 1989 god* [Chronicle of the life of nationalities on the eve of the collapse of the USSR: 1989]. Moscow: Institute of Ethnography and Anthropology, Russian Academy of Science, 1997.

Koroteeva, Viktoria. *Ekonomicheskie interesy i natsionalizm* [Economic Interests and Nationalism]. Moscow: Rossiiskii gosudarstvennyi gumanitarnyi universitet, 2000.

Kotkin, Stephen. *Armageddon Averted: The Soviet Collapse, 1970–2000*. Oxford: Oxford University Press, 2001.

Kryshtanovskaia, Olga V. "Transformation of the Old Nomenklatura into a New Russian Elite." *Russian Social Science Review* 37, no. 4 (July/August, 1996): 18–40.

Kto est' kto v Respublike Tatarstan [Who's Who in the Republic of Tatarstan]. Kazan: Izdatel' TOO Star, 1996.

Kudriavtsev, Alexei. "Democratic Values and Political Reality in Chechnya, 1991–1999." In *Democracy and Pluralism in Muslim Eurasia*, edited by Yaacov Ro'i, 359–373. N.Y.: Frank Cass, 2004.

Kuzhuget, A., and M. Tatarintseva. *Etnopoliticheskaia situatsiia v Respublike Tyva* [The Ethnopolitical Situation in the Republic of Tuva]. Moscow: Institute of Ethnography and Anthropology, Russian Academy of Sciences, 1994.

Laitin, David. "Language Games." *Comparative Politics* 20 (April 1988): 289–302.

——. "The Nationalist Uprisings in the Soviet Union." *World Politics* 44 (1991): 139–77.

——. "Language and Nationalism in the Post-Soviet Republics." *Post-Soviet Affairs* 12 (January–March 1996): 4–24.

——. *Nations, States, and Violence.* New York: Oxford University Press, 2007.

Lake, David, and Donald Rothchild. "Containing Fear: The Origins and Management of Ethnic Conflict." In *Nationalism and Ethnic Conflict,* edited by Michael Brown, Owen R. Cote, Jr., Sean M. Lynn-Jones, and Steven E. Miller, 3–25. Cambridge, Mass.: MIT Press, 1997.

——, eds. *The International Spread of Ethnic Conflict: Fear, Diffusion, and Escalation.* Princeton: Princeton University Press, 1998.

——. "Spreading Fear: The Genesis of Transnational Ethnic Conflict." In *The International Spread of Ethnic Conflict,* edited by David A. Lake and Donald Rothchild, 3–32. Princeton: Princeton University Press, 1998.

Lankina, Tomila. *Governing the Locals: Local Self-Government and Ethnic Mobilization in Russia.* Lanham, Md.: Rowman & Littlefield, 2004.

Lapidus, Gail W. "Asymmetrical Federalism and State Breakdown in Russia." *Post-Soviet Affairs* 15, no. 1 (January 1999): 74–82.

Lapidus, Gail W., and Edward W. Walker. "Nationalism, Regionalism, and Federalism: Center-Periphery Relations in Post-Communist Russia." In *The New Russia: Troubled Transformation,* edited by Gail W. Lapidus, 79–113. Boulder, Colo.: Westview Press, 1995.

Leff, Carol Skalnik. "Democratization and Disintegration in Multinational States: The Breakup of Communist Federations." *World Politics* 51, no. 2 (January 1999): 205–35.

Lewin, Moshe. *The Gorbachev Phenomenon: A Historical Interpretation.* Berkeley: University of California Press. 1988.

Linz, Juan J., and Alfred Stepan. "Political Identities and Electoral Sequences: Spain, the Soviet Union, and Yugoslavia." *Daedalus* 121, no. 2 (Spring 1992): 123–39.

Mansfield, Edward D., and Jack L. Snyder. *Electing to Fight: Why Emerging Democracies Go to War.* Cambridge, Mass.: MIT Press, 2005.

Martin, Terry. *The Affirmative Action Empire: Nations and Nationalism in the Soviet Union, 1923–1939.* Ithaca: Cornell University Press, 2001.

Mayer, Zald N. "Culture, Ideology and Strategic Framing." In *Comparative Perspectives on Social Movements: Political Opportunities, Mobilizing Structures, and Cultural Framings,* edited by Doug McAdam, John D. McCarthy, and Mayer N. Zald. New York: Cambridge University Press, 1996.

McAuley, Alastair, ed. *Soviet Federalism: Nationalism and Decentralisation.* New York: St. Martin's, 1991.

McAuley, Mary. *Russia's Politics of Uncertainty.* Cambridge: Cambridge University Press, 1997.

McCann, Leo. "Embeddedness, Markets, and the State: Observations from Tartarstan." In *Russian Transformations: Challenging the Global Narrative,* vol. 8, edited by Leo McCann, 173–90. New York: RoutledgeCurzon, 2004.

McCarthy, John D., and Mayer N. Zald. "Resource Mobilization and Social Movements: A Partial Theory." *American Journal of Sociology* 82 (1977): 1212–41.

McFaul, Michael, and Kathryn Stoner-Weiss. *After the Collapse of Communism: Comparative Lessons of Transition.* New York: Cambridge University Press, 2004.

McMullen, Ronald. "Tuva: Russia's Tibet or the Next Lithuania?" *European Security* 2, no. 3 (Autumn 1993): 451–60.

Morozov, N. "Tatarstan—Freedom Square Seethes." *Pravda,* October 17, 1991, 1.

———. "Tatarstan—A People's Militia is Being Created." *Pravda,* October 16, 1991, 1.

Moskalenko, Nelli. *Respublika Tyva [Tuva]—Spravochnik* [The Republic of Tyva (Tuva): Reference Book]. Moscow: Panorama, 1994.

Motyl, Alexander J., ed. *Thinking Theoretically about Soviet Nationalities: History and Comparison in the Study of the USSR.* New York: Columbia University Press, 1992.

Muller, Edward N., and Mitchell A. Seligson. "Inequality and Insurgency." *American Political Science Review* 81 (1987): 425–52.

Muller, Jerry Z. "Us and Them." *Foreign Affairs* 87, no. 2 (March/April 2008): 18–35.

Musina, Roza. "Etnokul'turnie orientatsii i mezhnatsionalnye otnosheniia: Analiz situatsii v gorodakh Respubliki Tatarstan" [Ethnocultural Orientation and Interethnic Relations: An Analysis of the Situation in the Cities of the Tatarstan Republic]. In *Sovremennye natsional'nye protsessy v Respublike Tatarstan,* edited by D. M. Iskhakov and R. N. Musina, Vol. 2, 46–58. Kazan: Tatarstan Academy of Sciences, 1994.

Mustafin, M. R., and R. G. Khuzeev. *Vse o Tatarstane: Ekonomiko-geograficheskii spravochnik* [All About Tatarstan: Handbook of Economy and Geography]. Kazan: Tatarskoe knizhnoe izdatel'stvo, 1994.

Muzaev, Timur. *Chechenskaia respublika: Organy vlasti i politicheskie sily* [The Chechen Republic: Organs of Power and Political Forces]. Moscow: Panorama, 1995.

———. *Etnicheskii separatizm v Rossii* [Ethnic Separatism in Russia]. Moscow: Panorama, 1999.

Nairn, Tom. *The Break-Up of Britain: Crisis and Neo-Nationalism.* London: New Left Books, 1977.

Narodnoe khoziaistvo Rossiiskoi Federatsii [The Economy of the Russian Federation]. Moscow: Goskomstat, 1990.

Nielsen, Francois. "The Flemish Movement in Belgium after World War II: A Dynamic Analysis." *American Sociological Review* 45 (1980): 76–94.

———. "Toward a Theory of Ethnic Solidarity in Modern Societies." *American Sociological Review* 50 (1985): 133–49.

Oberschall, Anthony. *Social Conflict and Social Movements.* Englewood Cliffs, N.J.: Prentice-Hall, 1973.

Olzak, Susan. *The Dynamics of Ethnic Competition and Conflict.* Stanford, Calif.: Stanford University Press, 1992.

Omrod, Jane. "The North Caucasus: Confederation in Conflict." In *New States, New Politics: Building the Post-Soviet Nations,* edited by Ian Bremmer and Ray Taras, 96–107. Cambridge: Cambridge University Press, 1997.

"Otchet o komplektovanii i rasstanovke kadrov aktsionernogo obshchestva KamAZa na 01.01.96 goda" [Report on the Organization and Composition of the Personnel of the Joint Stock Company KamAZ, January 1, 1996]. KamAZ Center for Sociological Research, Naberezhnye Chelny, 1996.

Pankhurst, Jerry G., and Michael Paul Sacks. *Contemporary Soviet Society: Sociological Perspectives.* New York: Praeger, 1980.

"Platforma Tatarskogo obshchestvennogo tsentra—Proekt" [Platform of the Tatar Public Center—Legislation]. Kazan, Tatarstan.

Platonov, Yu. V. "Spravka: Nekotorye aspekty mezhnatsional'nykh otnoshenii v kollektive AO KamAZa" [Information: Several Aspects of Interethnic Relations in the KamAZ Workforce]. KamAz Center for Sociological Research, Naberezhnye Chelny, 1991.

Platonov, Yu. V., and G. A. Kulakova. "Otchet po rezul'tatam oprosa obshchestven-nogo mneniia rabotnikov tatarskoi natsional'nosti po nekotorim problemam natsional'nogo razvitiia" [Report on the Results of a Public Opinion Survey of Tatar Workers on Issues of National Development]. KamAZ Center for Sociological Research, Naberezhnye Chelny, 1992.

Posen, Barry. "The Security Dilemma and Ethnic Conflict." *Survival* 35, no. 1 (Spring 1993): 27–47.

Professional'no-otraslevoi sostav intelligentsia naseleniia titul'noi i russkoi natsional'nostei absoliutnie znacheniia [Titular and Russian ethnic group composition of white-collar economic sectors]. Unpublished Goskomstat data from 1989 All-Union census.

"Programma Naberezhno-Chelninskogo otdeleniia Tatarskogo obshchestvennogo tsen-tra" [Program of the Naberezhnye Chelny Branch of the Tatar Public Center].

Ragin, Charles. "Class, Status, and 'Reactive Ethnic Cleavages': The Social Bases of Politi-cal Regionalism." *American Sociological Review* 42 (June 1979): 438–50.

Regiony Rossii: Statisticheskii sbornik [Regions of Russia: Statistical Handbook]. Moscow: Goskomstat, 1999.

"The Republic of Tatarstan: A Path-Breaker in Political and Economic Reform." Prospec-tus. Kazan: Chamber of Commerce and Industry of Tatarstan, 1996.

Rezoliutsiia s"ezda Bashkirskogo narodnogo tsentra "Ural." In M. N. Guboglo, *Bashkiria i Tatarstan: Paralleli etnopoliticheskogo razvitiia* [Bashkiria and Tatarstan: Parallels in Ethnopolitical Development], 77. Moscow: Institute of Ethnography and An-thropology, Russian Academy of Sciences, 1994.

Roeder, Philip G. "The Triumph of Nation-States: Lessons from the Collapse of the So-viet Union, Yugoslavia and Czechoslovakia." In *After the Collapse of Communism: Comparative Lessons of Transition,* edited by Michael McFaul and Kathryn Stoner-Weiss. New York: Cambridge University Press, 2004.

——. "Soviet Federalism and Ethnic Mobilization." *World Politics* 43, no. 2 (January 1991): 196–233.

——. *Where Nation-States Come From: Institutional Change in the Age of Nationalism.* Princeton: Princeton University Press, 2007.

Rorlich, Azade-Ayse. *The Volga Tatars: A Profile in National Resilience.* Stanford, Calif.: Hoover Institution Press, 1986.

Roth, Joseph. *The Radetzky March.* Woodstock, N.Y.: Overlook Press, 1974.

Sacks, Michael Paul. "Ethnic and Gender Divisions in the Work Force of Russia." *Post-Soviet Geography* 36, no. 1 (January 1995): 1–12.

Shabaev, Iurii. "National Movements in the Eastern Finnic Republics of Rossiia." *Anthro-pology and Archeology of Eurasia* 37, no. 2 (Fall 1998): 48–78.

——. "Peculiarities of Nation-Building in the Republic of Komi." In *Nation-Building and Common Values in Russia,* edited by Pal Kolsto and Helge Blakkisrud, 59–88. Lan-ham, Md.: Rowman & Littlefield, 2004.

Shadid, Anthony. "Divvying Up the Spoils of Political War." *New York Times,* June 27, 2010, 7.

Sharaftutdinova, Gulnaz. "Chechnya Versus Tatarstan: Understanding Ethnopolitics in Post-Communist Russia." *Problems of Post-Communism* 47, no. 2 (March/April 2000): 13–23.

Sharov, V. D. *Etnopoliticheskaia situatsiia v Respublike Marii El* [The Ethnopolitical Situ-ation in the Republic of Mari El]. Moscow: Institute of Ethnography and Anthro-pology, Russian Academy of Sciences, 1994.

Sheehy, Ann. "The All-Union and RSFSR Referendums of March 17." *RFE/RL Research Report*, March 29, 1991, 19–23.

———. "Russians the Target of Interethnic Violence in Tuva." *RFE-RL Research Report*, September 14, 1990, 13–17.

———. "Tatarstan Asserts Its Sovereignty." *RFE/RL Research Report*, April 3, 1992, 1–4.

———. "Tuva Adopts New Constitution." *RFE RL Daily Report*, October 26, 1993.

Shlapentokh, Vladimir, Roman Levita, and Mikhail Loiberg. *From Submission to Rebellion: The Provinces Versus the Center in Russia*. Boulder, Colo.: Westview, 1997.

Shnirelman, V. A. *Who Gets the Past?: Competition for Ancestors among Non-Russian Intellectuals in Russia*. Baltimore: Johns Hopkins University Press, 1996.

Simon, Gerhard. *Nationalism and Policy toward the Nationalities in the Soviet Union*. Boulder, Colo.: Westview Press, 1986.

Slater, Wendy. "No Victors in the Russian Referendum." *RFE/RL Research Report*, May 21, 1993, 10–19.

Slezkine, Yuri. "The USSR as a Communal Apartment, or How a Socialist State Promoted Ethnic Particularism." *Slavic Review* 53, no. 2 (Summer 1994): 413–52.

Slider, Darrell. "Federalism, Discord, and Accommodation: Intergovernmental Relations in Post-Soviet Russia." In *Local Power and Post-Soviet Politics*, edited by Theodore Friedgut and Jeffrey Hahn, 239–70. Armonk, N.Y.: M.E. Sharpe, 1994.

———. "The Soviet Union." *Electoral Studies* 9, no. 4 (1990): 295–301.

Smith, Anthony D. *The Ethnic Origins of Nations*. Oxford, U.K.: Basil Blackwell, 1986.

———. "The Ethnic Sources of Nationalism." In *Ethnic Conflict and International Security*, edited by Michael Brown, 27–42. Princeton: Princeton University Press, 1993.

Smith, Graham. "The Soviet State and Nationalities Policy." In *The Nationalities Question in the Post-Soviet States*, edited by Graham Smith, 2–22. New York: Longman, 1996.

Smith, Hedrick. *The Russians*. New York: Quadrangle/New York Times Book Co., 1976.

Snow, David A., and Robert D. Benford. "Master Frames and Cycles of Protest." In *Frontiers in Social Movement Theory*, edited by Aldon D. Morris and Carol McClurg Mueller, 133–55. New Haven: Yale University Press, 1992.

Snow, David A., E. Burke Rochford Jr., Steven K. Worden, and Robert D. Benford. "Frame Alignment Processes, Micromobilization, and Movement Participation." *American Sociological Review* 51, no. 4 (August 1986): 464–81.

Snyder, Jack L. *From Voting to Violence: Democratization and Nationalist Conflict*. New York: Norton, 2000.

Snyder, Jack. "Problems of Democratic Transition in Divided Societies." In *Domestic Perspectives on Contemporary Democracy*, edited by Peter F. Nardulli, 11–32. Urbana: University of Illinois Press, 2008.

Soldatova, G. U. "The Former Checheno-Ingushetia: Interethnic Relations and Ethnic Conflicts." *Anthropology and Archeology of Eurasia* 31, no. 4 (Spring 1993): 63–84.

Solnick, Steven. "Will Russia Survive? Center and Periphery and the Russian Federation." In *Post-Soviet Political Order: Conflict and State-Building*, edited by Barnett R. Rubin and Jack L. Snyder, 58–80. London: Routledge, 1998.

Standing, Guy. *Russian Unemployment and Enterprise Restructuring: Reviving Dead Souls*. New York: St. Martin's, 1996.

Statisticheskii ezhegodnik Respublika Tatarstan 1995 [Statistical Handbook of the Republic of Tatarstan 1995]. Kazan: Goskomstat Respubliki Tatarstan, 1996.

Stoner-Weiss, Kathryn. "Federalism and Regionalism." In *Developments in Russian Politics 4*, edited by Stephen White, Alex Pravda, and Zvi Y. Gitelman. Durham: Duke University Press, 1997.

Sullivan, Stefan. "Interethnic Relations in Post-Soviet Tuva." *Ethnic and Racial Studies* 18 (1995): 65–88.

Suny, Ronald Grigor. "Provisional Stabilities: The Politics of Identities in Post-Soviet Eurasia." *International Security* 24, no. 3 (Winter 1999–2000): 139–78.

——. *The Revenge of the Past: Nationalism, Revolution, and the Collapse of the Soviet Union.* Stanford, Calif.: Stanford University Press. 1993.

Tarrow, Sidney G. *Power in Movement: Social Movements and Contentious Politics.* Cambridge: Cambridge University Press, 1998.

Tatarstan: Na perekrestke mnenii [Tatarstan: At the Crossroads of Opinion]. Kazan: Tatarstan Supreme Soviet, 1993.

Teague, Elizabeth. "Center-Periphery Relations in the Russian Federation." In *National Identity and Ethnicity in Russia and the New States of Eurasia,* edited by Roman Szporluk, 21–57. Armonk, N.Y.: M.E. Sharpe, 1994.

——. "North-South Divide: Yeltsin and Russia's Provincial Leaders." *RFE/RL Research Report,* November 26, 1993, 7–23.

——. "Russia and Tatarstan Sign Power-Sharing Treaty." *RFE/RL Research Report,* April 8, 1994, 19–27.

Terent'eva, I. V., and A. S. Alishev, eds. "Sotsial'no-professional'nye gruppy i obrazovanie osnovnikh natsional'nostei" [Socioprofessional Groups and the Education of Major Nationalities]. In *Multiethnic Tartarstan,* 21–27. Kazan: Tatarstan Presidential Apparat, 1993.

Tilly, Charles. *From Mobilization to Revolution.* Reading, Mass.: Addison-Wesley Pub. Co., 1978.

Tishkov, Valery Aleksandrovich. *Chechnya: Life in a War-Torn Society.* Berkeley: University of California Press. 2004.

——. *Ethnicity, Nationalism and Conflict in and after the Soviet Union.* Thousand Oaks, Calif.: Sage, 1997.

——. "Materialy po problemam mezhnatsional'nikh otnoshenii v Rossiiskoi Federatsii" [Material on Issues of Interethnic Relations in the Russian Federation]. In *Rossiiskii Etnograf.* Moscow, 1993.

Toft, Monica Duffy. *The Geography of Ethnic Violence: Identity, Interests, and the Indivisibility of Territory.* Princeton: Princeton University Press, 2003.

Tolz, Vera. "Thorny Road toward Federalism in Russia." *RFE/RL Research Report,* December 3, 1993, 1–8.

Treisman, Daniel. *After the Deluge: Regional Crises and Political Consolidation in Russia.* Ann Arbor: University of Michigan Press, 1999.

——. "Russia's 'Ethnic Revival': The Separatist Activism of Regional Leaders in a Postcommunist Order." *World Politics* 49 (January 1997): 212–49.

Ustav, Souz Yakutskikh obshchestvennykh ob"edinenii i grazhdan "Sakha omuk" [Charter of the Union of Yakut Social and Civic Associations "Sakha omuk"]. August 10, 1990. Unpublished document personally provided by Marjorie Balzer.

Ustav, Erziansko-mokshanskogo obshchestvennogo dvizheniia Mastorava, g. Saransk [Charter of the Erzyan-Mokshan Popular Movement Mastorava]. 1989. Unpublished document.

Van Evera, Stephen. "Hypotheses on Nationalism and War." *International Security* 18, 4 (Spring, 1994): 5.

Walker, Edward W. *Dissolution: Sovereignty and the Breakup of the Soviet Union.* Lanham, Md.: Rowman & Littlefield, 2003.

——. "The Dog That Didn't Bark: Tatarstan and Asymmetrical Federalism in Russia." *Harriman Review* 9 (Winter 1996): 1–35.

White, Stephen, Graeme J. Gill, and Darrell Slider. *The Politics of Transition: Shaping a Post-Soviet Future.* Cambridge: Cambridge University Press, 1993.

Wixman, Ronald. "The Middle Volga: Ethnic Archipelago in a Russian Sea." In *Nations and Politics in the Soviet Successor States,* edited by Ian Bremmer and Ray Taras, 421–47. Cambridge: Cambridge University Press, 1993.

Yakubovich, Valery, and Irina Kozina. "The Changing Significance of Ties: An Exploration of the Hiring Channels in the Russian Transitional Labor Market." *International Sociology* 15, no. 3 (September 2000): 479–500.

Yeltsin, Boris. *Prezidentskii marafon.* Moscow: Izdatelstvo AST, 2000.

Young, M. Crawford. "The National and Colonial Question and Marxism: A View from the South." In *Thinking Theoretically about Soviet Nationalities: History and Comparison in the Study of the USSR,* edited by Alexander J. Motyl, 67–97. New York: Columbia University Press.

——. *The Politics of Cultural Pluralism.* Madison: University of Wisconsin Press, 1976.

Zakon Respubliki Tatarstan o iazikakh narodov Respubliki Tatarstan [Law on Languages of the Republic of Tatarstan]. June 8, 1992.

Zaslavsky, Victor. "Ethnic Group Divided: Social Stratification and Nationality Policy in the Soviet Union." In *The Soviet Union: Party and Society,* edited by Peter J. Potichnyj, 218–28. New York: Cambridge University Press, 1988.

——. "Nationalism and Democratic Transition in Postcommunist Societies." *Daedalus* 121, no. 2 (Spring 1992): 97.

——. *The Neo-Stalinist State: Class, Ethnicity, and Consensus in Soviet Society.* Armonk, N.Y.: M.E. Sharpe, 1982.

Zubkov, A. A., and V. V. Maras'ev. *Demograficheskie protsessy, etnicheskaia i sotsial'no-politicheskaia struktura Mordovii* [Demographic Processes, the Ethnic and Socio-political Structure of Mordova]. Moscow: Institute of Ethnography and Anthropology, Russian Academy of Sciences, 1994.

Zykov, F. M. "Etnopoliticheskaia situatsiia v Respublike Sakha do i posle vyborov 12 dekabria 1993 g" [The Ethnopolitical Situation in the Republic of Sakha before and after the Elections of December 1993]. Moscow: Institute of Ethnography and Anthropology, Russian Academy of Sciences, 1994.

Index

Note: Page numbers in *italics* indicate figures; those with a *t* indicate tables.